'THESE WERE EARTH'S BEST':
VOICES OF THE FIRST WORLD WAR

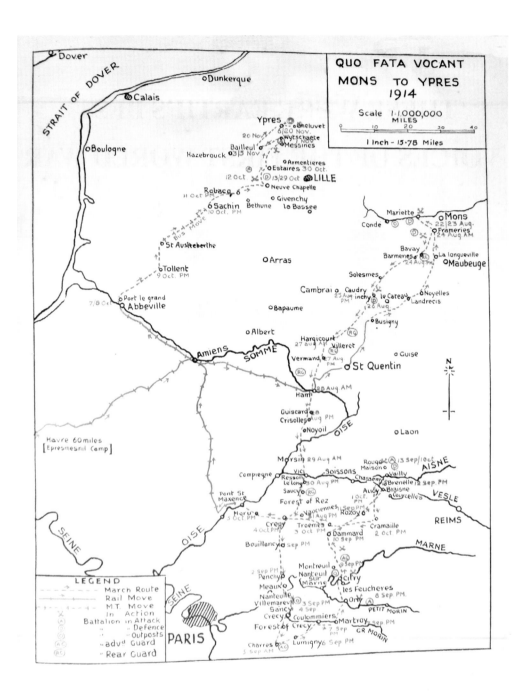

QUO FATA VOCANT
MONS TO YPRES
1914

Scale 1:1,000,000
MILES
10   20   30   40
1 Inch = 15.78 Miles

Dover

STRAIT OF DOVER

Dunkerque

Calais

Boulogne

Ypres ○Gheluvet
20 Nov. 6/20 Nov.
○Wytschaete
○ Bailleul 1 Nov.
Hazebrouck 3/5 Nov. ○Messines
○Armentieres
12 Oct. ○Estaires 30 Oct.
13/29 Oct. LILLE
Robacq ○ ○ Neuve Chapelle
11 Oct ○ Givenchy
○Sachin Bethune la Bassee
10 Oct. PM

Bus Move
St Austreberthe

○Arras

Tollent
9 Oct. PM

Port le grand
7/8 Oct. Abbeville

○Albert

Amiens SOMME

Mariette
Conde ○Mons
22/23 Aug.
○Frameries
24 Aug AM
Bavay
Barmeries ○La longueville
24 Aug PM ○Maubeuge
Solesmes
Cambrai ○ Caudry
25 Aug inchy ○ le Cateau ○Noyelles
PM Landrecis
26 Aug
○Busigny
Harqicourt RG
27 Aug AM Villeret
Vermand 27 Aug ○ Guise
RG St Quentin
Ham 28 Aug AM

○Bapaume

SEINE

Guiscayd
Crisolles Aug PM
○Noyoil OISE
○Laon

Havre 60 miles
[Epresmesnil Camp]

Morsin 29 Aug AM
Compiegne Vici Ressons Soissons
Le long 30 Aug PM
Saucy RG
Forest of Rez
Vauciennes Sep PM
Maru ○ Aug PM Rozoy
5 Oct PM Crepy Troemes ○
4 Oct PM 3 Oct PM
Bouillancy 1 Sep PM

Rouge 13 Sep/10 Oct AISNE
Maison ○
Chassemy ○Vailly
○Brenelle 12 Sep PM
Aücy ○Braisne
1 Oct. ○Courcelles VESLE
PM
Cramaille
Dammard 2 Oct PM
10 Sep PM MARNE

REIMS

OISE

Montreuil 3 Sep PM
2 Sep PM Nanteuil Cifry
Penchy Sur
Meaux Marne
Nanteuil les Feucheres
Villemarey Orly 8 Sep PM
Sancy 3 Sep PM
Crecy 4 Sep PETIT MORIN
Coulommiers
Forest of Crecy Martroy Sep PM
GR MORIN
Charres ○ 7 Sep PM
5 Sep AM Lumigny○ Sep PM

SEINE

PARIS

LEGEND
– – – March Route
Rail Move
M.T. Move
In Action
Battalion in Attack
"   " Defence
"   " Outposts
adv⁴ Guard
Rear Guard

N

'THESE WERE EARTH'S BEST':
VOICES OF THE FIRST WORLD WAR

Van Wilson

YORK ORAL HISTORY SOCIETY 2014

The title is paraphrased from a poem by Rupert Brooke

Book layout and cover design by Clare Brayshaw

Cover photographs supplied by Mike Race and Dom Williams

Prepared and printed by:

York Publishing Services Ltd
64 Hallfield Road
Layerthorpe
York YO31 7ZQ
Tel: 01904 431213

Website: www.yps-publishing.co.uk

CONTENTS

INTRODUCTION

In the late 1970s, Dr Alf Peacock, a Cambridge man who spent much of his life in York as warden of the York Educational Settlement, historian, connoisseur of Real Ale and jazz, and magistrate, decided to research the Battle of the Somme of 1916. His own father had experienced the battle and in later life shared his memories with his son. Dr Peacock found others who were veterans of the battle and the project snowballed as more men came forward to talk about their part in the First World War. Most had never told their families about

Alf Peacock
(Alf Peacock Collection)

what they saw and did. He made recordings of over 200 of the men on reel to reel tapes. Some of the men were visited many times and became friends. The tapes went to Cambridge University. After Alf's death in 2004, his partner Brenda Naylor told York Oral History Society about them. They had lain in a cupboard for many years so they were brought back to York and we were delighted to be able to have them digitised and transcribed.

Alf Peacock in France
(Alf Peacock Collection)

It has been a huge undertaking. The sheer bulk of the collection has meant that only extracts could be used in our book and CD, though our plan is to eventually make them publicly accessible. We have used every means possible to locate present day relatives of our veterans and have traced about a quarter of them. We have been pleased to present relatives with copies of the relevant recordings.

Today these veterans are no longer with us. Most died in the 1980s and '90s. When Harry Patch died in 2009, he was the 'last fighting Tommy', then the world's last combat veteran was Claude Choules, an Englishman who had been in the Royal Navy. He died in Australia aged 110 in May 2011, but it was not until 2012 that Florence Green, the last person to serve in the forces in the First World War, died at the age of 110. She served in the Women's Royal Air Force for a few months before the war ended.

This book is not a military history, it does not pretend to be a comprehensive history of the war, but it tells the stories, in their own words, of men, and one or two women, who experienced the war, whether in the army, navy or air force, on the home front or in prison for their pacifist beliefs.

EXPLANATION OF THE PROJECT BY DR ALF PEACOCK

In these interviews the lack of involvement [in the bigger picture] *of the common soldier comes over loud and clear, as does the lack of hatred for the enemy. They are human records of men representative of a wasted generation. Nearly all volunteered, some liked the army, all came out with a sense of terrible loss and belief that their experiences had been futile. After all they saw the Second World War too.*

Most were privates; some became corporals, lance corporals, sergeants, a few became officers. Many were wounded. Many were haunted by the recollections of the war. Others still suffered physical pain from their wounds. All were incredibly nice men.

ACKNOWLEDGEMENTS

We are particularly indebted to Dr Alf Peacock for the legacy of a collection of wonderful recordings, the result of his travels all over England, and to Wales and France, interviewing veterans of the First World War. We are very grateful to Brenda Naylor, Alf Peacock's partner, for donating the recordings to York Oral History Society, and for allowing us to copy photographs from the Alf Peacock Collection.

We would like to thank those relatives of our veterans that we have been able to trace, who have allowed us to copy photographs –

Charles Angus (son of William Angus), John Ayers (son in law of Thomas Nixon), John Blakeway (son of John Blakeway), Don Bowerman (son of Arthur Bowerman), Alan Bowman (grandson of Isaac Bowman), Stuart Broadley (great nephew of Walter Smalley), Jane Chimes (grand-daughter of Leonard Cavinder), Josephine Clampitt (daughter of Joseph Blades), Christine Clay (niece of Edward Cooper), Beryl Cockerill (daughter in law of Harry Cockerill), Alan Elsegood (grandson of William Shaw), Ann Firth (grand-daughter of Hugh Whitehead), Rosemary Fox (daughter of Jack Bouch), Julie Gifford (grand-daughter of Reg Gifford), Janet Hayton (daughter of Harry Shaw), Geoff Headley (son of Robert Headley), Robert Hey (son of Claud Hey), Karen Hyatt (grand-daughter of Edwin Bond), Jasper Kay (son of John and Guendolen Kay), Doug Kershaw (son of Bill Kershaw), Peter Lawson (son of John George Lawson), Nigel Loadman (grandson of Gilbert Loadman), Tina Milson (grand-daughter of Arthur Aylett), Chris Moorey (son of Ernest Moorey), Ted Newby (son of William Newby), Judith Reynolds (grand-daughter of Percy Fuller), Peter Roantree (son of Percy Roantree), Martin Roberts (grandson of George Harbard), Richard Seymour (son of Charles Seymour), Andy Simm (great grandson of George Ashurst), Mary Sylvester (daughter of Ernest Deighton), Marian Tate (grand-daughter of Ernest Newsome), Eileen Tutill (niece in law of Herbert Cussons), Jon Vause (grandson of Ernest Mackinder), Jeremy Ware (second cousin of Innes Ware), Mike Welsh (grandson in law of Jim Melody), Martyn Winn (grandson of Ernest Done), Tony Wood (grandson in law of Clarence Ward), Enid Worrell (grand-daughter of Harold Victor Shergold).

We would also like to thank the following for allowing us to use photos –

Borthwick Institute of Historical Research at University of York, Raymond Calpin, Joy Cann of York City Archives, Daphne and Peter Dench, Rita Freedman, Paul Harris of Helmsley Archive, Andrew Jackson of Accrington Pals Association, Liddle Collection at Brotherton Library, Leeds, John Lofthouse, Jenny and the late Alan Milner, Jill Murray, Richard Pollitt of York Mansion House, Chris Poole, David Rubenstein, Peter Sharp and Malcolm Walker.

For help with tracing relatives, thanks are due to the Bradford Telegraph and Argus, Chris Bouch, James Burton of the Hull Daily Mail, Keith Edmonds of the Western Front Association, Stephen Lewis of the York Press, Glynis Ludkin, Margaret Tadman of York Family History Society and the Yorkshire Post. We would like to thank David Grant of Soundabout for the excellent digitisation of the reel to reel tapes, and Carolyn Mumford, Vicki Peden, Janet Pigott, Philippa Pinder, Sue Platt, Therese Barton Rowan and Mary Varley for their hard and accurate work in transcribing difficult recordings.

For help with research I must thank – Ken and Linda Haywood, (whose knowledge of the First World War is vast), Anne Houson, Edith Jayne, Chris Litton, Peter Pigott, Sue Platt, and Andrew Jackson for help with searching First World War newspapers.

I would like to thank York Oral History Society trustees, Nigel Evamy and David Poole for help with research, Brian Freeborn for transcribing many recordings, Alan Hardwick for handling the financial side of the project and especially Mike Race for managing the project, overseeing the photographic collection, obtaining and copying photos, for research, and for reading the text and making useful suggestions.

This project (digitising, transcribing, producing a book, CD, exhibition, and a range of educational workshops) has been funded by the Heritage Lottery Fund. We are very grateful to them for their financial support, which has enabled us to bring this wonderful material to the public.

Our greatest debt of course is to the men and women who were interviewed by Dr Alf Peacock, who have shared their experiences of the First World War with us.

CHAPTER ONE

JOINING UP AND TRAINING

When war broke out in August 1914, the men in the regular army were already mobilised. Those who had joined the Territorials, or special reserve, also received calling up papers. They had been raised for home defence but were now needed to go overseas. But the army was small compared to that of Germany, for example, who sent 1,500,000 men to France and Belgium and 500,000 to the east.

So Lord Kitchener, the Secretary of State for War, appealed for a 'new army', and within days the first 100,000 had enlisted. As the war machine began to take its toll, Lord Derby devised a scheme in 1915 where men would 'promise to enlist' which meant attesting, or signing on, to be called up when needed. The advantage of this, so the poster said, was that men could join up together and be guaranteed to serve in their own groups of friends. This was persuasion on a grand scale. However the scheme did not succeed in getting enough volunteers, so the government brought in conscription in 1916 with the Military Service Act.

There were varied reactions to the announcement of war, just as there were varied expectations. Some men had no idea war was imminent. Others had been expecting it. Most people thought it would be over by Christmas. There was a general belief in patriotism and duty, the blind following of orders, and women selling kisses or giving out white feathers played their part. For young working class men, particularly agricultural labourers, working long hours for little pay, in dreadful conditions, joining the army seemed an exciting adventure. Philip Larkin in his poem '1914', talks of lines of men waiting patiently to join up, 'grinning as if it were all an August Bank Holiday lark'. But within a short time there was 'never such innocence again'.

William Angus was born in 1899 in Bingley, and remembers,

William Angus
(Charles Angus)

One summer morning my father came into my bedroom and he threw the Yorkshire Post on to my bed and I read that we were at war. I was fifteen and I felt excited. Obviously it was going to be bigger than those little Balkan Wars in 1912 and 1913. This was the Triple Alliance of Germany, Austria and Italy against the Triple Entente of Britain, France and Russia. All the big powers were involved. Italy switched to the Allied side in April 1915.

In the middle of September I went back to school and I learned that a contingent of the Officers Training Corps was being formed and I joined it on the very first day.

The war in the west began as a war of movement, the Germans broke in through Belgium and although they were held up to some extent by Belgian fortresses at Liege and Namur they passed through. On the Belgian frontier they came up against a British and French army at Mons and Charleroi and then the Allies retreated back down to the River Marne and there they were able to play tit for tat. Joffre [the French commander] brought out the Paris garrison mostly in taxi cabs and motor buses and outflanked the Germans so they were forced back on the Aisne and there the Germans dug in. That began a period of static trench warfare and before long there were trenches running all the way from the English Channel to the Alps.

On the whole in 1914/15 the Germans gained. They got the Russians out of Poland, Turkey came in on the German side in October 1914 and Bulgaria in October 1915, and after that the Germans had control of a band of territory running from the North Sea right across to the Persian Gulf and the Red Sea. It became apparent that the Russians needed all the aid we could give them. Their munition plants were not capable of supplying their armies on a large scale and our attempt to aid them by forcing the passage of the Dardanelles ended in failure. So did our invasion of Mesopotamia with the object of protecting our oil supplies from Persia. But the German colonies in Africa and Asia were mopped up by the British and the French and their allies the Japanese.

In September 1917, I joined Number 12 Officer Cadet Battalion at Newmarket. We lived in a hutted camp. There was a staff of officers and NCOs whose job it was to train those with active service experience and boys fresh from school like myself.

William Angus and others go to war
(Charles Angus)

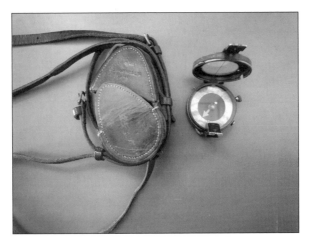

William Angus's compass
(Charles Angus)

We did a good deal of squad drill, open order drill, weapon training, physical jerks, plus officer training in tactics, map reading, military law, etiquette. It was hard work. We had Wednesday afternoons off for games. We worked hard in the evenings as well. It was a four month course but was cut to three and a half months because of the shortage of young officers and so we did an extra hour each day and in December we were parading in the dark.

Arthur Abel was

15 when the war broke out. I was big and strong even though I was young, I weighed 14 stone and I was over 6 feet. The road between Manchester and Derby was largely occupied that weekend by a West Riding division of territorials. It took all day for 22,000 troops, plus their equipment, to pass down the road.

There was a day of decision whether I should abandon my job and go in the army. My father said, "If you want to go, I suppose I better let you go". I just declared a false age.

George Ashurst was from a village near Wigan.

As lads we enjoyed ourselves because the country was lovely. No machines, motors or crowds of people. We could go out all day, take huge barm cakes with black treacle and we'd make our own pop out of meadowsweet and nettles. It was grand. Five or six boys in the village, out to the fields all day, come back at night as hungry as wolves and ready for bed. We never went on holidays but one summer's day somebody got a waggonette and one horse to take the children to Southport. That was a trip of a lifetime.

George joined the Special Reserve and went to camp once a year. But when war broke out, they were immediately called up and his life changed dramatically. He was a lance corporal in the 2nd Lancashire Fusiliers.

I reported at Bury Barracks at 10 o'clock on the 8th [August]. There were crowds outside. There were fellows walking in barracks drunk. Several of the women and children were crying. We went inside and were given tea. At 3 o'clock we marched to the station with the Bury Concertina Band in front, playing tunes. Oh what a day!

Arthur Bull

joined the Territorials in June 1912. History was one of my favourite subjects, anything like the Charge of the Light Brigade or the Zulu wars. They were heroes. The uniform attracted us, the music was good and I really enjoyed it. But I paid for it.

I joined the first South Midland mounted brigade. I was waiting, hoping the war would not be over before I got to it. The War Office said, "You'll be back home again in a month".

James Dunnett's

elder brother was in the militia so he got called up. I was in the boy scouts, there were ten in our group, we went to Ipswich drill hall and joined up. They said, "You're a fine lad but you'll have to be older than that if you want to go in the army". I told the other boys, some put their ages up one year, I put mine up two, and we all got in. I didn't think it would last a great while, not if we joined up and helped them.

Bill Busby was born in 1895 near Leamington Spa. He spent 42 years in the army and rose to the rank of Lieutenant Colonel.

It was 21st of August. A crowd of us from the village went down and the recruiting bloke said, "What unit do you want to join?" "Royal Warwicks". And he sent us away with a bob and told us to come back next night. We caught the train to Lichfield and by the time we got to the barracks, it was ten o'clock and lights out had gone. They put us in the guard room for the night. We didn't sleep, one of the chaps in the draft was a local bobby and he kept us laughing the whole night long. The old sergeant kept coming in and telling us to shut up. Next morning we went out onto the parade ground and found that we wasn't in the Warwicks at all, we were in the South Staffordshire Regiment. But we didn't give a damn, as long as we were all together.

We'd have one rifle between ten, the rest of us had broomsticks. The only uniform I had for a long time was a pair of puttees. But in my hurry checking knife, fork, spoon, razor, comb, shaving strop, I missed the puttees. So I went back for them. And this bloke who was Quartermaster, he told me to get the hell out of it.

Mr. Peter Mason, left, and Mr. William Busby look over books about the Great War battlefields.

Peter Mason and Bill Busby

(Alf Peacock Collection)

We were ordered Saturday afternoon drill and these two old soldiers said, "You don't want to stand for this. When he tells you to slope arms, chuck the damn rifles on the ground". Well he gave the order "slope arms". Down on the ground went all our rifles. We turned round. To our astonishment these two old soldiers had sloped arms and stood there rigidly to attention! Left us properly in the soup! They put us all under arrest and marched us back to barracks and we were in front of the commanding officer on Monday morning and he tried the whole lot of us. He said he didn't think for a minute we realised the seriousness of what we'd done, and we got away with ten days jankers. But he split the whole lot of us up, all over the regiment and that was the biggest punishment of all.

Taking the King's Shilling Exhibition Buildings 1914

(York Oral History Society)

We were sent to Grantham. We were under canvas. These old sweats used to go out to the pubs at night. I didn't drink much in those days. Those tents were made for eight and there were thirty of us! Poor devils near the door used to get their faces trod on. They eventually built some very good huts on the other side of the road. We stayed until June 1915.

We went to Surrey and were inspected by Kitchener and issued with tropical uniform. One in 50 of us could put it on properly. These old sweats made a fortune charging us a tanner a time to put our clobber on for us. We embarked at Liverpool, on the Empress of Ireland, and went to Egypt.

John Blakeway recalls,

There were soldiers going about. A couple stopped me between Easingwold and Tollerton, and asked if I would join. Of course I wasn't anxious to go. I put myself down as a farmer in the enquiry. However they said I must go into the army so I joined on 11ᵗʰ May 1916.

John Blakeway and friend at Tollerton 1917.
Friend went to France and was killed
(John Blakeway)

I went up to Richmond and they told me I was poor physique and not robust. I only weighed ten stone. I got into the farmers' regiment, the Kings' Royal Rifles. We went to Seaton Dellow on the north coast.

I was ailing most of the time I was there. I marched with a pair of new heavy shoes and a sock with a piece of wood chip in it, and it took the skin off. I was five or six weeks walking a mile every morning with these shoes on, going to see the doctor. I said I'd report sick in billet. And they sent a chap with some iodine, he clapped this on the raw wound and it got better. They'd have had me walking for I don't know how long if I had stopped in the billet. Then I was inoculated. But I got tonsillitis and they marched me between two soldiers, and I had to carry my pack, to Ashington, a temporary hospital. I was in there three or four days with tonsillitis but they had me out again. If there was anything I hated, it was drilling. I never knew left from right and I didn't get any better at being in the army.

But I got my marksman's badge. And that entitled me to a penny a week more. I'd missed one or two drafts with not being trained properly. I think they were tired of me and said, "You'll go with the next draft". We went from Southampton, we were nearly all seasick, and landed at Harfleur in a driving rainstorm.

John Blakeway 1917 Sunderland hospital with bandaged head on right
(John Blakeway)

Edwin Bond recalls,

Edwin Bond
(Karen Hyatt)

Medical boards could be falsified. I had a poisoned arm and went sick. I saw a private in front of me and his right arm was useless through being injured as a boy in an accident with a traction engine. The doctor used to get half a crown for every man that passed. He saw this arm, it was withered, like bone with skin on. The doctor said, "It's a shame", but got him in!

We proceeded to Norwood, south east London, billeted in empty houses. Then we was at Pennington Camp. We marched up in fours, and it was sixteen in a tent. Some of the blankets were wet where they'd been in leaking tents and it had been raining. In the morning the sergeant come round at six o'clock, Reveille. As we marched into this camp they'd be bringing the dead out on stretchers covered over with blankets. The tents was so full, you had food in the marquee. Them that was lucky could get on the tables and the form in front, but beyond that you had to stand up. They were admitting men at such a rate they couldn't cope with them. The first meal in the army, I got three cubes of fruit and two slices of bread and margarine and a mug of tea in a basin. The chap doling it out, if you wanted another cup you had to give him a cig.

Edwin Bond in later life

(Karen Hyatt)

I had two lumps on my wrist and under my arm, they were getting poisonous. I went to the medic's door. He took my name, "How long have you had in the army?" "Three days". He said, "What's your religion?" I thought, 'They're getting ready to put me away!". They put me down to have hot fermentations. But it was getting worse and I went sick again at two o'clock in the afternoon. And after waiting till 5pm for a doctor, I laid in the hallway of this house. I can remember the Medical Corps fellow, "Come on, get up". They took me into another room and a lot of fellows were in their blankets, three men were laid unconscious. Then an old soldier took charge of us and dismissed us. I went back again next day at nine o'clock. They put a man on the door with a bottle of iodine and a brush and as you come out, he said, "Paint his lumps with iodine"!

Horace Calvert was 15 when the war broke out.

I was going to work up Richmond Road in Bradford. There's a newsagent shop at the corner with a big placard out, 'War Declared'. And everything seemed to come to a standstill. There seemed to be such an air of excitement. In Carlisle Road there was a German pork butcher and they smashed his shop front. A lot of German wool merchants in Bradford had gone, cleared away.

At the end of September I enlisted and was given a shilling. I think they realised the British Expeditionary Force and the Indian army, which took a long time to bring over, would not be sufficient to cope with the huge German army, which was conscripts at that time.

Irving Camplin was born in 1896 near Barnsley and he and his brothers all joined up in 1916. He went to train in Bradford.

They were all volunteers in our family. We used to drill in the park. The barracks got that full that they drafted some of us into a big house opposite Manningham Station. We were trained with horses, and used to do gymnast training. We went to Woolwich Barracks and from there to Southampton, Le Havre and Boulogne. We had some terrible characters. There was one called Walters, he was a Cockney. They say they could tame anybody in t'army but they couldn't tame him. He flogged everything he could lay his hands on. He flogged all the company's bacon ration one day in Boulogne and they tied him to a gun wheel and the civvies got him drunk and when they untied him he fell on t'floor.

Binoculars advert
(The Graphic 1915)

Women of Britain Say Go

Harold Carson was born in 1897 in York. His father

was a caterer. We had the De Grey Rooms for a number of years and then he packed that up and we had a private hotel, Bootham House.

Everybody was in Exhibition Square waiting for the paper lads to come because there was no wireless then. There was a pork butcher, Steigmann, in Goodramgate, and he was interned. [Although he had lived in York for 34 years and was naturalised in 1898]. *Even at school Germany was behind people's minds all the time.*

There were three of us pals, Frank Kay, they had a goods shop in Parliament Street. His grandfather Robert Kay founded Old Priory. The other friend was Ted Wright of Wright's cycle and pram shop in Market Street. We all decided we would join the army. Ted got into mechanical transport. Frank and I went into the Exhibition [Hall] to join the Yorkshire Hussars. It was a

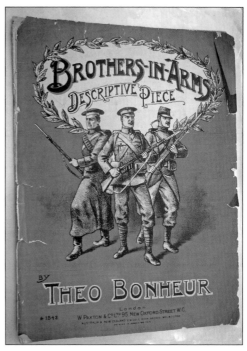

Brothers in Arms sheet music
(Chris Poole)

temporary recruiting place so they gave us papers and told us to go back in the afternoon to take the oath. When I got home I found that we hadn't joined the Yorkshire Hussars but the York Heavy Battery. I said, "We'll go up on the bar walls and burn the papers". So we did, and went to Castlegate, the HQ of the Yorkshire Hussars.

We went to Beverley to a riding school. We did musketry and manoeuvres. The range was on the railway embankment. When a train was signalled, they used to wave a red flag and we had to stop firing. In April 1915 we went to a village called Leven under canvas there. One day they called 15 names out, "You are going on a draft". We went by train to Plymouth and marched through, the band preceding us. In the high street there were no cars, everybody was doing their Saturday morning shopping, and they loaded us up with tobacco, sweets and fruit. I'll always remember that.

There was a converted troopship, the Caledonian. Four destroyers left with us, two came as far as Gibraltar. Then we set sail to the north coast of Africa. We were transferred to the Kings' Own Royal Lancs and went to Salonika.

Gilbert Loadman was born in Vine Street, York. His father was chief clerk at the parcels office on the railway.

Gilbert Loadman 1914
(Nigel Loadman)

I volunteered in the early days of the war. I was 22. I joined the 2/5th West Yorks Territorials. After a few months I got a job in the quartermaster's store and kept accounts, ordering food and ordnances and in fact I was quartermaster's chief clerk.

I did requisitions for food for the battalion in the quartermaster's general service wagon. I went all over the place in France. It was a really interesting job. We'd be seven or eight miles behind the line. I'd take the rations up in a limber wagon, two small wagons joined together. I had to see they were carried into the trenches. We took turns, there were two of us, I drove one night, the next night I'd rest. When they were shelling, I'd take shelter in an old shell hole. I'd see the quarter master sergeant, and collect any messages they had back to base.

I think the West Yorks training was the best. We always did as we were told. We'd take the horses up night after night. The horses were doing what they were told, same as everyone else. But sometimes they stampeded, broke loose. [Because of the shellfire].

I remember going through Belgium and into Germany. We drove them back to Cologne and the Rhine and that's where we stopped. [He was there until 1919]. *I got discharged before the troops because I got an injury to my leg. Several of my friends were killed. I can picture them now.*

Oh it's a Lovely War, sheet music
(Chris Poole)

Alfred Chapman came from Lincolnshire and had been to grammar school, then worked for Doncaster Council.

I was not quite 18. I was going to Helmsley, the Earl of Feversham formed a battalion. I arrived at Helmsley and I walked up to the big house and slept my first night in the army on the concrete floor above the horses. It was mainly composed of the agricultural community was the Yeoman Rifles. There were troughs in the paddock and we'd have to go and smash up the ice and get a drop of water and get washed. At Duncombe Park it was square bashing, chasing the deer out of the park and rounding them up sometimes, which we enjoyed.

I didn't like it in the army. I'm not going to pretend I did. I did what I was asked to do and smiled.

21st Yeoman Rifles reunion – Alf Chapman, 3rd left, Bill Poucher, 7th left, Frank Arnold, 3rd right, Harry Shaw 4th right, Dick Smith fifth right.

(Helmsley Archives)

Harry Cockerill

joined up on December 26th and I was put back a year. I had a bit of a murmur of the heart.

There was a scare on, they were getting badly beaten, knocked about. And we had to go across at very short notice. We crossed over from Dover. There was thousands. I'd never had any training because it was about February when I went abroad and there was no time. I didn't even know how to fire a rifle. I was clerical.

I was put in charge of a battery behind a six inch howitzer. We were just chucked in. We realised that we were in for some trouble the first night we got to within a mile or two of Ypres. We'd never experienced any fighting. And the officer said "Look lads, get down into them ditches", and they were dropping bombs at the side. That was my first baptism. I'd only been in France a day.

Bill Harrison

volunteered at Pocklington but I had an impediment in my speech. They said, "We'll send for you", and they did, the impediment in my speech didn't count after that. We thought it was a lark. We had no idea what it was going to be. We used to see the pictures, the Pathe Gazette, [newsreel at the cinema] *with our lads walking about and thought, 'It will be grand'. We soon found out it was different. We joined up in February, a rimy frosty morning.*

Tobacco advert with face of Kitchener

(The Graphic)

It was Trainee Reserve Battalion, TRB on our epaulettes. We went to Northumberland and had proper training there. There were two lads from Pocklington in the same hut, Sid Fields and Billy Hunter. It was very nice to have two lads that you knew, because it was strange. Beds were three boards and two trestles, a straw mattress and a straw pillow, blankets and your overcoat. Different from your feather bed at home.

Edward Cooper

saw the advertisements on the hoardings about the types of infantry in the British army and I was attracted by this particular uniform, green with black buttons. I was asked my age and date of birth. I said 1896 and I was told that recruiting was now 19 and they couldn't accept me.

I was leaving the building and an old soldier who knew me said, "Have you joined up, Edward?" "No, I was too young." "Well, that's a pity. But there's nothing to stop you having another birthday". I didn't know what he meant at first but I went back. "How old are you?" "19," and I was in.

You were given a fitness test, I was passed as A1. Then you went in front of a sergeant and an officer and you had to attest that you would be a true and loyal subject and citizen of the King.

At the depot at Winchester they were receiving anything up to 3,000 men a day because there was three battalions that used that depot as their headquarters. There was no facilities for feeding, you just went into a barrack room and you were given half a loaf and a pot of jam between three of you. You had to provide your own receptacle for a cup of tea.

There was some open land just outside Bisley where they put canvas up and we did our first training. We were in civilian clothes, drawn from all quarters of the population, some were in plus fours, some in corduroy trousers, some were in working clothes, some were in straw hats, some with caps. Some had boots, some hadn't. By the end of the winter we were in a very sorry state.

We went out in June 1915, the first to go up to France as a division. Others had gone out as brigades or battalions. We were very highly trained, a magnificent body of men.

Gerald Dennis

was at Hull Teacher Training College. A County Durham lad from Spennymoor enlisted, came back and told us about a marvellous staff sergeant on the Hull City steps, in a green uniform, with black buttons, and a red piece of cloth behind his cap badge, the Yeoman Rifles. So we enlisted. But it wasn't mounted after all, we were in the infantry, which we regretted.

I had a weak heart from when I was about ten. I had to play no games, do no gymnastics. But I persuaded him to let me through. He said, "Well, it'll kill or cure you."

Nine men from the college went up to Helmsley in 1915. The Earl of Feversham had formed the Yeoman Rifles, and we trained until January 1916. Footwork, section work, platoon work, battalion work, route marches, getting fitted with uniforms. Then down to Aldershot. A regimental band met us. When we got to the barracks the order was, "Kits off, draw buckets of water, soap and brushes from the canteen and get busy". So we scrubbed all the barracks out! We were in the army at last! In Helmsley, we'd been known as feather-bed soldiers, because we'd come down from the park huts, which were found to be unfit, and the people put us up in feather beds.

We started in seriously, Reveille half past six, gun fire quarter to seven. Gunfire was hot tea or coffee and biscuits if you got up in time. Then 7 o'clock drill, eight to half past was breakfast, 9 o'clock to 12 parades, 2pm to 5 was parades, 6 to 8 parades. It was morning, afternoon and night. I bought all the infantry training books and various manuals, and set to real training. Sections were formed, bombers, snipers, scouts. We didn't have idle hands or idle minds. Route marches, towards the end of the training, were about 20 miles in full pack. We weren't mollycoddled. May 5th we entrained at Aldershot, went to Southampton, and went across at night-time, with the destroyers flashing their lights and nursing us across the Channel.

Leeds Teacher Training College athletics team, Claud Hey back far right 1919

(Robert Hey)

Reunion at Duncombe Park. Claud Hey at back far right

(Robert Hey)

Claud Hey

went to Tadcaster Grammar School. I decided to go in for teaching and went to Leeds City Training College. It was the year the war broke out. It was taken as a hospital. Half the hostels were taken over by the army so we had to go down into Leeds to Thoresby High School.

After a year of listening to the wounded soldiers walking about the college grounds and listening to their jibes of, "Give him a stick and a balloon. Why don't you get to the war?", a lot of us decided to join the army.

The Earl of Feversham was colonel of the Yeoman Rifles. He stated emphatically that he wanted men of good character. He wanted chaps with academic qualifications, and yeomen, every quality you could find. He got one of the finest battalions ever raised.

We had a wonderful send off from Leeds College and arrived in Helmsley. I slept under a billiard table the first night. We trained there before we moved to Aldershot, then to France on a paddle steamer La Marguerite.

(For more about Claud, see the chapter on Artillery). Gerald Dennis and Claud Hey were both in the original Yeoman Rifles, the 21st battalion King's Royal Rifles. Only 170 men survived out of 2999. They were two of the four remaining in 1989 when they met together for the last time in the private chapel at Duncombe Park. They had met every year for 60 years apart from during the Second World War. They had their own service in the chapel followed by tea with Lord and Lady Feversham. Claud died in 1990.

Herbert Evans was born in 1897.

Me and my pal joined the Territorials when we were 16, the 1st/6th West Yorkshires. Of course we gave wrong ages. We went to camp in 1913, did night manoeuvres. When the war broke out we were going to Scarborough for a fortnight's camp, but instead we moved into billets at Selby, then to Strensall Common. And then into York where we trained on Bootham Asylum field. We went to Folkestone on 15th April 1915. There was submarines in the channel. They was going to hold us up but they decided to rush us across. We just saw a cruiser in front and one behind. We landed at Boulogne. When we went in at Neuve Chapelle, we had to bury a few of the dead that was laid out in our own line. I think they were Royal Scots.

Tom Fidler was in the Church Lads' Brigade.

I was about 17. One Sunday morning we'd been on church parade and everybody was wondering when war was going to be declared. Kilden Wright was there with the Church Lads' Brigade, and he was an officer in the Derbyshire Yeomanry. We couldn't move because the trains were requisitioned for the troops, so we had to stay there for a few days. I couldn't settle down. I went to several different recruiting meetings for Kitchener's Army. It was patriotism as much as anything. We formed up as a body, all the Church Lads Brigade. They didn't ask any questions, and one or two of the lads were only 16.

Jim Gill explains

Let's really be honest. I had this feeling that, if we didn't join up and get an army, that our parents and people would suffer. And we had got to fight the Germans.

Arthur Gladwin

was born in 1895. We came to York in 1912. I got an appointment with Yorkshire Insurance Company, and was studying accountancy amongst other part time studies. I went into the army in 1915 with the East Yorkshires at Hornsea. Wherever one went there was great posters with Lord Kitchener's hand, "Your country needs you". And there was a great surge of young fellows wanting to join the forces because none of us had any idea what war meant. A lot of the officers had no previous experience of war. They were coming straight from the cadet corps.

We were doing simple drills in Hornsea. Learning about the construction of firearms, how to use them and clean and maintain them. It was as a precautionary duty, walking the cliffs day and night on coastal guard. It was very nice in the day but at night I came precious near to falling over the edge of the cliffs on more than one occasion. I remained a private soldier for three years then I was commissioned. This was with the 10th battalion East Yorkshires.

William Gray was born in 1897. He joined the army in 1913. He was an agricultural labourer but

couldn't get a job at that time. With no work, I fancied the army. They recruited at Kempton Barracks, Bedford, the recruiting sergeant used to come every year, part of the horse fair. He took me in, "Here's a lad wishing to join the army". "How old are you sonny?" I said, "18 last August", but I wasn't even 17. He put his hand round me chin, he said, "You haven't started shaving yet", then turned to the sergeant. "Is this man 18, sergeant?" "Yes sir, I've seen his birth certificate".

We used to do PT. You'd start early morning, do a few hours of parade. Come home, wash, shave, have your breakfast. You had about an hour, musketry course, rifles, a quarter of an hour break, then everyone had to head to the gymnasium. After I'd been in the army three months I went on a firing course and I was a rifleman. I passed out first class.

Eric Haylock was

due to report on the Monday. But there's about sixty there at the Corn Exchange, Cambridge. And they phoned through to Bury St. Edmonds, told them that they'd got sixty people wanting to join. And Bury said they couldn't take us, they were full up. They asked us to go home. But we'd given up our jobs, nobody wanted to go home. So they went and got a load of straw in the Corn Exchange, and we laid like a load of pigs for about a week in our own clothes. Used to go out and do a bit of training. We were in our own civvies for three months. They give us twelve bob for the use of them in the finish. And then we didn't get khaki, we got kits in blue.

Then they suddenly decided we're going to move to Ripon in Yorkshire, in tents on the racecourse.

William Angus

joined the 3ʳᵈ North Staffords, the reserve battalion of the North Staffordshire Regiment, as a newly gazetted second lieutenant.

We were stationed at Mablethorpe on the Lincolnshire coast, billeted in empty houses. We had our meals and such social life as there was. It was a friendly and courteous society although not intellectual. A good deal of time was spent on training 18 year old recruits but I felt very green beside senior men and men with active service experience. Because the manpower shortage was getting rather acute they decided that we would get Christmas leave and then join our battalions in January.

On 3rd April 1918 I crossed to France and reported to the 'K' infantry base at Calais. I joined the 2ⁿᵈ/5ᵗʰ North Staffords just outside Poperinghe. The 59ᵗʰ Division had been smashed to bits and was now being made up with a mixed bag, men who had been on leave, reinforcements from England, people from other units. There was poor cohesion, discipline was not good, morale was low and some of the men were not physically fit.

As we moved up a road towards the front we met refugees coming back, grey haired old ladies in long black dresses and black bonnets sitting on a pile of baggage on a farm cart drawn by a horse with a man walking at the side, or perhaps nothing better than a wheelbarrow between a man and his wife. One evening we were in a farmhouse and one of our officers went round the farmyard shooting at the hens with his service revolver until he killed one for our dinner. There was not much sign of the enemy.

Fred Horner joined up on

27ᵗʰ of August 1914. Everybody was enthusiastic. They thought the war were going to be over in a very short time. I went up and attested and when I come back she knew where I'd been, my grandmother, she were crying.

We had a very strict examination. They put us through the mill. And they even examined for corns on our feet. I tried to get in to the Mechanical Engineers. I got a promise, if I joined the Norfolks they'd transfer me. But it never occurred. I was stuck in the infantry.

We went by train from Norwich to Shorncliffe. The barracks were full up with the regular soldiers. Our lot had bell tents on the barrack room square. It was a blooming stiff training, get up at six o'clock, get into your shorts and run down to the sea, into the sea for half an hour and run back again. But the people of Shorncliffe were exceptionally good to us. We went to the Mayor's for tea sometimes.

The pub were very nice and at night-time there used to be the gamblers' school. They had two packs of cards and our sergeant major were a right trickster. We'd play pontoon and he'd be shuffling the cards underneath the table. He damn well beat us all the time. I got pally with an old chap from the next village, a big property owner. We used to go coursing with him with his greyhounds.

When we got to Aldershot, it were absolutely choc-a-bloc with the troops. You bunked down on the floor doing the best you can, but the training were exceptionally stiff, with manoeuvres, shooting, bayonet practice, a lot of mock battles.

John George 'Algy' Lawson recalls

There was recruiting at the barracks and in Parliament Street, York. An empty shop had been taken on. 'COME AND JOIN UP HERE'. When I was 19 I was there like billy-o.

I had a few pals in the Territorials. They got their uniforms straight away. But if you went in Kitchener's Army they just gave you a navy blue jacket, a pair of navy trousers and a badge to wear on your arm. I joined the Garrison Artillery in Burton Stone Lane, York.

Peter Mason

had worked for my Dad for two years. On August 4th war broke out and in a railway carriage at Middlesbrough, there were eight or nine men and I sat next to the quartermaster sergeant of the yeomanry, a man called Clive Mildred.

He asked, "What about it lads? It looks as if we're going to be wanted, there's going to be this war and we have to do something about it". I said, "If we are going to be invaded, if our navy gets beaten we'll be in trouble. Put me down for foreign service".

I wanted to go into the yeomanry. We went to the Talbot Hotel, Malton, for the medical then along to camp. Some of us had breeches and they were given a tunic. Some were in long trousers and they had to ride the horses. It was extraordinary really, a cosmopolitan crowd. Eventually we were all equipped with uniforms, service caps, spurs, puttees and then we started squadron drill, mounted drill, musketry training. We moved to Harlow in Essex. Our OC had been up to the War Office wanting to know when we were going to France, and during our Christmas dinner when the loyal toast was given, he declared that he'd said, "We'll go out on our hands and knees if necessary".

I was only a lad and my elder sister Alice was a trained nurse and she knew that I hadn't the experience of an older man with regard to the facts of life. She was afraid that if I got in contact with foreign women, I may contract some disease which would last me for the rest of my life and she did not want this to happen and I was very glad to have that advice.

We went by train then to Meuville. I was given about twelve of the men's water bottles to fill in the standpipes in the station yard and other people were taking the canvas buckets to water the horses. The yard was full of wounded men waiting for hospital trains. Some had badly injured legs and arms and bandages with blood. It made you sick to see so much of it. It upset me and I nearly fainted. They had to lift me into the truck.

Jim Melody was born in York in 1894. He joined up in

1914. I was fit, I used to do amateur boxing and I was a swimmer and a footballer, and a runner. I joined the West Yorkshire Regiment, 5th battalion. I was made because I was given a job of physical instructing at Strensall. There was just wooden huts, big stove in the centre and iron beds. The parade ground was all sand, hard work it was. We had to do our firing on the range. I acted as gym instructor because I'd done a course at Rowntree's. I was acting sergeant major.

Histon where Alf Peacock was born
(Alf Peacock Collection)

We went to the front at Laventie. We had to travel on those cobbles. We had some who had been in the Boer War and they'd say to take your boots off, and get your feet into cold water, maybe out of the ponds, and I did that regular and thank God I have good feet.

Alf Peacock's father Alfred Peacock, was

called up for a medical for army service. He was unwell but the nation desperately needed men. He was graded fit for service at home only. But within a very short space of time he found himself in the Ypres salient in Belgian Flanders with the 8th battalion of the Kings' Own Yorkshire Light Infantry.

Alf Peacock Senior
(Alf Peacock Collection)

Arthur Pierse was from York. He recalls

We were big-headed, young and silly, we wanted to kill the Germans. We didn't know the consequences and we wanted to follow the other boys to join up.

Arthur Pierse
(Borthwick Institute)

When I went into the recruiting office at Darlington he said, "Your age?" I said, "16 and a half". He said, "You're 16 and a half today and you're 18 tomorrow". We did all the grooming, cleaning the stables out, then water and feed before breakfast. We'd get the bugle sound and fall in for inspection. We'd ride round the ground bareback and then we'd get harnessed up for taking guns out onto the Knavesmire and drill.

When we left Newcastle we got nothing to eat, nothing to drink till we got to Le Havre. And there were 22 of us in one little tent and there was a big hall where we had corned beef and pickled onions and they were frozen to your plate. We were there a few days and then we were shipped up to the front. As we got nearer it was all desolate, all barren, and you could hear the guns going and soldiers coming down and ambulances going up all the time.

Chris Rogers was born in 1891 and living in Godmanchester when the war broke out.

We thought that it's going to only last about six months. Two mates and myself decided to join up. We thought we was going to have a nice uniform for nothing, and pay with it. Board and lodgings for nothing. But after we joined up, it was months before we got any khaki. We joined the 8th Lincolns, training at Grimsby. We had Mills hand bombs and they'd stick old sacks up on a linen line and fill them with straw. You'd got to rush forward and stick your bayonet through there, and make believe that's a German's body.

In September 1915 we marched to Ascot, through Maidenhead. That's when Lord Kitchener went at the side of us, on a white charger!

Victor Shergold joined

Victor Shergold, secondfrom right
(Enid Worrell)

the Territorial army, the Isle of Wight Rifles. I was nearly 17 when war broke out. I joined on the 15th August to go with the village cricket team. We did rifle training, and making clay bombs and throwing them. We were on the last trip of the Aquitania. We had to wheel the crew on board, they were all boozed up. We had to find a fatigue party to fire the boilers. We landed at Mudros [a Greek port on Lemnos]. Then they told me the papers had come to release me. I was under age! Victor Seely told me to go out, come back in again and I should be old enough. A lot of things were ignored.

Cecil Slack

got a letter from the 4th East Yorks Territorials saying I had been given a commission. But I had already joined as a private. I wrote to the Commanding Officer of the 10th Yorks, saying that I had now got a commission in the 4th East Yorks and wouldn't be turning up as private in the 10th. But then a squad of men came to my home to arrest me for desertion! It was all settled and in the end I got double pay – a fortnight's pay as a private in the regulars and a subaltern's pay in the 4th East Yorks!

The young officers that came along, they'd no skills at all. We expected when we got to France that we'd have three or four weeks preening, getting used to the environment. Instead we were in action in two days.

John Slingsby

was very anxious to go. In those days I thought one Englishman was equal to a dozen foreigners! We just did what we thought was our duty. We were proud at the fact that we were members of the British army.

Bill Smedley recalls

The German shops near us were absolutely finished. Windows broken, stock spoilt. In fact a friend of ours was a German violin maker, he came from Germany because he didn't like the military life, he was a quiet pacifist. A piano was thrown through the bedroom window, over the shop. I can hear it now, the strings and all the keys breaking on the road. The police couldn't do anything. Anybody with foreign names was for it. It was the commoner crowd. In more high class areas you wouldn't see that at all.

Harry Smith felt

It's class-ridden all through is the army, and we used to get annoyed when they'd send young subalterns that had been in the OTC, [Officer Training Corps] coming and telling you what to do, and we'd had nearly a year's experience of it. If you didn't do these things you were put on a charge sheet. We were on parade and something funny happened with a dog. I burst out laughing and I were put on a charge! I was only a PBI (poor bloody infantryman).

Soldiers marching
(Mike Race)

Ernie Nicholson remembers

Joining up at Helmsley. I went to Duncombe Park and there was a man, obviously a country lad, had a great big apple pie. And he gave us a little of it each. It was bitterly cold, the first night we slept in the saddle room. We kept changing billets, and the people in Helmsley were extraordinarily kind to us. There was a Mrs Barton, of gracious memory, on the roadside where the river runs, she had a little café and we'd go there for tea and we could eat as much as we liked for ninepence. And she had a room with a piano and she let us stay there at night for a singsong. That really was marvellous. We went to the Primitive Chapel and a lot of us went in the choir. We were going to sing Hymn of Praise, very ambitious, and we got word that we were moving. It nearly broke his heart, the choirmaster and organist. So one of our men said, "Look I'll play the organ for you. We'll sing the first chorus and you shall conduct". Then we went.

Harry Tate

joined the oldest regiment in the world, the Royal Scots.

I was transferred into the drummers and I went out one evening when they were having their practice and someone was trying to blow a bugle. In a jokey way I said, "I'll show you how to blow it George". He was trying to eat the thing. Well, he give me his bugle and I rattled off a few calls which I gained from being a bugler in the Boys' Brigade.

Next morning I was told to get ready for orderly room and I wondered what I was going to get. The drum sergeant was there and they marched me in in front of the CO, "Do you want to go in as a bugler? We've been looking for one for a long time".

Clarence Ward

went to Exhibition Square in York, Monday morning. There was 60 or 70 Kitchener's men. The doctor got you to touch your toes, and he touched your shoulder, that was your examination. I got signed in about quarter to 12, and we was on parade at half past two.

We used to march round York. We was in the nurses' home from the hospital, three storeys high, then moved to York barracks where we got some horses which had come straight from Canada. There was stables there where a horse trainer used to break horses in. Every day we'd groom them, water and feed them and then after breakfast we'd take them for exercise.

Clarence Ward
(Tony Wood)

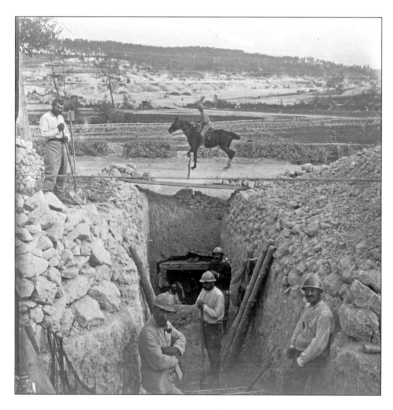

Trench building in Champagne
(Daphne Dench)

Colonel Innes Ware was a well-known figure in York, where he was born in 1896. He became the city coroner in later life. His father was a solicitor and paternal grandfather the vicar of Clifton.

I joined the first West Riding Heavy Battery, and did my first camp at Budden in June 1914, having received my commission. My first training was to learn how to take down and put together a breech block of a 4.7 gun. We were young fellows enjoying life, and war never crossed our minds. It's a beautiful sight, a 4.7 gun being hauled by eight horses. We had our drills on Saturday afternoons and took our guns out on marches. We had two non-commissioned officers from the regular army who trained us, and the territorial battery was quite a large affair because we had our own band and I got a full dress uniform as well as my khaki and equipment.

The commission read,

> 'You are therefore carefully and diligently to discharge your duty in the rank of Second Lieutenant or on such a higher rank as we may from time to time hereafter be pleased to promote or appoint you, of which a notification will be made in the London Gazette. You are at all times to exercise and well discipline in arms both the inferior officers and men serving under you and use your best endeavours to keep them in good order and discipline. And we do hereby command them to obey you as a superior officer and you to observe and follow such orders and directions as from time to time you shall receive from us or any superior officer according to the rules and disciplines of war. In pursuance of the trust hereby reposed in you given at our Court of St James the 30th day of May 1914 in the 5th year of our reign'.

On 4th August the brigade major from Northern Command was with us playing tennis, in the days when houses all had their own private courts. And a message came through and he said, "Young Ware, you'd better get your boots and spurs on and get down to the barracks and get the embodiment notices out". And by that night we had the whole of our men in the barracks.

We had horse buyers and they got the most magnificent shire horses, from John Smith's Brewery. My first job was to go to Selby, to the ordnance depot and collect the ammunition, which I did with Staff Sergeant Sadler who seemed to know all the pubs on the way from York to Selby. The other job which amused me was to take officers' swords to have them sharpened.

Harry Webb

had two brothers. We thought the war were going to come here so we enlisted. We had 18 to 20 in the army at the little village green. My brother went first. He got up to acting sergeant major and he got killed before he was twenty one.

They said we could join the Suffolks and we'd be able to get a transfer later on. But this old quartermaster sergeant said, "You'll get no transfer here". One of the blokes said, "What about a pillow?" So he said, "Do you want to bring your bloody mother with you or what?"

PALS BATTALIONS

General Henry Rawlinson and Lord Derby decided that men would be more willing to enlist if they were going with their friends and colleagues. All sorts of units were formed by workplaces, public schools, sports teams and associations. But the Pals battalions were formed in towns and cities, mainly in the North of England, and young men were urged to have pride in their home town. The first one was in Liverpool.

Harry Kilkenny

belonged to the Manchester Pals at Heaton Park. We had blue uniform and silver buttons, beautiful. We went together to Salisbury Plain early in '15 to get ready for the Somme offensive.

I got wounded early. Talk about a barrage, it was like cutting corn down. I was peppered all over with pieces of shrapnel and little bullets. I went into Number 8 General at Rouen, a convent hospital run by the sisters.

Ernest Brook was born in 1897.

I were 17. Joined the Bradford Pals. 18th West Yorkshires. It were a gimmick. The First Bradford Pals were oversubscribed, so they formed the Second Pals in the roller skating rink on Manningham Lane. Eventually they put us under canvas and there were wounded soldiers who said, "Whatever you do lad, don't go to France". Well of course I went. I was an officer's servant.

On July 1st, 1916 I was detailed off as a ration carrier. The first wave went over and we were in the communications trench going down and they sent a heavy shell. My pal got wounded. I got down to the front line and we were just going to get over the top when they were coming back. They says, "Get back, it's off". They'd cancelled it, they'd killed that many men with machine guns.

George Robinson was born in 1894 in Harrogate. He was a photographic apprentice on the Harrogate Advertiser in 1914.

I joined one of the Pals Battalions, at the Drill Hall at Harrogate. There were about 200 of us, Harrogate businessmen's sons and that sort of thing. On September 14th I received orders to report to the depot at York. We was in billets in the Railway Institute near the railway and had battalion drill on the Knavesmire.

James Atkinson joined

the First Bradford Pals in Bowling Park. [After the Somme] *there were seven left out of the whole battalion. I was very badly wounded. You were shot down as fast as you got up. I was lucky to be shot in the leg. If I'd been shot in the head I'd be finished.*

Arthur Britton was

born in Leeds but I joined the Bradford Pals because I was only 16. I couldn't join in Leeds because too many people knew me. I'd been a bugler, but in the army a bugler's called a drummer. You had to sound at night the Last Post, then Reveille in the morning. You got into all sorts of trouble unintentionally. I remember being stood in a ring. The old drum major in the centre said, "Britton we haven't heard anything from you lately". I said, "What would you like sir?" Immediately he turned red, pulled in two men and said, "Away to the guardroom with him", I was on a charge of insubordination. Apparently our drum major liked a drink or two and I'd said, "What would you like?" The titter that went round!

Bill Kershaw remembers

the Bradford Pals whilst I was still at school. The Bradford wool men had provided them with blue uniforms until there was sufficient khaki.

We'd see them marching across the top of our playground on these route marches. They used to go round Heaton Woods. No band at that time but they were usually whistling 'Viva la Compagnie', it was quite poignant because that would be 1915 and they didn't realise, and neither did we, that most of them had little more than 12 months to live.

Tom West explains

In 1916 was the Battle of the Somme and the Bradford Pals were absolutely annihilated. It was the blackest day that Bradford's ever experienced, blacker even than when Cromwell shelled it. [The two sieges of Bradford in 1642 and 1643].

Walter Aust

used to pass Paragon Station, and I saw that the latest blurb was 'HULL COMMERCIALS. 950 RECRUITED. WILL DEFINITELY CLOSE TODAY'. So instead of going home to my dinner, I went straight through onto Anlaby Road, got on a tramcar and went down to Wenlock Barracks.

"When were you born?" "1895." "You're too young laddie. Go and have a walk around the barrack yard and if you find it's '94, come back". So I came back and said it was '94, and I was in.

Tommy Oughton who was a miner, was born in 1896 in Wombwell.

They agreed to form a battalion at Barnsley, the Barnsley Pals. There was a recruiting meeting in the Wesleyan Room. I was on afternoons at work, and the meeting was at seven at night and the thing uppermost in my mind was going to that meeting. (As things turned out at the pit, we were waiting for empty tubs, some accident had happened). I went and it was a full house. They got talking about serious things, the Germans and atrocities that had been committed and a lot were exaggerated as we know now. Then Colonel Hewitt got up and talked about raising this battalion. And he was with us all the time, the regular colonel.

The town hall were about 200 yards from Wombwell station and we met there. It meant paying the fare from Wombwell to Barnsley. So I happened to say, "When t'other recruits have been going to Pontefract, they've been taken free. We're going for king and country, are we to pay our own fares?" Then this local man says, "Take this, that will pay your fares", and it were a gold sovereign. We set off for t'station and there's Railway Hotel. Beer was threepence a pint. I were teetotal but we went in and he served the others and I got five packets of Woodbines.

When the train pulled in, two first class carriages was in front of us. We thought, "We're riding first class for once". When they come for t'tickets, they found out and t'train must have been held up ten minutes or quarter of an hour. The stationmaster come. "I'll have to take your names", and we never thought no more about it. You can bet there were near a hundred to be sworn in.

It'd be a month after and my name were called out and there were a charge [about travelling first class]. *Had we anything to say? Colonel Hewitt had been there so we got some sympathy. I told him the tale and mentioned this man at Wombwell who give us the pound. Colonel Hewitt looked at the adjutant and says, "Well, if Mr so and so could afford that pound I don't think the railway company has owt to grumble about". And it passed off at that.*

Stanley Bewsher was born in 1895 in Markington near Ripon. He went to join the Accrington Pals, the East Lancashire regiment.

There was the usual hullabaloo going on, all the men wanting to go. I said to my pals, "Well we'd better join up hadn't we?" We had no uniform. We trained in civilian clothes. They fitted us with boots. We'd no rifles, we learnt to slow fire with broomsticks.

Stanley went to Port Said and Suez with the Pals but then back to France and the trenches.

The tragedy about these Pals battalions was that when they were decimated, on the Somme for example, whole towns and villages were affected. There were communities where all the young men went off to war and very few returned, and those left behind never really recovered from their sorrow and grief.

CHAPTER TWO

A CHILD'S EYE VIEW

Children who were too young to fight in the war were still affected, by fathers and brothers joining up, by Zeppelin air raids and by rationing.

Hilda Carr, born in 1903, was from a farming family in Wheldrake, near York.

We were playing down North Lane and a farmer came up to us and said, "Get yoursen off home as sharp as you can, there's a war started". The village hall was full of wounded soldiers, my mother had four at a time billeted on her. She used to say, "They're all somebody's lads". These lads had the blue hospital uniform on. My father wasn't well but he joined the Red Cross.

Zeppelins? We saw more than we wanted to see. The buzzers went, or the special constables would come round, "Get that light out".

In Wheldrake they seemed to all want to be volunteers and get the war over. My brother joined the West Yorkshires and he was wounded three times. He was on the Somme. I remember my father fetching me out of bed and my mother says, "I know my lad's wounded, he's waving a green flag on a hill". So I had to help my father to get her back into bed. I had to stop at home next day and all she could say was, "My lad's wounded". [And he was]. They sent word to say he was somewhere down south. They couldn't go, there was me younger sister and me at home. They got field cards to say he was a little bit better. He'd had his left ankle blown out, saving his officer's life from heavy shell fire. He got a citation and my mother had it framed.

Mother used to knit socks, and we had to do socks and scarves at school. My brother didn't like to talk much about the war, he said it was too horrible. My cousin George Britton, a tram driver in Alma Terrace, was the first Fulford lad to be killed, the second day the war started. He'd gone through the Boer War.

Farming just before the war
(York Oral History Society)

Village children 1915
(York Oral History Society)

Bill Kershaw 1971,
at Alhambra where he worked 1914

(Doug Kershaw)

George William Kershaw, known as Bill, was born in London in 1901 but moved to Bradford and became a call boy at the Alhambra Theatre. His father and uncle had been comedians in music hall theatre. He was too young to join up but recalls the war atmosphere.

The newspapers had tiny little maps of a very small area that seemed to indicate significant gains. We at home hadn't a clue as to the extent of the slaughter. Douglas Haig is one of my pet aversions. At the Alhambra, before conscription came in, occasionally you'd get somebody in the audience shouting out to these turns on the stage, "Why aren't you in khaki?"

Some of the staff, they'd be 40-ish, said, "I'd be off in a crack if I was younger." And then as the call for men got keener and they began to get apprehensive, they'd go to the central baths for medicals, and be drinking strong coffee, swallowing salt pills – anything to try and make themselves seem off colour so that they wouldn't pass!

I saw the young men gradually enlisting and showing up a few weeks later in their new heavy boots and ill-fitting uniforms and grinning. The whole atmosphere was one of inducing young men to join. These young girls singing, "We don't want to lose you but we think you ought to go". And another one, "On Monday she walks out with a soldier. Tuesday she walks out with a Tar". Actually I took part in one of these because, "On Thursday she's out with a baby boy scout", and I had to put a boy scout's uniform on and take her arm. We all walked across to the other side of the stage. Well that was worth a quid to me!

Bill Kershaw in 1920s

(Doug Kershaw)

I joined in that feeling. My formative years were in the heyday of the British Empire. Just as there was a sun in the sky there was a British Empire. And we British were the salt of the earth. I hung around Valley Parade where the soldiers were and when they'd fall out, we'd run for ice-cream sandwiches for them. I remember artillery being pulled onto Manningham Park by trams for gunnery drill.

Doug and Bill Kershaw 1962
(Doug Kershaw)

For the second half of the war I was down in Shropshire. One of the first jobs I had was carting cider to the harvest field for farm labourers. The war had drifted into its dreary endless state and there were land girls on this farm and elderly soldiers, artillery men who were being recalled to the army one by one, as the greedy sausage machine wanted them.

I was 17. I went to Ludlow where they were recruiting and I was always very young for my age. And this grizzled old sergeant says, "What do you want" "I want to join the army". "Have you got your calling up papers?" "No I haven't". He says, "Get off, if I see you around here again I'll kick your arse". Soon after that the war finished. I'd got a job as a grocery and bread roundsman. We knew the day before that the Armistice was going to be signed and that the church bells were going to ring at eleven o'clock. I delayed my departure until the church bells rang and then I set off. For my first few calls, I was the carrier of the news that the Armistice had been signed. It was a time of hugging and kissing and drinks and what have you, until, as I gradually got further round, the news had beaten me.

CHAPTER THREE

CYCLIST BATTALIONS AND MOTOR DESPATCH RIDERS

The British territorial force had four cyclist battalions before the First World War started, situated in Kent, Huntingdonshire, the North and the Highlands. The Army Cyclist Corps was formed in 1914, but infantry battalions also included cyclists for observation and reconnaissance. But bicycles were no use for the conditions in France, with its mud and pock marked roads, or Gallipoli and Egypt in the sand.

Bill Busby was part of

a cyclist battalion. When we landed in Gallipoli, they were no damn good and the whole lot were in a pile and left there to rot. An enormous pile of brand new cycles.

William Marsh was

transferred to the 2ⁿᵈ/1ˢᵗ Essex Cyclists. Every man had a cycle. They was army bicycles, green and heavy and they had a proper fitting on for your rifle.

Gaythorne Kettlewell joined up at 16 at the Drill Hall, Colliergate, York and was told to go out and come back aged 19. He later had an amazing experience.

Jerry [the Germans] was bombarding this particular part. I was cycling on an army bike to a canteen, and I saw this coin on the road. I picked it up and it had my initials GHK. The fact that I stopped there, I missed a direct hit on the canteen. I'd have been there! And I've never lost that coin. A pal said, "Why don't you put it on your key ring? I'll bore a hole in for you". And that's where I put it.

Tom West

joined up in April 1917. We went to a place near Hull called Skirlaugh then with the cycles down to Skegness. Some of them could hardly ride a cycle all the time they were in, they were useless, falling in the dykes at the side of the road. Now a motor-cyclist could work wonders in a battalion. He could be off with messages and get there and back quickly. But I know for a fact they weighed about 49lbs these bikes, they were shockers. And you put your rifle across the cross-bar. We were in the Northern Cycles, but they disbanded. The next minute we were bonded into the Northumberland Fusiliers and out to France.

Claud Hey in sidecar 1917
(Robert Hey)

Cycling unit in Champagne
(Daphne Dench)

Cyclists on Somme
(York Oral History Society)

A MOTOR MACHINE GUN BATTERY: A FIGHTING UNIT THAT HELPED IN THE GREAT ADVANCE

Motor Machine Gun Battery
(The Graphic 1915)

Motorbike
(Mike Race)

Alfred Terry was born in 1888 in Burnley. When war broke out,

The whole town was very excited. I was a keen motorcyclist and in those days there were very few. It was the equivalent of being a racing driver today. Somebody told me that the army was building up a signals' detachment and they would have despatch riders. So I wrote to the War Office in a youthful enthusiasm, and heard nothing. The regular army by this time were decimated after the Battle of the Marne and they were appealing for people to join. Suddenly I had a telegram telling me to report to Old Trafford [to join the Royal Engineers signallers' section]. *There was a sergeant there, "So you're one of them motorcyclists? We have a chap here to see if you're any good." It turned out to be a man who was, in much later years, BBC sportsman for the Isle of Man TT.*

There was a big drill yard but in the centre they'd built a great mound. And he went round and round this thing, and then suddenly up the mound and over the top. I followed, and I didn't know where I was going to land, but I landed at the other end, and we got round. "Right, sign here". Within an hour I'd seen the doctor, been examined, sworn in, got a shilling and I was in the army.

First of all you had to have a motorbike of your own, that ruled out most people. They bought it from you, I got £56, and you never saw it again. We got a train down to Fenny Stratford in Bedfordshire. And they brought a damn great BSA out for me. No kick starter, you had to push it and then flop on your belly on the saddle and trust to luck. It were bigger than me was this bike, a big, ugly thing. And I pushed it and it fired and I flopped on, and then gradually found my feet. Then we went to this big field with army tents. Some chaps come down with goggles round their necks and a uniform, I recognised one of them straightaway. He'd been a friend of mine in Burnley, a keen motorcyclist. So we had quite a reunion and he found me a place in a tent. We were given the rank of corporal. And then the fun started. We never had rifles, we had revolvers. We went to a proper unit of engineers and were trained in map reading and went out all over Bedfordshire. Then we were inoculated and they fainted by the dozen. You were riding one handed for a day or two. My friend was in front of me in the queue and he fainted, and he's six foot up.

There was a delivery of new Triumphs all in crates, and we were set to unpack them, and get them ready, and that's when we really got going. We rode down to

Southampton in a column, about December 1914. The roads were choking and we were covered in dust when we got to Windsor. In Southampton there was a boat, we slung our bikes aboard and it took us all night to get to Rouen. And we were all agog in case the war was over before we got there. When we landed we had to ride straight north towards the front, and it was beautiful. We stopped many times to raid orchards. It was a large and lovely country. But when we got further up, south of Arras, things began to look a bit mucky. And we got to a very nice little village called Bapaume and headquarters had set up its signals' division. We got a farm building. The upper storey was quite clear, so we made trestle beds out of timber, scrounged all over the place. We were the newly-formed Third Army, a mixed up crowd, excited, enthusiastic, and longing to help to win the war. As despatch riders, we had our own mess, and it was better than the sergeant majors' mess. We bought our stuff from the big canteens and looked after ourselves pretty well.

I remember going to Amiens in freezing rain, and very carefully bringing back a haversack full of stuff from this mail head, and finding to my disgust when I got back, there was the commanding officer waiting for me, because I was bringing some fish that they had coming by King's Messenger for their mess. All they were anxious about was this fish, it just shows you how they could use you, taking advantage of the opportunity!

On one of these trips to brigade headquarters, we were looking out over no man's land, and one of the fellows said, "There's a chap over there, he's never moved." You could see the head and shoulders of this German. It took them a day before it was quiet enough to get across. It was a German despatch rider who had run into mud, got stuck there and got a bullet through the head. He was riding a Harley-Davidson, a prized possession. They managed to get his body and this Harley-Davidson back. And we had this for several weeks, before the authorities found out and took it.

The war started at Mons and for me it finished at Mons. There was a road there, it'd been behind the German lines all through the war. I was riding along and I saw three fellows in rags, their feet tied up in sacking, a dejected lot. I said, "Who are you chaps?" They had been prisoners of war in forced labour in Germany and the Germans just let them loose. No provisions for them. I asked, "Where do you come from?" One said, "From Lancashire. I worked for John & Abel Terry." I said,

"That's my uncle." I told him I came from the same place. He was so rundown, he cried.

I had to go from Arras to Bapaume along the front line to GHQ, which was St Omer. It took half a day. At Arras the shellfire was very heavy, a lot of stuff flying around. And I was picking my way in the dark along ruined streets, and something hit me. I thought, "I've had it". Everything went black, I flew one way and the machine another. And I lay there quite a while wondering how bad I was, or what heaven was like. Then a voice down below, "Are you all right mate?" And I couldn't see anything. It was the remains of a shop. They'd backed a field gun into the ruins and this gun had fired, and blew me off. "Stop where you are, we're coming out for you." So they dragged me down into this cellar and they made tea and we swapped yarns, then they brought the bike back. It took four men to carry it down some steps, and examine it and see if everything was all right, then I went on my way.

Despatch riders 1915
(York Oral History Society)

CHAPTER FOUR

HORSES AND CAVALRY

From ancient times, through the Middle Ages to the days of Henry V at Agincourt, up to the 20th century, Britain has been renowned for its horsemanship in war. Its cavalry saw action in the Napoleonic wars and the French revolutionary wars, as well as Crimea in the 19th century. When the First World War began, Britain would again decide to fight with cavalry. But it was a different war and the cost to both men and horses was huge.

A government census of horses was taken in 1913. When war broke out, the army was able to acquire 140,000 in the first fortnight which had a devastating effect on farmers and small businesses. The army used dragoons, mounted cavalry, hussars, which were light cavalry, and the lancers. Although horses were initially part of the fighting unit, they gradually moved into use as transportation. In 1916 British and Indian cavalry again took part, this time north of the Somme. But they could not destroy German defences. By 1917 thousands of horses had to be imported from the USA.

Horses on York Cattle Market, which was taken over by army
(York Oral History Society)

The Veterinary Corps played a large part in the war. Over two million animals received treatment and eight million horses died. Britain lost a quarter of a million animals. And for the first time, medals were awarded to animals such as horses, dogs and pigeons for their part in the conflict.

At the end of the war, 85,000 horses were shot for meat, and half a million sold to farmers in France and Belgium.

William Angus recalls seeing the cavalry.

It was a glorious drive, a lovely September afternoon, bright sunshine. I sat on the front of an ambulance van beside the driver and had a grand view of all the stuff going up the line. Guns, ammunition limbers, [a two wheeled vehicle to which a gun is attached], lorries and cavalry. The cavalry weren't much use anywhere where there was a lot of wire. They were also subject to attack by machine guns. Their one real advantage was that they could move more quickly than the infantry and wouldn't get tired so easily.

Harry Kilkenny remembers

the Indian Cavalry and Bengal Lancers moving up. That was on the Somme. With them big beards hanging down and the swords and lances, what a sight they was.

William Marsh was

Household cavalry
(Mike Race)

put into the Hertfordshire Yeomanry. We went to Sevenoaks camp in Kent. We had our horse with a rifle one side and a sword the other. We'd trot first, then gallop, jump over jumps and then got to the stage of charging and that was the most exciting thing I've ever done. A row of horses stretching right across the field and when you got the command, you all charged and the bugle sounded and you shouted and swished your sword in an imitation of a real thing. It was wonderful but it would have been terrible if we'd been charging with machine guns firing at us.

They had cavalry in France in early 1914 but when I went in 1917 there was no sign of cavalry then.

Peter Mason explains

We slept behind the horses each night for two or three weeks, then moved to Sailly sur Lys [three miles from Bethune]. *We used to swim there on the afternoons.*

Horses on the plain with gun carriages
(Ann Firth)

We had to join a concentration of cavalry prior to the Battle of Festubert. There was thousands assembled together for a breakthrough if it happened. An aeroplane had seen that the German wire had been changed, on a long stretch of front which was needed for a breakthrough by thousands of cavalrymen, and the wire was much thicker and could not have been cut by our wire cutters. Even if our shellfire had destroyed a lot of the wire, there would have still been patches preventing the passing through of mounted troops. Thank God we were saved, it would have been a massacre. Instead of an order to advance we were retired back to camp. We saw signs of war because down the road came many of the Royal Irish Rifles wounded.

Harold Carson trained in Beverley then went to Salonika.

There must have been a thousand of us on the boat. We landed at Salonika and marched to the base camp at Summerhill. The idea was to stop the Bulgars coming into Greece. There was only a country lane, no good for motor lorries, so the Royal Engineers set about making a road for 70 miles.

First I went with two horses, Sal and Jock, and then two beautiful grey mules. They said, "You're going to be the Colonel's mounted orderly", and I was for the rest of the war. Best job I ever had. The colonel had two horses, he had a groom and when he dismounted, I used to ride forward to hold his horse. An infantryman got his shilling, but a cavalryman got one and threepence for buying polish for your saddle and suchlike.

In Salonika there were some wells, and we had a water boy. He had two mules and two cans on either side, and all day he did nothing but go and fetch water. We set off one night through Bulgaria, we were by the side of Lake Dorian and the Bulgars shelled us all day but fortunately they were poor shots! We marched along and came to a most beautiful valley. And across a stream there was a field of tomatoes on sticks. We hadn't seen a tomato for two years.

We were supposed to be going out at dawn one morning. The colonel ordered his horses for three o'clock. We were told to keep quiet, but then there was a lot of singing and shouting and the Bulgars had signed an armistice. We were a month in Bulgaria and it rained all the time. Groundsheets made into a cape is all we had. It was so bad that even the colonel went into hospital. I got that flu that was sweeping the world. Then I went on a hospital boat. That was heaven. I'd never had a hot bath in two years.

Frank Arnold was born in 1894 and grew up,

Farming and ploughing with horses. I joined the King's Royal Rifles at York barracks and they were decked out in all red ribbons. It was a battalion that was going to be farmers and farmers' sons. They couldn't get plenty so they had to open it out. I was sent on a course on shoeing. 14 weeks and I could get home every weekend. I finished out as a shoeing smith. Then to Aldershot, across to Dover, then on to Dickebusch in 1916.

Frank moved to 21ˢᵗ Yeomanry Rifles.

I liked to go to the horse lines, groom them and that. There was maybe 40 horses, two on each limber. One man and a breaksman. I had to take rations, and I stopped runaway horses belonging to the fusilier, they were galloping too much. I think my luck was in because I got in front of them, facing the horses. They were treading on my toes but they kept down the middle of the road or it would have been curtains for me as the pole end sticks out in front. The officer in charge said he would recommend me [for a medal] but I never heard another thing about it. I was breaksman with general service wagons, maybe three mile behind the line. We had some casualties in the first few days. There was my twin cousins, Crossleys. They was lined up out of Dickebusch Wood for rifle inspection and Jerry come across and dropped a bomb. Killed the twin brothers and sergeant.

Reg Gifford joined the Sussex Yeomanry, a mounted regiment in 1915.

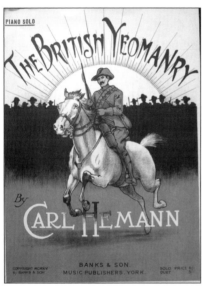

British Yeomanry sheet music
(Mike Race)

We'd do our training up in Coleford Park, a grand old place, all the old stables there and we were billeted in the surrounding villages. We did cavalry drill, we got the horses at Colchester. We went to Maresfield Park in Sussex and there we handed the horses in. We went out to the Suffolk Yeomanry but a lot were drafted to the infantry to make them up to strength.

Reg wore

The broken spur badge, that would be all the yeomanry regiments.

Wilfred Hunt

decided on the cavalry. It was a holiday I wanted. We thought it would have lasted about five or six months.

I went into the 10/18th Hussars. They used to get horses from Canada, remounts, and I got one with a very hard mouth. After a while, they'd get used to the various trumpet calls, and one time there was an order to charge. My horse turned sideways, it just wanted to go in front of everybody, it skittled two or three chaps who was kneeling down and firing blank pistols at us.

"PALS" in the R. F. A.

RFA postcard
(Mike Race)

Another time I went on a manoeuvre and we came to a river and he said, "Let your horse have a drink now". Well, my horse walked into the middle of the thing and laid down with me on it. Another time I had to take it to the vet because there was something wrong, and he said, "It's got colic", and he put something down its throat. He told me to walk it back. An old soldier said, "When you get over that hillside, get on and make it jump over every blessed hedge", and it cured it lovely. I was 18. And I was put into a camp there with the Warwickshires. I were more or less a mascot for them. They called me Yorkie.

Wilf then transferred to the infantry and went to the Dardanelles.

Arthur Bull

got the call up papers on Wednesday [6th August 1914]. *I was at the barracks waiting to get in. The yeomanry had a lot of moneyed people, farmers.*

I was in the 5th Cavalry Brigade. The officers were strict disciplinarians but they were gentlemen. They made the best officers, they knew how to treat men. The Duke of Beaufort, an honorary colonel, reviewed us at Sandringham. He said, "You're going to be sent where cavalry can be used".

We went to Gallipoli. We only had one destroyer to protect us. We were loaded with horses and most of the officers, and she was a big boat. The portholes had to be shut up at night, we weren't allowed to smoke on deck. The food we had was curried stew, mutton stew, thick porridge, no milk and sugar. The boat, the SS Minneapolis, was torpedoed [on 23 March 1916. The cargo and passengers were all saved and taken off by tugs and the destroyer. Twelve crew died].

Arthur Pierse recalls a cavalry charge.

As we were drawing into Lens, with our guns, we passed the Bengal Lancers riding their horses and the sergeant was leading with his flag. They made a full gallop. There were a hundred of them. Eventually as they got nearer and nearer to the Germans, one went that way, another that way, and I thought, 'There'll not be many of these come back', because the barbed wire entanglements were about 15 to 20 yards wide. It was terrible, you couldn't get through and I knew the horses couldn't jump them.

Eventually I saw one of the Bengal Lancers. He had the sergeant laid over the horse and it happened to be white. The blood was running down the side of the horse and that was the only one that came back in that attack.

John Pratt

stood in High Wood, and watched them down on my right, the Greys on their horses. They were doing battle and those poor horses just couldn't do anything, they were all entangled with barbed wire. At one period they were losing so many horses that rations come up at night time, not during the day.

I saw the cavalry. It was thick as smoke, explosions of shells and everything. They were slashing out, in blue tunics, brass plates on front and back, long red plume on the brass helmets and a brass chain. The Canadians were knocked out and they brought the cavalry in to block the gap. You couldn't see anything on my left for smoke. But I thought of those poor fellas. The chap that passed me was a big heavy fellow, on his horse with his plume.

I think he was about finished.

Tom Scott was born in 1895 near Leeds but he moved to York as a boy. His father had worked with horses.

That's where I get my love of horses from. In 1914, if you had anything about you, you volunteered. I tried to get into a cavalry regiment, they told me they were all full up. The war was going to end by Christmas they said! So I went to Hull and found Walton Street barracks where there was a riding school. It looked as though the Kaiser would overrun Belgium and France, and Britain naturally stepped into the breach.

They opened the door into the riding school and there's a grey mare saddled up. I got up and the mare knew all the orders, 'ride walk, ride trot, ride canter' and I managed to stick on. This was the York and East Riding of Yorkshire Yeomanry. They were billeting troops in Hull, and I had some relatives in a butcher's shop. They were delighted to see me.

Eventually we embarked for the Dardanelles. We were fighting the Turks and the landings were never properly made and they called the whole thing off and we went on to Alexandria. In Palestine the Turks were well armed. I was once on a cavalry charge against some Turkish guns. We came on these chaps over a ridge, they all opened up and we had to retreat until we got into a cavalry charge line and we charged these guns. They gave up resisting, threw up their hands and appealed for mercy. There was very little killing, it was more we hit them with the flat of the sword and took them prisoner. It was quite exhilarating.

We had a big problem with water for the horses. Near the coast we could dig down and come to water, which was brackish but fresh. We had canvas troughs and the engineers put up pumps and we'd fill these troughs with water. When the British advance got under way properly, the Turks were driven back. Gaza was pretty well fortified. That was dismounted action. While the battle was on, you're a foot soldier. It was pretty severe but not to be compared with France. The town of Gaza gradually fell and we went on to Beersheba.

Then they took our horses away and sent us to France. We became the 101ˢᵗ Battalion Mobile Machine Gun Corps. When we got rid of our horses, that was heartbreaking, we left them all in Egypt. Colonel Wilson was very upset and he got up some fund to try and buy back as many as he could because the Egyptians hadn't much thought for animals.

John George 'Algy' Lawson, bombardier on horse

(Peter Lawson)

I was wounded on November 5ᵗʰ 1918. I was very fortunate, it just missed my spine, a piece of shrapnel, and they called it a right buttock wound. The stitching was very crude in those days, although they looked after you well enough.

Oscar Bell was born in York in 1892. He joined the Territorials but left, though this meant he was 'on reserve'.

I wanted to join the 17th Lancers, but got my papers before then. When I reported on the Monday morning, my unit had moved. I went with a friend in the blacksmith's shop on the green at Acomb. Mr. Richardson was a horse dealer and farmer, right at the end of the village. He was buying horses and I started pulling shoes off and then dressing the feet and then fit a shoe. It didn't take me long. The hardest job was nailing one on. I passed out and I had to report to Lumley Barracks.

We went to York station, the horses, wagons and everything, straight for Southampton. I was a farrier to the Medical Corps Transport. In between any odd jobs, "Go here, go there, go and seek a vet", because one horse had a broken leg.

[As Oscar got nearer the battlefield] *I might tell you I had the wind up, that first do, because the shelling was all shrapnel, just like a big cloud burst, it all rained down. We went through Poperinghe. They used to shell it every day two or three times. We'd go into Ypres with our wagons collecting bricks to make stands for*

Supply wagons in France
(Daphne Dench)

the horses. There was two of us sat together on our heels at the side of a tree, and all of a sudden we heard an explosion. Talk about a hole! If it had been another three or four yards to the left it could have taken all the horses!

There was horse ambulances, great big clumsy things. They were well sprung, they'd go on rough ground, they shook you to pieces. We had tents in the wood for the ambulance men, and they'd spotted us from observation balloons, and we moved right up to the Arras front. It was very cold, by it was bitter. You'd got to be handy for drawing rations and to supply the dressing stations. If there was a convoy going out, I'd ride behind that. The sergeant in charge would be in front. It was banging [with shells] *behind our heels all the way. When I first went into Ypres, a few houses were damaged but they didn't half shell that place. I think the worst place I saw was Rheims. They had tried to clean it up, to make some roads through but there wasn't a brick standing.*

My job was exercising the officers' mounts. We got a horse down and it got its leg broken. I had to go and find the vet and he shot it. Then we had to skin it. You'd seen that many dead, you just got hardened to it. We went to Évin Malmaison collecting German wounded prisoners. I was driving the ambulance then because the man that was 'A' Section went down with flu. We lost a horse there with colic. I had to cut that up and after I skinned it, they got some straw and the civilians were hanging round, and the vet says, "They want this, it's good flesh". I give 'em all chunks of meat, and we had some.

The second battle of the Somme, we got a remount, and when they tried to pair it with this other horse, it kicked the front in, so they took it out. Next morning, everybody had to be on pins and needles, and they put this horse in. It was a GS [general service] *wagon, and the driver was on the box and sergeant major shouts to me, "Here, take this." I jumped onto the box, picked up the reins and whip and said, "Let her go". Just as we're going through this wood, a big naval gun went BANG. The horses was frightened. They just danced about. We went trotting up the line and I've never known so many guns in my life. Lines and lines of guns and new artillery.*

[Oscar was wounded a second time] *in May 1915 with a bit of shrapnel. My cap broke it, just at the front, and after that they started to get some tin helmets because you hadn't a chance with no shelter. I could have got in a mouse-hole that day. If it had been big enough I would have.*

Tom Bell was born in Warkworth, Northumberland. He joined the army at 17, telling them he was 19. He had been

a horsing man. We were at Bakewell, and we got 14 rear mounts. The lads knew nothing about them so I chose one, and we got it back next morning saddled up.

French soldier on horse
(Alf Peacock Collection)

Douglas Haig riding at Chantilly
(Daphne Dench)

Usually you prepared a mount and as soon as I got on its back I knew for a fact she'd never been broken, she kicked and bucked up in the ash yard and I said to the officer, "If we don't get out of here soon we'll have a ploughed field!" Major Foster says, "They tell me you can ride so I'm going to promote you to be my groom, you get another sixpence a day". That was a lot of money in those days!

We were in the heavy battery, 60 pounder guns. Eventually we went to France. In December I went from feather beds in Northampton to a tent with one blanket. When we left Southampton we had 200 horses on the boat, and the guns and two battalions of infantry. I was in charge of officers' horses. We went to a village just outside Doullens and in that village we lost 20 horses. Frozen stiff. There was snow on the ground, anything up to a foot deep when we got up the next morning.

In early 1918 I was Major's valet. I was in the 62nd division, we had six horses per team, a gun team with a driver. Then a gun team in the rear and a pair of horses in the middle. We finished up at Boulogne Wood and the battery was at the gun line. We were knee deep in mud. We had the infantry behind us and the Germans were coming over at one point and we were firing point blank at them as they came over, we killed thousands.

I went up in charge of the gun teams at night. I had a young lad, and 22 miles the other side of Cambrai, Jerry started shelling and there was heavy battery in a wood behind there. The roads were between the howitzers and the 18 pounders and Jerry dropped a shell right underneath the horse I was riding. Poor devil dropped down and I borrowed a revolver off an officer, and I shot this horse.

I was in Etaples when I got wounded. The French had lost about 200 horses, all dead in one corner, it was shocking. The smell was terrible. I dashed across and Jerry dropped his shell and buried me in the soil. I went into this dugout, there was sand bags, a sheet of corrugated iron with a bit of soil on and Jerry had dropped a pipsqueak shell and hit the sergeant major dead in the forehead and his brains were laid behind him. I dashed in and found out it was full of gas. We got in an ambulance down into Cambrai and I sat with my right leg across the seat. I was wounded on the 4th

Ypres

(Mike Race)

of November and I was in Birmingham by half past one on the 8th, sat up having eggs and bacon.

George Gledhill

(George Gledhill)

George Gledhill

was nearly four years on the Somme and Ypres. My job was with horses and mules, getting rations up to the lads in the trenches. I volunteered because others were. When you're young you don't think much about it. I was put on transport because I had poor eyesight, and I was left handed and they didn't allow men to shoot left handed.

We landed in France 15th of April, 1915. I can see now all the trucks and guns being swung up over the top and we got on with the horses and mules. I went out with a pair of mules I had for the first eight months. They would go anywhere for me.

George Gledhill 1998
(George Gledhill)

Ypres was a quarter of a mile of one big bog. How those men had managed to get these double sleepers across, I'll never know. There were dead horses and mules and wagons all the way up the side. One afternoon I was leading and we took these pack horses. We got to the end of this double sleeper track and it was a complete turn left onto a single track and you had to be careful. If you slipped off you'd had it. We just got nicely across, and there was a burst up in the air. We heard shrapnel dropping, but it didn't get any of us. I never hesitated, and I think animals know what kind of people are in charge of them. We got across and the others followed and we got our rations delivered and back out safely. We were kept busy. Wet cold nights, coming back with the horses and mules, we had to tie the poor beggars up to a rope. Just lifted them up, tied a hay net for them, and the mud was all they had to lie in.

I remember coming on leave after nine months. I had a pair of mules which I loved and I wanted to get back to them but I fell ill at home and never saw them again. I'd got right attached to that pair of mules. Then I had a pair of horses I got to like very much.

Frederick Sharp with mules in Egypt, 2nd left at back
(Peter Sharp)

Eventually George got a bullet wound in the thigh in 1916 which required hospital treatment.

Bill Hairsine had

always been breaking horses in and breeding them. Horses were part and parcel of our living. Young lads round about joined the yeomanry and suggested I did. It sounded exciting.

It was East Riding of Yorkshire Imperial Yeomanry. Everyone took his own horse but for those who couldn't, they found mounts for them. I was called up with my own horses. They were requisitioned and very cheaply bought, a sharp practice one could imagine. They only gave £50 for a good mare. It wasn't a fair price. Thoroughbreds were a bit more.

We went drilling in Beverley. We were billeted in public houses but we couldn't sleep in the bars while the pubs turned out at night. Then coast guarding became necessary so the yeomanry regiments nearly ringed the whole of the coast to keep a watch out to sea.

The east coast from Withernsea to Hornsea, that was our squadron's allotted place. They sent us back into the country to Kilnwick Percy and we did the mounted training there. My own horse didn't go abroad. It was classed as 'left in England'. It was a very nice mare but she couldn't walk fast enough. She was a coach bred animal. I was sad to lose her, but I got two other mounts. The training was as much for the horse as ourselves. New Zealand and Australia sent a tremendous lot of horses over, I got one of those in the finish. We were drafted to different places along the coast, doing troop drill, musketry and horse management. The army way of managing horses was different to ours.

It went on for months till the shelling of Scarborough. We were mobilised in case of an attempted landing or sabotage. We hadn't swords then, we had a rifle on the back and bayonet in an old fashioned rifle bucket. We were inspected by King George himself at Newcastle, a big parade of all sorts of troops. We were training on different heaths and sand. Then spent three or four weeks at Filey drilling on the flat wide beach. They could get the whole regiment abreast at low tide.

Robert Headley in centre. 1916
(Geoff Headley)

Mr and Mrs Headley in 1970s
(Geoff Headley)

Robert Headley tag
(Geoff Headley)

We had an old fashioned sword in the early stages, for when knights stood still and slashed at each other. The impact of a charge was to be at the gallop and use his sword as a spear. It's very manoeuvrable, more than a lance. We got the new sword, the cavalry bucket and a long bayonet.

Robert Headley was born in 1893 and was a horseman when the war broke out. He was initially exempt, but when he found out that his brother Tom had joined up, he wanted to go to France.

I come to York and this chap saw me papers. He says, "Horseman. Royal Field Artillery driver." And that was it. I'd passed my riding and driving and I was ready for off.

I went to Salisbury Plain and that was when we started war, riding and driving. And then to France. We were just led down like cattle in the bottom of the ship. It was snowing and freezing like the devil and it went on for about six weeks. We were in Bray then went upline into the ammunition column. We supplied batteries, supplied infantry and we worked for the engineers. My job was lead driver.

The first time I went out with a load, I was frightened to death. I could hear guns and see them flashing. When you couldn't get wagons through, you'd take pack horses. But we had mules at finish. You had to cross country sometimes, but if you got onto a road, that was where they used to shell mostly, it was a devil to get through. You risked your life every minute. There'd be maybe 40 horses in a sub section. Six horses pulled the limber, and they come down to four.

And when you're shifted on rail you had ordinary cattle wagons and you tied horses at the end. You were made to sit in the middle. We did gallop through Ypres. What frightened me most was going over a pontoon bridge. I used to take my feet out of the stirrups and I couldn't swim. It put the wind up me. You had to ride them across bridges or else they would never have gone. And

Arthur Aylett's cigarette tin

(Tina Milson)

we saw that retreat of civilians, the road was blocked completely with the few things that they could get in a wheelbarrow or a perambulator or on their back.

We didn't mind turning out at night and packing ammunition, that was what we'd gone for, but cleaning harness and grooming horses, it broke our hearts. The harness was just rough and ready. The brass buckles they could see a mile away. It was ridiculous. But they didn't value men's lives then. You were gun fodder and that was all. I always said, if a shell had your number on you would get it. But I prayed.

Arthur Aylett was born in 1893 at Cherry Burton near Beverley and spent all his working life on farms.

Arthur Aylett 2nd left at reunion
(Tina Milson)

In January 1914 I joined the Waggoner's Reserves. I got a badge [in silver metal with a horse's head]. *We had horses on the farms and we used to go to Market Weighton and Pocklington shows to drive on a figure of 8 for prizes.*

The competitions were a celebrated event and in 1913 there were 50 teams competing, with over 2000 spectators. This training was ideal for what they would face in France. Unlike other Territorials, the Waggoners' agreed to serve overseas when they joined.

Sir Mark Sykes of Sledmere, [in East Yorkshire] got 1100 of us. He gave us a pound to be on the Waggoner's Reserves. They called it the 'silly quid'. They came one Saturday night to Market Weighton to recruit. I joined up, then I was on a farm, we was harvesting and the postman came into t'field to give me the calling up papers. We had to go to Bradford. They marched us to the station, brass band afore us. All our horses and pontoons got on board ship straight to France.

We marched to Mons and the Germans was coming in at other end. So we had to turn round and retreat. We had trestle wagons with pontoons on top. We landed at Campagnie Forest. We was cut off, no food or anything for a week. All we had was fruit we pulled off trees. We got out of the forest and pulled in at a place, the Germans came past during the night. Our major says, "Keep quiet". We was on the side of a hill and down below there were the French infantry and the Germans collared them all.

Arthur Aylett's medals
(Tina Milson)

Arthur Aylett
(Tina Milson)

When we turned back from Mons, we put three pontoons into t'river and the Germans had a range on it and they smashed them all up. Next night we went five mile up river. We took the bridge down there. There was hundreds went over. They were marching but that was a job with the trestle wagons. Horses shoved at one another because they could see the water. After that we got to know to gallop. We weren't allowed but we used to do it across the bridges. I was in the second train, that was 15 pontoons, 50 wagons. We had six horses on a team. My brother was the leader. I was a wheel.

Then we landed at Rouen. Sir Mark Sykes came out to find us. We were reported missing or captured. He came and spoke to us, asked if there was anything we wanted. Oh yes, we wanted shirts, socks, tobacco, cigarettes. He said he would send it and he did. We set off and landed up near Paris, we bridged the River Seine in different places and we used to take sappers up to the front. They was mining underneath Germans' trenches.

There was some gas, and soldiers laid dead both sides of the road. We had to run over the soldiers with wagon wheels because you couldn't miss them. That was worst I ever saw with gas. They gave us muslin with cotton wool with some stuff on it. Used to tie it round our mouth and nose, fasten to the top of our heads, you'd think everybody had toothache.

We landed at one place and we couldn't get up this hill, our horses kept slipping. And a farmer yoked his cattle and he pulled our wagons up. Then we went to the Somme. There were horses and men on both sides of the road. Horses had been there five or six days or more. Legs were out, blown up. All you could do was smell dead. It's a sickly feeling. We was up one night, and there was a bayonet charge. It was soldiers five mile away screaming and shouting. By, it was terrible.

In 1916 we could go back. I says, "I'm going back onto the farm". My brother took £15 and had a month's leave and they shoved him into the Duke of Wellington's infantry. He was buried with this shell and lost use of his finger and thumb.

I went onto the farm and I got married. They kept calling me up but the farmer kept going to tribunals and getting me off. And before I had to go, the war stopped.

The Sledmere memorial reads,

Lt. Col. Sir Mark Sykes, Bart. M.P, designed this monument and set it up as a remembrance of the gallant service rendered in the Great War 1914-1919 by The Waggoner's Reserve, a corps of 1000 drivers raised by him on the Yorkshire Wolds farms, in the year 1912.

Sledmere memorial
(Don Bowerman)

The Waggoners' Reserve Monument
of 1920 at Sledmere
(Mike Race)

CHAPTER FIVE

THE WESTERN FRONT

Any romantic view of war or a sense that men were fighting for honour and glory soon dissipated once they got to the Western Front. Soldiers could expect to be in the front line for several days, then on reserve for several days, where they would spend time cleaning weapons, training, perhaps marching, and then they would get a few days' rest behind the lines. Then it all began again.

There were many long battles during the war, but those which stood out were the First Ypres in 1914, Second Ypres, Loos and Festubert in 1915, the Battle of the Somme which continued for much of 1916, Vimy Ridge, the Third Ypres and Passchendaele in 1917.

Edwin Lofthouse recalls,

Just imagine a military band marching down the street in bright uniforms and playing stirring tunes. One's eyes took in the regular pattern of the uniform and the precise steps of the soldiers, and one's heart started beating to the music, so that one's feet were marching along with the soldiers. In this atmosphere the crowd was drawn to some central recruiting place and on the platform were some beautiful ladies who, as their part in the war effort, were prepared to give every man who joined a kiss. This was the path which eventually led me straight into hell itself.

I was born in 1899 at West Hartlepool. We moved to York where I went to Park Grove School and I enlisted at Fulford Barracks. I was sent to the KOYLI's [King's Own Yorkshire Light Infantry] barracks at Pontefract.

In France we were living in trenches with a blue sky overhead or an old corrugated sheet for a covering, or we were laying out in the open in shell holes half full of water or we would be standing in a bay of the trenches looking out into no man's land. Here we were, a band of men who lived in those trenches for days at a time, expecting every minute a whizz bang or a bullet would be dropping and would send one to Blighty, or would add another name to the already long list of unfinished life beneath us, whose dreams of a better world had ended so abruptly. Yet in spite of all this, a spirit of comradeship and good humour kept us alive and we could joke with one another, in the words of [the cartoonist] Captain Bruce Bairnsfather, "If you know of a better hole, go to it". We could not go to any pictures or dances. No wireless, no shops, money had no value to us in the trenches. The rations were brought up, bully beef, biscuits, sometimes cheese and jam, a smoke and a tot of rum. Yet what was it all for? Those men believed that they were there to do their duty, a task which had been allotted to them in order to bring the war to an end and secure a peace which would end all future wars.

Charlie Minett

travelled over the Channel at night, 18 hours on that boat before we could land because a German submarine was chasing us backwards and forwards. But we landed at Le Havre and went to St Martin's Camp, up on the cliffs and it was freezing sharp. Then we went up to Voormezeele near St Eloi [in the Ypres salient]. *That was where we had our first casualty. We got the doctor, he says, "You can bury him, he won't be no good". We dug the hole and we see him start moving. A bullet had hit him in the nape of the neck and just knocked him out!*

Charlie Minett
(Borthwick Institute)

There was no billet, only little dug outs in the ground. When we was at Ypres all we did was sit on a fire step and pull a waterproof sheet over us and sleep in the pouring rain. The German trenches in those days, they was a rabbit warren under the earth. They went down 30 feet.

You might have a day when all you'd hear is a few rifle shots. But then you might be nice and quiet and all of a sudden all hell would break loose. Before the offensive on the Somme, it was a living hell. They must have had all the guns from the British army there. It was enough to burst your eardrums.

I went home, got married in December '17, and then in February 1918, I went out again.

When we left Felixstowe, there was 250 of us, from all sorts of regiments. These young officers tried to bully us and get us into formation but they'd never been abroad. The majority of us was going up the road arm in arm, singing and hollering. One of these young officers lost his temper and tried to put us in shape. Sergeant Major Snowy Adams said, "If you want to get these men on that train keep quiet, otherwise you might not be alive. You're dealing with men who've been out there and fought in the trenches. Not with recruits."

The majority of the boys hadn't got any fear, they wasn't old enough to fear. I was only in France a month and I was wounded and back home again. At three o'clock in the morning the Jerries broke through. We had a call to say we'd got to spread ourselves out across the fields and dig ourselves in with a little entrenching tool. I got down on a field roadway and there was a sniper from the communication trenches. That bullet went in the thick part of the arm. It broke all the ribs, went through the lung, the frothy blood was running out of my mouth and I see the doctor shake his head. I said, "I ain't gone yet. I'm one of the old bulldog breed."

They said they wasn't discharging me but sending me on to a farm to work to recuperate, down in Suffolk. I says, "My father is a bailiff between an 800 and 900 acre farm. Why can't I go with him? I'm a young married man, I've got two homes to keep". I took out two half crowns and laid them on the table in front of that officer and he picked them up. He phoned through to Mr Doggett and he accepted me. I wasn't a fit man but I worked on the farm for eight months. When the war finished I went to Thetford to get my discharge. They granted me 8s 3d a week pension but I never received it. After a fortnight they sent me £52.10s, take it or leave it. And it took me five years to get over this wound.

George Ashurst recalls

In between the lines was a little row of cottages. There was even stuff in the cellars, like turnips. There used to be a real scrap for these cottages. We got them at the finish and Jerry was in a house near us! We had a fireplace and a chimney and we were cooking our dinner in a big pan, bully beef and potatoes. Of course there's smoke coming out of the chimney and Jerry must have guessed what we were playing at. He opened out on this chimney. Bricks and soot came down, filled this pan and knocked it all over the kitchen. That was our dinner! So we run in the back and we shouted and cursed. That wasn't the front line. That was just an outpost!

In the trenches we had to keep bailing out if it rained. We fried bacon and made tea by sticking a peg in the side of the clay and hanging a canteen on it by the handle, and then putting pieces of wood under it. You don't make smoke, that was one of the biggest targets for artillery, so it took an hour to make a canteen of hot water.

Lea and Perrins sauce
(The Graphic)

Gong Soups advert
(The Graphic)

Advert for periscope
(The Graphic)

We cut a hole in the sides of the trench and we used to curl up in it. While I'd been asleep like this my feet had dropped out and when I woke up it was freezing. We got back to the village and in the morning you should have seen my feet. They placed me against the stove. It was frozen feet. They cut my shoes off and then I was in hospital. I had to catch a train and go to Boulogne. I was on the luggage rack on top. It was made into a bed. There were four in a compartment. My head was right against the little window and I was laid there, no pain, and nurses came in now and again to give us a drink. I was with one who was sick and two wounded. I could see the rain and snow battering on the window. And I thought, "I'm here with two dead feet but I'm better off than them poor buggers up there".

We got to the Canadian hospital. It was a hotel up on the cliffs. When you've frozen feet you sleep in bed with your feet cocked up and no clothes on them, because you can't bear them once they start to recover. The doctor used to come round every morning and rub your toes. All the time he was shoving in a little needle. He knew the minute you reacted that you were getting better. There was a little fellow in the next room who had to have both his feet off. He said, "I don't care, I've finished going up yonder." I thought, "But two feet, it's no joke". Gangrene had set in. We had to go down a long corridor on hands and knees to the toilet at the bottom. I'd be going and another fellow would be coming back and when he got to me he'd go, "Woof, woof!" The nurses used to laugh like anything.

Going into the line

(The Graphic 1915)

In 1915 I was badly gassed. I thought I was dead and so did everybody else. They issued NCOs with red flannelette and black elastic and you'd to fold it about four times, stitch the elastic on and round it would go. But when the gas came it was all still in my haversack. We never bothered. It looked like yellow smoke so we hopped it. We were running as fast as bullets. We reached Ypres and some French soldiers were giving us salt and water. We were gasping for breath and this water wouldn't go down. We got on the road to Poperinghe and there was a ditch at the side and we laid down. Then an ambulance picked us up. We couldn't eat, couldn't drink, couldn't smoke, that was a horrible thing.

They took us to Bailleul and we went in front of the doctor and he pinned a label on us, 'Down the line'.

They would only give us a cup to spit in and a drink of milk. I was sweating, I couldn't lift my hand up. Then one morning the doctor let me have a thin slice of bread and butter and I got it down. The following morning the nurses come to fix me up, I'm away down to the docks and rushed on the boat. They put us down below. I never felt as queer in all my life. They took me up on deck. That was what I wanted. I was laid looking out at the back of the boat. I said to the officer, "Do you know there's a red light following us?" "Yes, it wants to do, it's our escort."

Walter Stubbings was born in 1895 near Cambridge.

There was an appeal in our village for recruits and we thought we ought to get in and be there at the time we were needed. I was a lance corporal and promoted sergeant a couple of months later. We went to Le Havre on an old cattle boat. A lot of the boys were seasick. We got off and had to march to the camp. We were issued with some animal's coat like sheepskin and the smell was terrible.

When we got to Ypres, it was a beautiful day and the whole of the market square was full of stalls. The town had been blasted and Jerry had been driven back and we thought everything was going lovely. Two days later the place was finished off properly. Market square was littered with dead and horses with their insides out. When we got into the front line, all you could see was a huge sheet of flame from Ypres.

I remember we camped at a little village. It was a lovely afternoon and the troops were playing football and running about and all of a sudden there was a huge green cloud come up over the tops of the trees. We couldn't make out what it was. The next thing we saw were Algerian soldiers coming down the road, they'd left the guns and the other vehicles behind and they'd got away on the horses and they'd got handkerchiefs round their mouths. Then we got the order, "Gas". We'd got no protection, our instructions were to dip our handkerchief in water, urinate on it and put it round your mouth.

In the trenches, an hour before sunrise you get the order to 'stand to', to be on the alert. Then you stand down when it's daylight. You'd have sentries at a certain distance apart, and other people would be sitting on the fire step, eighteen inches high. You had the daily routine. Some troops were working, building up the trench, repairs and that sort of thing or if there are dugouts, having a nap. You had to clear the rats out first. We had raiding parties going out over the wire at night. They got suspicious about Jerry preparing for an attack and they wanted the information, whether the wire was secure.

Street scene, Clermont, children playing regardless of war
(Daphne Dench)

I'd lost my platoon commander. I had to take charge of the platoon and the first wave that went over. We were to form up at three o'clock and the first barrage would be on the German wire. We had to move forward 50 yards. When it lifted onto the support trench of the Germans we were to jump in, which we did very successfully. We captured a whole lot of prisoners. Once we got in the trench, a lot of them gave themselves up. The battalion on our right was the Black Watch and they got the brunt of the German machine guns. They were blasting them to hell.

Walter got the DCM for this action.

The CO said, "The brigade wants you to go back to England and take an officer's course". I wasn't interested but they talked us round. I was posted to 5th Officers Cadet Battalion at Trinity College, Cambridge, and commissioned to the Bedfordshire Regiment as second lieutenant. Then I got wounded and sent home and I went back again. At Lens I had to take charge of a working party to do some repairs. I'd only gone about a couple of hundred yards when a whizz bang came down and dropped just outside the trench and a great lump landed on my foot. After I got over the wound I was sent on a PT course

British soldiers with gas maks
(Mike Race)

and then appointed PT officer for six months. Then back to Cambrai. But I got the flu in November. I didn't come home until March 1919. I'll never forget it. When there's anything on the television, and Armistice time, you relive all those things. And you think of your pals cut off at the age of 18, some even younger.

Arthur Britton was

billeted in this dilapidated barn and I had my 48 hour iron rations in a white bag and it contained bully beef, some hard biscuits and an oval tin divided in the centre with tea and sugar. This barn was infested with rats and I thought, 'I'm not going to let those rats get my iron rations, I might be wanting these very badly'. There was a long beam, and I got a bit of string over this and I suspended my rations about five foot above floor level, and I laid down underneath. I woke in the early hours by a bump on my chest. My eyes slowly got accustomed to the dark, and right along this beam were a long line of rats. The rat nearest to my string come down it, put his teeth into the canvas bag, shook it, and eventually it came away. And the rat dropping on me was the bump. They were queuing up, and doing it in an orderly manner. We'd one or two people in the trenches that had their ear lobes eaten away. You were so exhausted, you just couldn't keep your eyes open any longer and the rats seemed to actually like the lobe of the ear.

Ernest Moorey

Ernest Moorey on right
(Chris Moorey)

went over from Folkestone to Boulogne. We got off the boat about 11 and went into a camp on the cliffs and it was a long march with a full pack and about 250 rounds of ammunition.

We got a lay down and most of us were marching about before three o'clock the next morning, it was so cold. They moved us up in cattle trucks to a farm amongst the straw which was luxury. But another couple of days and they took us up near Poperinghe, in London buses. There was no trenches, just open land. And we marched in artillery formation and casualties were very heavy. We were ordered to dig in with our entrenching tools. Then to our surprise we were ordered to retreat into a sort of wood, and spent a night in pouring rain.

Some of the lads started to light little fires to boil the dixies and one stray shell came over and killed one of the chaps. There were seven of our lads, then 200 of the rank and file either killed or wounded the first day! I was just a week out from Newcastle.

Ernest recalls an attack on 1st May 1915.

A shell must have burst just above us and it really wiped out the whole of my section. There was dead and wounded lying in a pile. Three of my school pals from Helperby were killed instantly and the other two died two days after. One laddie from Bedale was laid by me, badly wounded, and he died.

Ernest Moorey
(Chris Moorey)

I was wounded in the left shoulder. When I came to, I lay in the trench for a couple of hours. I jammed my balaclava helmet into the wound to stop the flow of blood and I could feel the artery thump, thump, thump, and I thought I'd had it.

I got the last seat in the ambulance, hanging with the right arm. They gave me a jab and took me to Bailleul. Then on the Red Cross train, I was in the top tier, and I was in Manchester for eight months and then in a convalescent home. The surgeon, Dr Platts, reputed to be one of the best, his skill must have saved my arm

Ernest Moorey 3rd from left at back, and colleagues

(Chris Moorey)

Ernest's father Edward Moorey built the war memorial in Helperby.

A lot of the village lads had joined up eventually. It was so sad. I read the names on the monument and it makes my heart ache. What good did it all mean?

John Blakeway recalls

I was only in the trenches a short time. We went through Rouen up into the lines, in one of the villages we were two nights in bivouacs, going up for an attack on 15th September. The first day the tanks were used, I saw those in front of us. We'd had a lecture the night before from a doctor. He said our water bottle was our best friend if we were wounded.

Early on the 15th it was misty. At the attack we went across no man's land. We were told that if there was any turning back, we'd be shot. There were dead and wounded lying about. We had to leapfrog over the trenches. We were weighted down. I had three bandoliers of bullets, pockets full of hand grenades. We had bandages, rations, a little entrenching tool (it wasn't much good). We went down into the German trenches then met machine gun fire. I went into a shell hole with a Lewis gunner and he was shot through the wrist. I had a spare bandage so I wrapped it up. He went and then before I knew where I was, I was sailing in the air. I was hit in the head. I didn't lose consciousness, but was concussed. My eyes cleared and I felt blood running down my face. I took off the helmet and a piece of shell was stuck through the front.

I bandaged myself up best I could, threw all my tackle off except the water bottle. I set off, and got on a mound and must have lost consciousness. I didn't know anymore until I was being carried to a field ambulance on a stretcher. I remember being in an ambulance train then to the operating theatre at Rouen.

Next day I was on the way back to Harfleur and a hospital ship to Southampton. I recovered but had a big gaping hole in my skull. I got Christmas leave at home in Tollerton then they drafted me to Sheerness to a small naval barracks. They were drafting them out again to France. I got into trouble, I went out with another lad and the military police caught me. I had to go before the colonel and he was told I was wasting time and "eating good men's rations". He says, "Find him some work to do. He'll have to keep out of mischief". But then I was discharged.

I started to work on the land, helped to get the crops in. But there was an operation for head wounds. I had this bone graft, they took a piece off my leg for it. Dr Morrison was the chap in control. We were more or less guinea pigs.

Percy Fuller was born in 1894 in Soham. When he enlisted in 1914,

We went to Bury and they were full up with recruits and they give us some blankets and we had got somehow to lay out in a meadow. It was getting winter time and stood out in the middle of the meadow was a tub and that was what we'd got to wash in. It was so thick with soap suds you could put a stick in it and it wouldn't fall over. They never changed it.

I was a sergeant early. I was always rather keen. I was in the army to fight the war and that's all I thought of. And I done all my best to keep the army regulations. We went to Armentieres. The sergeant said, "We're going out on listening patrol tonight, are you coming?" "Yes it's what I came down here for". We crawled on our bodies and we laid in a round circle with our feet touching each other. All our toes was in the middle, you just got a tap of your comrade's toes and let him know you seen him. It was rather exciting.

We would be 150 to 170 yards apart, we could hear the Germans. One sergeant wouldn't come and Sergeant Noone said, "As soon as you get back there, that bloke will want to know everything. Don't you tell him nothing! If he hasn't got the guts to come out, don't let him pick your brains". Sometimes you went out as a fighting patrol, there'd be about 16 of you. But an ordinary patrol was one NCO and three men. There was a lot of shelling and a lot of search light beaming all

Percy Fuller
(Judith Reynolds)

night long. You'd move like a snake. Sometimes the Germans would walk right by us. That was nerve wracking. We lay there clutching each other but just before they came to where we lay, they dispersed which was lucky. We went in and out regularly from Armentieres. Later on, we went to the Somme.

We were ready to go, and a sergeant of the East Yorkshire regiment came running in to the trench, "Every man out". This man meant his own regiment but when you're all standing there, then every Tom, Dick and Harry were ready to go out. You was so sewn up with nerves, so highly strung. I had to take my gas mask off and I had to shout because I had no men left. That's where I got my gas. If I hadn't took my helmet off I wouldn't have had a man left in the trench at all. I still maintain if we'd prepared to go forward and take advantage of that crater, I'm quite sure it would have shortened the war a lot. But we did what we were ordered.

James Dunnett

had leave and went to Wadham College at Oxford on a four month course for a commission. I worked hard because I had no education really. They posted me to the Duke of Wellington's.

I used to do patrol work. My batman lived near Nottingham, he was double my age, he used to come with me, and three other fellas. I led one or two attacks. We went onto Hill 60 for a spell, and then the La Bassée front. I'd take a party to help the engineers in tunnelling.

Not long after I got back, we attacked a place in front of Albert. With my platoon, I actually captured a redoubt. We had to say, "Come out with your hands up", and 57 of them came out! I wanted their maps and compasses to send to battalion headquarters. I sent them into Henencourt Wood, and I posted two or three men there. Then a bomb hit me in the arm. I went back to the company headquarters, they gave me a good stiff whisky, sent me back in the Red Cross van to first aid, and I had an operation to get it out the next day.

I stayed on that front until we marched in Germany. After the war finished, I was acting captain but I couldn't carry a captain's rank because there were too many in England. The chaps that had had a cushy job in England, they came out there and took over. I got the Military Cross and Bar. They had recommended me and I didn't know anything about it.

Fred Horner

went on a forced march to Armentieres and 13 men died on that march. It was a bloomin' hot day, and you couldn't get any breath, and the poor devils were falling like nine-pins. It was all right for the officers because they had horses. In Armentieres we got billeted in an old corn mill.

I was a pretty good shot, and they put me on sniping. And I fixed a lot of rifles in a trench on a certain position where I thought the Germans would come over, and every so often during the night I used to let these off to see if we can cop anybody.

Then our captain asked if I'd like to apply for a commission, and I thought, "They're all public schoolboys", and I refused. And he sent me down to an army school behind the lines to train as a bombing instructor. We'd get the bombs delivered in an old hut. I'd take a squad of men to detonate them, but anybody who were rough putting a detonator in, it could go off and the whole blooming lot would go up. I had to take the recruits on live practice, and there's only five seconds by the time you pull the pin out to the time it explodes. And one dope hit his hand at the back of this trench and dropped the bomb! Luckily I were able to snatch it up and throw it over the trench before it exploded.

I went to Loos. We lost loads of men down there. It were French's [Field Marshal Sir John French] fault. He didn't bring the reserves up quick enough. It were bad organisation. Those people had taken the trenches and got massacred. It were so bad that several of the lads went mental. There was a little wood copse behind our lines, and there were any amount going and playing and dancing about. They didn't last five minutes! If there weren't any cover, you'd had it.

The Prince of Wales come up to the front line trenches and it's the only time I'd seen any generals. He picked up a periscope and he had a look at the German lines, put it down, walked along the trench and went. And if you'd read the press after, you'd think he'd won the war single-handed.

We marched a fairly long distance, to an old broken down village, and stopped there for a meal, and just as they were dishing the bully beef out, a blooming shell come and we copped it there, all the bunch of us. I got hit in the left thigh and in my shoulder. I made a dive for this dugout. And I bandaged my thigh and asked these fellas if they'd bandage my shoulder. I made my way onto the road and I found a dressing station, in a big house in a cellar. My tunic was all in ribbons, because it'd taken the full force of the shell. I stopped in there till it were dark, then we got onto an old Ford ambulance and got down the line and come back to England.

I went out again and got wounded at Passchendaele. I got a right packet in me arm, and wounded in my side. The biggest drawback was getting back to the dressing station. There's a huge salient and it's absolutely pitted with shell holes, full of blooming water. And this blooming bone's knocking together at the time, I had my nerves severed as well. It must've taken us two or three hours to walk back. That was the end of the war for me.

Isaac Bowman was near Ypres

in September 1916. The old Cloth Hall was burning. And when we got onto the Menin Road, there was trees up the side of it and we had to go under these because they could see us. We went into the front line there, Sanctuary Wood. The artillery were sending whizz bangs. They were travelling sharper than sound.

Devastation at Arras
(Daphne Dench)

I was put on sentry there, and a man had a shot at me straight away. I heard the gun go off and I felt it whizz by me. You was up to your knees in water. I felt I was walking on something. And there was four dead soldiers had been killed at that post, under the water and mud. After dark we dug some holes and buried them. We don't know who it was.

At Passchendaele, we were down in this hole for six days. When we came out, you could hardly see any flesh on my feet. They started to swell. There were four of us with trench feet. They couldn't send us all, so I was the one they kept. I was expecting my first leave, but I didn't get it.

The Germans had a machine gun. We had to go and take that. We got right up to them, and they all put their hands up. But our officer, he took his eye off the Germans and one got his hand down at the back and fired his revolver and killed him. But they never had chance to kill any more. The bayonet was through all six of them.

I was running back and a shell come whizzing past me, and before I knew anything I was hit with three pieces of shrapnel. One in my tummy, another in my groin and another in my thigh. That was the size of a pea. The doctor said, "You were lucky, if it had been bigger, you would have got the DSO". (Not the medal. The same as Lady Chatterley's husband)!

Isaac Bowman in later life
(Alan Bowman)

I had a bit of sick leave. But then we bore the brunt of that battle, from Saint Quentin. There was a big dug-out in a railway embankment, they reckoned it would hold 1,000 men. There were three or four wire beds above one another. We were in there and that night, 21ˢᵗ March, the officer had been having a look round. I saw him go down the railway line and he'd left a light burning. We split up, two of us down the line and two of us inside. And when we got there, there wasn't a soul in. We found six bottles of whisky. We drunk that, the five of us. I think the sergeant had half of it.

Isaac Bowman convalescing at Morton Banks hospital 1915, seated far right

(Alan Bowman)

Isaac was in an attack when his close friend, a Londoner, was hit. He went into no man's land in full view of the Germans, found his pal who had a bullet in his leg and took him to a little railway for the wounded. But just as they reached it, a German plane overhead machine-gunned them. His friend was hit between the shoulder blades and was killed. Isaac fired at the plane but it disappeared.

We ended up into Malplaquet and the Germans were running out at the other end. The French come out

General Joffre, President Poincarre, King George V, General (later Marshal) Foch, General (later Field Marshal) Haig

(Daphne Dench)

cuddling and kissing us. And an airman turned out. He'd been in there a long time, they'd had him hid. That was the end of the war. I took my second leave, and then I got demobbed on 9th February.

Arthur Bowerman was born in 1898. His eldest brother was in the army.

He said, "Don't have nowt to do with this lot. Keep out as long as you can because it will be no good to you", which it wasn't. But I was called up in 1917. I joined the 2nd/5th West Yorks.

I was at Cambrai and Bourlon Wood and Havrincourt. I'd been out there a bit and an officer from Harrogate took a fancy to me, he asked me to be his batman. He worked for the division, looked after water supplies. We was at Bucquoy in 1918, the retreat, you never saw nothing like it. All the guns on the roadside all gleaming and shining, all the artillery.

He was all right was my boss, he used to give me a bob or two. But I never could make his shoes shine. I don't know whether it was grease or dirt or what. I should

Arthur Bowerman 2nd from right
(Borthwick Institute)

have given them a good soak in hot water and a right good scrub. He had a horse and he got thrown and broke his shoulder. I had to pack all his kit up and send it to England. I had to take it right the way down to Etaples myself and keep getting lifts there. I remember I put my coat on a heap of top coats and packs. And next time I looked they'd all gone up in fire, Jerry had shelled them.

Donald Berwick was born in 1897.

I joined the King's Own Royal Lancaster's, 51st Division. In November 1916 they suddenly said, "You're going to France", and the next thing I knew I was in the frontline at Ypres, and I joined the remnants of my battalion which had been in the Somme and they were all very upset. Only one third of them had come back out.

Can you imagine a street dug up on a wet day, putting mains down, all muck and slush and boards you could walk on? And you were stuck in these trenches. No Man's Land was in front and the rations used to come up from the rear lines. It was terrible on a frosty night, your feet got stuck in this green mud. You'd be looking across the trenches and every now and again a party would go over the top and cut the wire. The first one I went on you were supplied with Mills bombs, like a brown egg, and you threw them.

I've never seen so many rats in my life, they were just in swarms all over. They'd got a good feeding ground in the trenches. There were frogs by the thousand. When you'd been on the march you got tired and weary and then one of the local bands would come out and play a bit of cheerful music. We put words to it but I won't repeat them.

It was such a bad winter in 1916/17, that often if you got some beer or a drink it was frozen before you could get back with it. I stayed in some underground places at the side of the Menin Gate itself on one occasion, the shells were going every few minutes and the place used to rock up and down and you're wondering how you'll ever come through it.

We went in July 1917 for the Passchendaele advance. I think it was the biggest bombardment the war had had. We waited at dawn and it was pouring with rain and we went over the top, and people were being shot down with machine gun bullets and blown up with shells.

I'd exceptionally good eyesight with one eye but I was born with deficient sight in the other. Unfortunately the good eye got hit and that ruined my career for the rest of my life.

They said it was the war to end wars, did you ever hear such rubbish? I got a disablement pension but the government in the 1980s said, "We're going to take twenty per cent off before you can claim anything". That was the last straw.

Jack Bouch recalls

I volunteered and they said, "You're six feet, you might get into the guards!" Just imagine – you could have a busby, and all the glory that goes there. So into the Foot Guards I went, the Coldstream Guards.

Bouch family 1910, Jack on right
with father, and brothers
Reg and Wilfred

(Rosemary Fox)

Now I expected, (surprising how childlike you can be) that when we got there we'd be met by the regiment, "Hoorah, they're here! The help, they're here!" Instead of which we met a colonel with a long face who proceeded to tell us that if the Germans didn't kill us, the British would, because we should be found guilty of this, that and the other. In other words it looked a very grim business. But we survived the training.

We could see the German wire, very close. And first thing in the morning there was a big placard put up, "Gott mit uns", the first propaganda that I'd seen, because of course we'd had a word from the padre before we went up the line that God was on our side! Our lads managed to splinter one of the stakes at the side, and it went down. It was a game of sniping, which went on all the time. We had no helmets, just ordinary service caps. Then suddenly a call, "Stretcher bearers!" It strikes a cold chill down your back. And in due course it came back, "Bennett's got one through the napper". They carted him off on a stretcher, but he was dead.

The old soldiers, the regulars, they looked down upon us rookies. They'd say, "I didn't see you, you weren't there", in other words, they were at Mons, we weren't there. But we said to them, "You only joined the army because you got a girl in the family way, or the police were after you".

I got one mark on my conduct sheet, I was booked for improperly shaving on parade, and I got seven days fatigues! As soon as we got out of the line, however filthy and muddied you were,

Soldier de lousing in trench

(Daphne Dench)

you'd to start scraping and cleaning. We were issued with waders. They were all right for a few hours, but then the condensation in your legs meant that your socks were wet through with perspiration, and your feet were colder.

Our two constant companions in the line were rats and body lice. The rats were bold and hungry. But the lice! It's a little flat creature. It does not hop, it doesn't jump, it just goes steadily on and when you get warm, it starts to bite. It also lays tiny white eggs down the seams of your clothing. If you could get the end of a candle, and it was summer, you got your shirt and ran up the seam with a candle flame and they all popped as you frizzled them. When we got a fresh change of shirts, and they got warm they hatched out. Boots the chemist produced a little brown powder, 'Vermin in the Trenches'. My parents sent me one or two lots. If you put the powder down the back of your neck, it put the wind up the lice who were active and alive and moving and they immediately took refuge by going further down. Having got them down towards the bottom you then tried to kill them. They were one of our perpetual troubles!

We were down in a place called Happy Valley. We were coming through the indescribable havoc of the country, and there was a fellow with two large horses. He said to me, "Where's Happy Valley? Get up and show me". I got on this horse which was about as high as a house and I thought, "If it does anything I shall cling on to its neck". And we went down to Happy Valley, with these heavy artillery horses. And we were invited to see a new weapon, the first tanks. I wrote in my diary, 'We saw the mastodons'. We were told that the tanks were going through in front of us, and they would break the line. I never saw a tank until well on in the afternoon and then we saw one away on our left chuffing away, and I think he'd got bogged down.

Jack and Edith Bouch with Rosemary, John and Bill and friend

(Rosemary Fox)

Edward Cooper recalls

When you got into an area where there was constant activity, you had to go out at night as listening patrol to try and listen to any conversation and try and judge how many men were there. The Bavarians would put up notices, "We don't want to fight, why don't you go home, Tommy?" But it was frowned on by the officers who used to retaliate by putting something rude up.

I was very fond of rabbit pie and my mother sent me a tin of Australian rabbit, and I carried this for over two months saying that will be my Christmas dinner. The rations came up, there was one loaf of bread between seven, the rest were bully beef and jam and butter. That was our Christmas dinner. My friends knew this tin of rabbit was available and we made all the preparations, got our bayonets out and opened the tin, and it was that salty we couldn't eat it. So I wasn't very popular!

Edward Cooper on right, when still a
sergeant
(Christine Clay)

Our first battle was the Battle of Guillemont. It was a village that had held out since the early part of the Somme offensive and we were about the fifth division to have a go at it and we eventually captured it. The Ulster Division had been in this attack and they'd been decimated and we were sent up to relieve them. We were not allowed to fire, to give away our positions. It was a couple of days before the attack was launched.

In August 1917 we went forward to positions in front of Langemarck, that was our objective. I was now a sergeant. A very formidable obstacle to negotiate was a stream called the Steenbeek. It had been so heavily shelled and the banks grown down that it was, in some places, hundreds of yards wide. We had to carry wooden bridges forward. I had a young officer with me. He'd come straight from university and he'd had no previous experience and he relied on me a lot. We knew that the Steenbeek was in the Germans' barrage line. I'd persuaded him not to wait for the second phase of the barrage but to go over with the first and just line up at the other side. We did this without a casualty and were complimenting ourselves. But we found that the battalion who was supposed to make good our positions had failed to advance far enough to clear the pillboxes standing in our way. They were held up and there was men all over the place, no cover. If anybody moved there was fire from the Jerry armies, and the colonel was wounded, three officers killed, sergeant major had gone and all of the sergeants in the company.

We're now held up with this blockhouse. It was firing at a tangent, and I knew that if I got at a certain point he couldn't fire at me. I went across his flank and got out of the range of the machine gun. I ran forward and got behind the blockhouse and I put a couple of bombs in and called on them to surrender. There were two openings and the first German came out of one. I was terrified. I had the officer's revolver in my hand, I'd never had hold of a revolver before, I pointed it at him and the damn thing went off! The Germans pushed back into the blockhouse to start again. So I decided that I'd rely on my rifle and bayonet. And I'm stood in there, called on them to surrender and eventually the next man comes out. As he passed I just cuffed him across the ears and kicked him up the pants. And then all the others came out. And to my surprise there was 45 prisoners and seven machine guns. Instead of taking them round the front I kept them at the back where the Germans could see what was happening. That was a fatal mistake. I then waved my men forward but the Germans opened up, killed seven of their own men and wounded three of mine. A German corporal had left the blockhouse with a machine gun.

So I ordered the Germans to pick up the casualties and my wounded men. By then I had got my men together. I'd got word back to the headquarters that we'd had these casualties and the adjutant came. We'd got into the wrong line of advance and there was nobody on my right and the adjutant was giving me a ticking off on the battlefield in front of my men, who were having a good laugh at me and I said, "I've just captured this blockhouse and there's seven machine guns and 45 prisoners". And he never said a word, just went off after them.

Edward Cooper VC
(Christine Clay)

I was sent on leave a few months later. Outside King's Cross Station was a YMCA hut where the troops got a cup of tea and a bun free. I sat down and saw a newspaper. I read about 'Ten new VCs'. And my name and number was second. I got on the train going north and sat in a corner and I could hear everybody on the train talking about Sergeant Cooper, some professing to know him. I learned afterwards that on the hoardings in the station, the national newspapers had found out that I was in progress from France to Stockton and to report to their office but I never saw it. I got to Darlington to change trains, and somebody threw their arms around me. It was my father and brother. And we sat on the train packed with troops. And my father couldn't contain himself, "This is my son, he's won the VC". They all knew.

In Stockton there was a big reception waiting for him. When he returned to France, he was sent back to get a commission. He had refused once, saying,

"I have no private income. I'm just an ordinary working man". The general said, "You're the type of man we want for officer material. And that's an order, you are not going back to the trenches".

Jack Dawson was

at Armentières. The officer would come round and we'd take our boots off and we had an issue of whale oil. We'd have to rub that on our bare feet. He'd see that we'd done it because if you got trench feet, it was a crime.

Just in front of Albert they'd keep throwing these minenwerfers, a trench mortar, they were terrible things. I've seen one drop in a bay, where there was four chaps, and it blew 'em to pieces. And it got so bad that the sentry on the fire step, would watch out for those. They'd leave a little trail of light so you could see whether it was coming straight towards you. And you had to dash either right or left to let it explode.

Gerald Dennis

went into Ploegsteert Wood. What astounded me most, the headquarters was in a farmhouse where the French farmer and his wife still lived. We slept in a barn, and all was peaceful and calm at the rear of the wood. It was cut across the middle with a barricade, trenches, sandbags and wickerwork. In the wood there were duckboard tracks, 'The Strand, Regent Street, Piccadilly, Hyde Park Corner'. London troops had been there earlier and named them. The Medical Corps were there, at 'Iodine Manor'. Yet at the same time, you went about normally, I gathered strawberries and wild flowers.

I collapsed on February 27th, my foot broke down. I was carried off in an ambulance. Then in March I travelled to Marseilles, and I missed the 21st push. The battalion arrived behind the Somme on 16th March and was disbanded. There were 165 men and five officers, out of 2,999.

I had a medical exam where I was found totally unfit for the line. I ought never to have been there. It was lovely news. I was moved to a prisoner of war camp, but quickly changed into a new battalion coming from Scotland. I was dressed in a kilt and joined the Cameron Highlanders and we went up to the front!

Reg Gifford recalls

There was a cherry orchard in no man's land and we took the haversack, climbed up the trees nice and quietly and got a haversack full of cherries, each of us. We took them back into the officers' mess and the old colonel said, "Where did you get those?" "There's a crop out there Sir". He said, "The cherries are very nice but don't go out there and get any more".

Walter Greenhalgh remembers

about the 2nd of March 1917, sitting in a café just outside Colchester, and we knew we were going out very quickly. By April 4th it was pouring with rain and we were towards Loos. It was 'stand to' in the evening, and the captain came along whom we despised most horribly. He was obviously under the influence of drink. He sees our seven rifles and handed them to his batman and they took them away. About midnight, he summoned us to his dugout, and said he'd saved our lives by stealing our rifles. That night they sent us on special duty. We stole a lot of duck boards and broke them up and made fires and next day he had us up in the order room. He said, "Admit that you're a fool, say yes". I was the last one and I said, "No". He said, "Put Greenhalgh's name down for a court martial," and I knew that was rubbish. The colonel came along, a very fine man. I was on a charge.

My platoon sergeant said, "Be very careful what you say," because I had said that I was going to denounce the captain. The colonel lectured me a bit, and then, "Right, stop seven days' pay". But they never put it in my paybook, and nothing happened. In fact, people started being very nice to me because they hated this captain who was incompetent. I was on good terms with the other officers.

The Germans were putting shells over, and this captain came out of his dugout and summoned the signallers. He said there was a shell landed on top, that it was a whizz bang or something, "Go and find it". They all crowded on top and another whizz bang came and killed two and wounded two, and wounded the captain very badly. He should never have done that. He was finished. He had 21 pieces of shrapnel in him.

Adam Gordon

was born near Enniskillen. My father was with Lord Eniskillen's grouse moors. We came to England then I went back to Ireland to train as a falconer's assistant. Eventually I came to Lord Feversham's Helmsley estate. War broke out and he went out to France. He was killed there. I went out at the same time and after the war I came back as head keeper to take over the whole Games Park. I was always interested in natural history and taxidermy and I'm also a botanist.

Lord Helmsley formed the Yorkshire Hussars Foreign Service Regiment and most of them were farmers' sons. We did cavalry drill. They sent a few old sweats to knock the stuffing out of us. We went to Harlow then out to France. I was a sergeant and was put on as a scout, creeping out at night into no man's land. I was used to it as a keeper, night watching poachers. It's no use saying I wasn't afraid but I managed and I had seven or eight men and they escaped a lot of other duties. When we were dismounted, it broke the hearts of a lot of them, giving up their horses. I found it a dash easier. I'd only myself to look after.

I was attached to the Aussies for a bit. Four of us were sent to their camp with our horses and the idea was to learn them to ride. I thought everybody from Australia rode but they didn't. They were born storytellers, spinning us yarns about enormous snakes that could swallow a cow and kangaroos that wanted to box, how dangerous they were.

I was wounded on my last scouting patrol. The brigade consisted of two Canadian regiments and the West Yorks. The Canadians led the attack on this front, it had all been hush hush. Only the senior officers knew about it. The planners got it from aerial photographs. If they got to this place they were to stop and we followed on. Well we got there and no sign of them. The brigadier from the rear had to hold the whole thing up, stop the artillery or they'd shell the Canadians. We hunted all around and they sent officers out. Then in the finish, "Send the Scouts out". I went a mile and a half to the railway lines and found them. That saved the day. I got wounded though and that's how I got the DCM. I was hit in the neck with a bullet off a sniper. They bandaged me up and got the

Adam and Minnie Gordon
(Helmsley Archives)

iodine out and poured it over me and I could see the bullet. They wanted to pull it out and I wouldn't let them touch it. It saved my life, not touching it. The doctor said, "The missile not to be removed except by a qualified surgeon". That was the end of the war for me.

Claud Hey explains

When you're out on rest you couldn't rest because in the huts they were all rat infested. I had half a sleeve eaten away. Somebody in England brought out Harrison's Pomade which was a kind of ointment, and you rubbed it all over and the lice didn't like it. On a midsummer day when it's very hot and tight puttees on and you've got lice, you nearly go mad.

I remember Christmas time we had no water, they'd put a shell through the water tank. So we used to make cocoa with snow in the billy can.

Maurice Jowett was born in 1895 and went to France in 1916.

The Germans had a good Very light system. They sent what they called floaters up, out of a pistol, like a star they'd burst, a lingering light. And they fired at anything that moved. So you stopped and tried to imitate a tree. I got my hat stuck fast in our own barbed wire and I couldn't get that back. I thought, 'If I stop here while daylight I'm going to be mincemeat', so by hook or by crook I got free.

One morning a gas shell came over and the nose blew off and the liquid flew out, splashed all over on the ground and then it dried and evaporated and the gas came up. I were pretty nifty at the gas mask drill, I could get mine on quick. But then the fun started. We were saturated with the liquid but it evaporated and it were the gas that came off it that did the damage. It were drying off on you, you couldn't get away from it. We set off for the first aid post, then my mate said, "I'm going blind". We hadn't been going long before I went blind. So we just stood there shouting out. And they came and took us down to the field hospital. They injected something in your spine. I was burnt from head to foot. I was bandaged up like these tyre men that you see in the paper. You couldn't talk and you couldn't see.

I gradually got my sight back, but my lungs were bad and the funny part about it was they puts us in an asylum. Like mental cases. I've been in all sorts of places but I'd never slept in a padded cell before. But I came out and we had to be outside in tents for the air, we couldn't breathe you see.

William Law

went straight in as a private in the 5th Cameron Highlanders. I got jaundice and I was out of the line at Festubert and I was coming back down the line and who did I meet but a staff officer and a tiny little Prince of Wales. They asked me what it was like and I said, "Keep your head down Sir, because they are popping at us". When I went back down, the colonel said, "I hear they've got the heir to the throne up in my front line. I'm getting on to the War Office." He was naturally worried. If they'd got hold of him at that particular incident it would have been very bad.

We had the kilts. When they got wet they scarred your knees, it was very uncomfortable. But we got ourselves little trews after a while. We were not supposed to wear them but we did get them. There was a bit of fraternising. For example at Hill 60, they used to shout across, "We're going out Jock, the Prussians is coming in. God help you." They knew who we were.

Lord Seafield came up to Hill 60. [This was James Ogilvie-Grant, 11th Earl of Seafield, a captain attached to 5th Battalion Cameron Highlanders]. *He was shot through the head. We carried him down on a few sheets and we gave him his last drink. He said, "Thanks awfully." He died in my arms. Lady Seafield wrote to me.*

Later William returned to London on leave and got his commission.

I changed into my uniform and went back with the Sam Browne and went into the Somme as a second lieutenant. I can still remember going through Longueval afterwards and the Highlanders, their white flesh, their kilts all over the place, lying dead along the main street. We were covered all the time by South Africans who were the Delville Wood boys, they were magnificent shots. One night we were creeping about listening, and a young German boy walked right into me and he started to cry. I took him down the line.

Ernest Done

was born in Hong Kong in 1898. His father was a regular soldier.

I joined the Territorials when I was 15. We went to France when I was 16. I was a driver. We had our horses and mules to look after all the way. I remember landing in an orchard. Got the horses and mules put tidy for the night, put a groundsheet down, and a blanket over, and we spent our first night in France like that.

Ernest Done with wife Ivy, daughter Maureen on holiday late 30s

(Martyn Winn)

We were taking ammunition up to the line. We had mules with packs on, but if the mule went down in the mud and couldn't get out, it had to be shot. We were bombed going up, and bombed coming back. In the day we'd be grooming, cleaning up, getting ready for the next road.

We were on the Somme in 1916 and in 1917 up at Passchendaele. People in England knew more than we did. We arrived in front of Poperinghe, our wagon lines. We had to dig out a hole in the bank to kip down. One beautiful morning, "Ooh, what's that nice smell?" We could sniff aniseed. It was gas, so we had to troop in front of the doctor.

German soldiers in Flanders

(Daphne Dench)

Five o'clock in the morning the Germans broke through, and we were just near Cambrai. We were running all over the place, we went back for 14 days, till one of the Jocks got his pipes out and started playing, and got the fellows together somehow. After that we kept going forward till we finished up. Two cyclists came down the road, and shouted, "Armistice!" You couldn't believe it after four years.

Arthur Pierse recalls,

We had gas masks for horses. You put your own on first and then them. There was plenty of mustard gas. It was yellow, like sulphur and thick and the shell holes used to fill up with water. It was all green and yellow and many a time we would have to skim the top off to wash. They'd send an ordinary shell and put a pineapple gas in between so that it was that strong and that beautiful you wanted to take your mask off to have a good feel of it!

Charles Seymour was born in Lincolnshire in 1896, the son of a blacksmith. He became an apprentice tailor.

I was a bound apprentice for 5 years, but the war started in 1914 after two years of my apprenticeship and I volunteered. I was 17 and only 5ft 2¼ and you'd got to be 5ft 2½ and I got onto my toes to give me another quarter. It was exciting, everybody was very pent up with patriotism for the country and most of those volunteers went to get away from their environment. Nobody thought it was going to be a long war. After a month in France we went into our sections, some in support, some in reserve. We had to walk miles and then fight, then shoot, we were half dead before we started.

Charles Seymour

(Richard Seymour)

Once I stood at the back of the parados, it had been built up from the earth. And we started to shave and a bullet went by my throat. A sniper had seen me, and missed me by a 16ᵗʰ of an inch. I should have been killed and I felt it, the heat of that bullet.

A gas shell exploded close to my chest and I'd got my jacket open and I got blistered. It wasn't enough to put me out. Those people who were in the middle of it, where there was a density of gas, they suffocate, it fetched their insides out. One time I picked up a beautiful Colt revolver, put it into my haversack and kept quiet about it. When we got out of the line I thoroughly cleaned it. It had five cartridges in the barrel. And I took it into the line and I was quite cocky about this revolver. The sergeant was half asleep in the dugout and a sapper saw the revolver in my haversack. He says, "Does it work? Let's see it". So I pulled the trigger but I shot the sergeant right through his leg and he went straight back to England. And our officers, after they told me off, said, "Seymour if you shoot me in the leg I'll give you 500 francs". When we came out of the line, of course I was court martialled. They sentenced me to ten days. But they were very sympathetic towards me and the captain gave me a 10 franc note to buy myself some coffee sometime.

In the trenches, I was on any dangerous job there was [as punishment]. There'd been a terrific bombardment of shells over our front line. It was about two in the morning. We kept our heads down. Then we heard somebody scuttling about in the front. I crawled out and I saw a chap fastened up in our wire. He'd thrown his equipment and his rifle away. So I grabbed hold of him and took him down to our headquarters, this German sergeant major. They sent him further back for information. Incidentally, these Military Medals, we used to sneer at them, there

Charles Seymour and his wife Beatrice
(Richard Seymour)

were so many of them. My name went down for a Military Medal but because I'd just done ten days jankers [for shooting the sergeant] I didn't get it.

But I had a lucky war really.

Cecil Slack recalls,

Our faces, hands, everything, all skin was blackened with burnt cork, all equipment on our rifles was dulled so that it didn't shine when the bit of light went up. Our bayonets were shortened, that was my idea. And I had two revolvers.

All the other men had wrist watches underneath so they didn't shine, that was for them to come back in time if they didn't hear my whistle. At a certain time we were to get up to the German trench, our own artillery would fire over our heads at the Germans' second line whilst we'd take prisoners, and blow up some sort of installation that had been there, which I never found. When 20 minutes was up I was to blow my whistle and if I didn't blow mine the sergeant was to blow his and if he didn't blow his, the men were to come back.

When we were about 20 yards short of a German line a shell landed. One of our own! Then more shells. Our own people were firing short! So I stopped crawling, I just jumped up and ran forward into the German trench. I heard a movement behind me, shone my flash lamp and there was one of my own men. There was hell going on by this time, machine guns all over the place of which we'd never been told, and it was absolutely disconcerting. There was another raid on our left. They got fired at too by their own guns. We had an inquest about that later.

I said to this private, "You and I will go along this way", and the trench was a zig zag and when you go down there, you are supposed to throw a bomb over. I said, "You've got your bayonet and rifle, I'll throw the bomb over and you go forward". "I can't move Sir", and he couldn't. I left him and went on my own, the revolver ready and I went 50 yards and heard a lot of shouting above all the noise that was going on. It was the Germans' second line. I looked at my watch and found I was five or ten minutes overdue. So I got out on top, blew my siren whistle and started going back. I ought to have been blown up time and again. I got back to the wire and got tangled up in that and then I fell. In the end I was absolutely broke from exhaustion.

Harry Smith was

at a place near Ypres, Essex Farm. I remember once getting some water, it must've been poisoned, to make some tea, and I rolled about in the cow shed practically all day with colic. It was just a few buildings and they'd made it into a dressing station.

Then the Battle of Neuve Chapelle was on, and we were rushed there. There were some Indian troops there, Sikhs. There were dead men wherever you looked, they started decomposing, and if you tried to lift them you pulled their arms out or their legs. If you wanted to move them you had to put your oil sheet down, roll them over, so you could carry 'em away. And the smell! We didn't want anything to eat, all we wanted was something to smoke. And there was an extra ration of cigarettes. At one time we got some Portuguese attached to us for instruction. If they were on sentry, they'd go and wake somebody up that were having a sleep, to ask them what time it were, and they'd get a right mouthful for it.

Indian soldiers
(Daphne Dench)

I were standing in a sunken road, and the lads were all there, and we were talking. And one of these 'Jack Johnsons' came over, it burst up the road and a piece hit my tin hat on the edge of the brim and it bent it down over me ear. We had to have our overcoats because we'd no blankets. And a piece went right through my overcoat, and hit my tin hat. And one knocked the rifle out of my hands and sent me spinning and I were down on the floor, but only my ear were bleeding.

We'd nothing to eat for four days and a plane came over and dropped a box of bully beef and the Germans mustn't have known a thing about it. And they put water on the stoves in the houses and the men went with barrows and came back and they'd sacks of potatoes with them. We had them that night, it were a godsend.

Jim Watters

was born in 1892 at Inveramsay in Scotland. I joined the territorials, 6th battalion Gordon Highlanders in 1912.

There was some of them trenches with seven foot of water in 'em. That was where our lads were drowned. You'd go out in the dark and they had to go into the turnip

Memorial to
Gordon Highlanders
(Mike Race)

field and you were sliding all over the place, over the tops of them. And if they fell in they couldn't get out, the weight of the kilts. And we went with spats on as well. We'd to wait for boots coming, and short puttees. With our kilts, the Germans called us 'the women from hell'.

We came down to Dieppe to make up the strength after Neuve Chappelle. Out of about 600 there was 60 or 70 left. I got shot through the foot. You'd to be careful getting down to the Field Dressing Station, there was dead lying all over the place and it was hot. And there were black flies all over. An ambulance came and I landed at Rouen and they operated on me. I went to York. I was nine months in hospital and five months on crutches.

Herbert Evans recalls

You couldn't explain what Passchendaele were like. No man could find his way, it was one massive big shell hole. There wasn't a tree standing, nothing, desolation.

We asked for a stretcher and they had none. We passed lines of our troops, laid out, the moon shining on them. And we set off to try to find our company. We ran into some troops, this officer said, "Who are you?" "We're C Company, we've been down for a stretcher". We went back with them and they had to cut the boots off some of the men. Their feet had swelled with the water. And the Colonel cried when he saw his men come from Passchendaele.

On the 19th December our Colonel came round, "We're expecting gas". We didn't take much notice of that but we were in the front line and all at once they gassed us from the cylinders. Our SOS went up, three different coloured lights to the artillery and they opened up but a lot of them were gassed.

We'd only a simple gas mask, it was like a Ku Klux Klan thing with two eye pieces that you screwed in and a piece that went into your mouth. And these masks were impregnated with what you put films in to develop. You had to put this in your mouth and then open your tunic and push the ends of that down. We all were gassed and turned all sorts of colours and them that got a bit of gas, tried to pull the masks off to get fresh air. We had to hold them and stop them pulling their helmets off. We all lost our voices. They had to withdraw us to be reinforced and they marched us down to Calais.

We were at Cambrai and we attacked. They sent us without a barrage, simply with our rifles. And Jerry opened up with the machine guns. But we got them on the run, and suddenly tanks came. The officer told us to attack again, with just our rifles against the tanks. Well they forced us back to our own positions. I stayed out with the men that had been wounded and that's where I got the DCM.

'His Majesty the King has been most graciously pleased to approve the award and distinguished medal to Corporal H Evans for acts of gallantry and devotion to duty whilst in the field. He attended to the wounded in the face of heavy fire from hostile tanks. He showed great courage and coolness on all occasions'.

Jim Melody recalls

Down the Menin Road, at Hellfire Corner, they were shelling, you had to run over, not walk, or you was buggered. And it teemed down until we got to our positions.

We had to go over to the ridge of Passchendaele. They were giving us some stick. The barrage had started and we were slipping and sliding, men

Jim Melody on left
(Mike Welsh)

were drowning in shell holes, it was hellish. A Canadian sergeant said, "We're taking over", and they got the worst because they was waiting for them. We had to withdraw and take the wounded back the best way we could. Brigadier MacFarlane was a nice chap, he was a Scotsman, he met us on the Menin Road, and he had soup kitchens there. We were starved and wet through. We had to rest on the road, dry ourselves and then got moved back into camp.

We re-equipped and was in bivouacs in fields, about 39 men. The others was lost. We went to Nieuwpoort. They used to drop the small shells and they hit the trench board and down you went. It was a good job we were swimmers. He gave us the biggest mustard gas shell that we ever had, I lost my voice for over a fortnight and was semi blind.

In towns and cities in England, stately homes, schools, halls, and other large venues were requisitioned to be used as military hospitals. In France a number of British titled ladies set up hospitals, such as Millicent Leveson-Gower, the Duchess of Sutherland, at Calais, and Constance Edwina Lewes, the Duchess of Westminster, who sponsored a hospital in a casino at Le Touquet. Many upper and middle class young ladies enlisted as VADs (Voluntary Aid Detachment) to nurse at the front.

Harry Dyson

was born in 1889 and joined the West Yorks. At Passchendaele Ridge there were pillboxes, they used them to shoot all over the ridge, and didn't half shift some troops. We got part of the way up the ridge and I got knocked out.

A shell came right across the middle of my jaw, and took it all away. It took my upper lip right across and ripped part of the throat. It took two and a half years to mend. They had to start at the beginning with bone and skin grafts. You got bone put in the jaw and flesh from my shoulders and my back. We had tubes up our nostrils, and down our throat. Food was all ground up. You had a tube and you can suck food. It's amazing.

I lost a great deal of friends, thinking about the people that I was with. When I got back from hospital, there was a lot of places that I never saw again.

Thomas Flint

went over t'top on t' Somme. And they sent me back to England to Woking, it was a disused prison. And they had to cut my leg off at finish. They had to send for my parents because I very near snuffed it. The daughter of one of the hoteliers in Woking used to take us all about, we'd maybe go to the theatre, and we had a real good time. I went to Leeds to get an artificial leg. My pension was 19 shillings and three pence.

Arthur Hemp

was in hospital in Le Havre, I got friendly with a young German. He spoke broken English and we often used to chat together. He admitted that he didn't want to fight at all. He drank vinegar and port wine to give him palpitations. And his first bombing raid, he gave himself up. And in that hospital the Germans had beds as good as we had. In fact one German used to shave me. They were glad to be out of it. And this young man, he was the only one to see me off when I came on the ambulance.

Ernest Mackinder joined up at 16.

When you was in the support trenches you had to go back for rations for the frontline battalion. We were in a shocking state, and the officer said, "Don't bother about yourself but clean your rifles".

When I got wounded, there was a big bang on my shoulder and I went flying. I picked myself up and my fingers were dropping off. I got one in the shoulder and a big one in the hip and then the hand. A whizz bang had come across. They weighed a pound and a half and they were made of aluminium. The doctors were pulling it out of me months afterwards. They issued us with sun blinds at the back of your cap and you had to put them on with elastic to protect you from the sun. And one piece of shrapnel cut that sun blind in two. Didn't touch my head and didn't touch the

Ernest Mackinder
(Jon Vause)

wire, it come straight through, it were really miraculous. I kept that for years. If it had been a quarter of an inch either way, the back of my head would have been blown off.

I went to the London hospital. In five days I had three operations and they saved the hand. I went back there and they operated on the hip. The shrapnel had gone in, in the shape of a penny and it had banged against the bone and the bone was stronger than the shrapnel and it broke away. We were told we were going convalescent to Tunbridge Wells. It was just before Christmas and the gentry did all sorts to comfort us. There were Christmas parties and we went to all the big houses.

I didn't want discharging so I came home on a month's leave. Then I reported to the Belle Vue Barracks. We got the train to Lincolnshire and they were supposed to be guarding the Lincolnshire coast. If you'd seen all the old men there, they could have guarded nothing, it took all their time to guard themselves. I was about six weeks there. I knew they couldn't put me down for the front again with this hand. Then they called me 'the gramophone corporal', I had to look after the gramophone and go down to Tetney Lock with the rations.

Tom West

was somewhere between Arras and Cambrai. We were walking along behind the barrage at dawn. It was getting lighter all the time, smoke and smelly acrid fumes. And all of a sudden, I felt like I'd been hit with a mallet in both knees. The bullet went through. I crawled to a shell hole. We went to a casualty clearing station. And then to a sort of hospital. I went back with a German boy and he'd been shot very severely in the arm. I says, "How old are you?" And he says, "Siebzehn". Seventeen. And he was a beautiful looking lad and I've never forgot his face. We were pals for a kilometre-and-a-half. When I got back to this base, there was tea in huge dixies. And, "Here you are chum". I just turned to this fella. "What about this Jerry?" "He's not getting any". I said, "What are you talking about? Give him it, he's finished has this lad. He might have his arm off for all I know". And I got me way and he said, "Danke". And if anybody had said to me they wouldn't have done that for a German, I'd say "You don't know until you're in the same position". He was a human being like myself.

Henry Bendall recalls a gas attack.

They marched us back from the front line, right down the communication trenches into a place named Boise Grenay. There were some old buildings there full of straw. They put us all into that, like little pigs, but it was somewhere to shelter. As we settled down, we had a gas alarm, we didn't get the full effects of it but I've had asthma ever since.

Alfred Scott felt

the gas was lethal, it did away with the throat. It'd come over in soft shells and you never heard them burst. It eased off for two or three years, and then I started having chest trouble. The doctor says, "You've got the gas in your system and you'll never get it out". I had to resort to Potters' cigarettes. Never went without them.

Clarence Ward was in Ypres in

March 1918 and I got kicked in the face by my sergeant's horse, he was a bit frisky. They took me on another horse to a casualty clearing station, gave me a tetanus injection. And there was a chap called Pickering, he used to be a jockey, he used to ride at York. There was a scabies hospital a bit further down that road in a French camp. I says, "Scratch between your fingers and we'll go to the scabies hospital," and they took us in.

Clarence & Annie Ward
(Tony Wood)

It were lovely and warm in there and you sat in your pyjamas and outside there was a tobacco factory and they'd bring a bucket full of shag tobacco, oh we had a good time there. We got sent to a Canadian camp and they were parading every morning so I says to Pick, "Get a sweeping brush, when they all go, start sweeping up." The sergeant major kept looking at us, he didn't know what to say so we had about three days of that. Then he says, "You two, you're never on parade," I says, "We're never off, we're always sweeping up here". "Well I'll put you up the line," and I went off in a box wagon.

Edwin Bond was in a tank crew.

We named our tank Hydra, 'many heads' in Greek mythology, how true that turned out to be. The Battle of Ypres was just coming to a climax and we were sent there for our first commission. The tank workshops were great big four sided tents.

There was eight of us in a crew including the officer, two machine gunners at each side. But on a six pounder unit, it has a loader at each side. Then there was two gearsmen. Nobody liked this job, the gears rotated with the track. To put one track out of commission you had to pull your gear out of joint. When the driver signalled that he wanted to be into neutral, you'd pull this gear over and it went round the sprocket and it moved it from its shaft out of gear and then that track ran free. You swung your gun round, it was on a mounting slide and it had a slit down the armour plating turret. You fired it with a trigger.

We had steel masks, with slits where your eyes would be. They were covered inside with wash leather. From the face down was chain mail. I've seen some fellows come out of action and they've had blood all over but they weren't badly injured.

I saw one driver who had the two portholes at the front, and a bullet come and hit the sloping thing and he had a face mask on and it dented this in his eye and blacked his eye but it saved him.

Edwin was later instrumental in saving a colleague who got trapped in the tank.

Life on the Western Front was not all trench warfare.

Irving Camplin joined the Royal Army Service Corps. They were mainly transporting ammunition and rations.

The first baptism we got were Ypres. I've never seen owt like it, talk about making you sick. Poperinghe, Pilckem Ridge, Hellfire Corner, Mousetrap Avenue, Dickebusch. The worst thing were the devastation. Roads were all water and mud and it had been shelled that often you had big ditches. And you'd see a leg stuck up, sometimes it would be a man and sometimes it would be a horse. It were a hell hole.

Passchendaele, the roads were that bad and swampy, we had to make a track of railway sleepers. On this particular day, at t'side of the road were an old steam roller that had been abandoned. All the gang of us were busy and four planes come along. They says, "They must be ours, look how low they are", but they were bloody Jerries. You'd see us dive under this old steam roller. There were machine gun bullets flying all over. People were used to diving anyhow they could, at a given moment they just vanished.

Devastation on the western front
(Daphne Dench)

I was glad when I got away from Ypres. The Somme was a picture palace at side of Ypres. We got more shellfire than t'infantry. Once they were in the trench, they weren't so bad. But we were at it all day and night. Sometimes we got hardly any sleep. Just outside Vlamertinghe, they dropped a shell and killed eighteen horses. We had them to bury and it were hard work, there were no mechanical diggers in them days.

John Graham also joined the RASC.

It was changing from horses to vehicles so we mixed among cavalrymen for a while. We travelled by train, in trucks labelled 'Quarante hommes, huit chevaux'. [40 men or eight horses]. You could get in them at night and shut the door and they were jolly warm. The train trundled along very steadily over points and crossings and precious little signalling until we came to the railhead at Doullens.

During the night you could hardly sleep for guns. We were allocated to ammunition dumps to take shells up to the guns. They were on sunken roads, they used to dig a pit at the side, put the big timbers down and then run the gun in so that its muzzle was peeping above the land. We had to put nine inch shells into these things. We brought the ammunition in three packages. One had gun cotton or TNT charges, the next had some other kind of primer and then a little box with detonators in. And nothing would go off until all these three were together. The gunners unscrewed the hook at the end, put in the nose cap and then the detonator and it was timed to go off so many seconds after touching the ground.

The dumps were as much as five miles behind the guns and they had thousands of shells in piles. Jerry was by then burning all his ammunition dumps. We even came across a dump of liquor and we sampled that all right. And then all at once the war was over and the mess of tidying up began.

On the night before the Armistice, I was trying to get up the line with a lorry. The whole Army Corps was pulling out and the road was choc-a-bloc. They cut down hedges outside in the fields and horses could get over the soil and the vehicles keep to the road. It took three hours for a division to pass. My lorry was finding its way along, and there was Sir Douglas Haig walking in the road to keep warm. And his Rolls Royce was there. How he got back to base, to be in at the signing of the Armistice at 11am on the 11th of November isn't clear to me, but he must have managed it!

William Shaw

William Shaw as farrier

(Alan Elsegood)

was on transport. We had to take two horses to Vignacourt. We got into an estaminet [a café bar] and had a drink and they wouldn't let us keep the horses in the yard so we put them under a railway bridge. At half-past one in t'morning we tramps back. It was a lovely night. There was four of us in a tent and the guards' tent was next with a lot of ammunition in. There was a parcel from home with cakes and tobacco and all sorts. I had two bits of candle and I stood them on this rucksack and reads my letter. Goes to sleep and it sets the rucksack afire and then the tents. And the guards spotted it and they come with buckets of water. There was one chap, he had a milk business in Harrogate after the war, he were nearly drowned with water. I couldn't help but laugh. But if we'd got killed!

I stayed in transport until I got nephritis. I was the colonel's groom and they wanted two horses so I takes them and then I reported to the doctor. He gave me M & B tablets [before antibiotics]. *I still had to work. But my legs was twice the size they should have been. I went to pick the horses up and I'd had to take my puttees off.*

Colonel Wood says, "How is it you aren't properly dressed?" "I couldn't put me puttees on Sir". "Why haven't you been sick?" I says, "I reported sick this morning. He gave me M & B". "With legs like that?" So he played pop with the doctor. They moved me to hospital. I got eventually to Cheltenham and I was there twenty weeks and I went to Ripon camp to convalesce.

William Shaw at 90
(Alan Elsegood)

William went back to France in

September 1918. There was two dips in the road. And we'd to go to the second dip and wait while the French got up on our right. And they was dropping like mad. There was three of us left, the officer, a corporal and myself. They'd sent for reinforcements and they hadn't come. So we just laid at the back of a broken wall that'd been shelled and bullets was flying past us all t'time. So the officer said, "We might as well try to get back". There was bullets coming that fast, I dropped in a shell hole and the officer dropped in on top of me. The corporal got hit in the leg. The Germans came and they took me into hospital. I was taken prisoner and I was there when the war ended.

CHAPTER SIX

FREE TIME AND ENTERTAINMENT

Free time was very important to the soldiers. Once they came out of the front line on 'rest', they needed to find ways to forget the reality of war, and enjoy themselves in any way they could.

William Angus

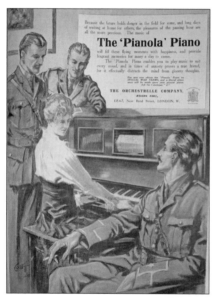

The Pianola
(The Graphic 1915)

went out to Vaudricourt Wood where we had a battalion mess. We did training, we had baths, there was the concert party in the evening. The 'principal girl' in the Whizz Bangs concert party was on my platoon roll but I never saw him off the stage. So we led a fairly peaceful and orderly life.

George Ashurst recalls,

We'd no money, I'd only a franc in my pocket. I waltzed down a main road with shops and a church. I could have done with a lovely feed and a drink, but a franc wasn't much. I twisted round and I hit two women, knocked them both to the floor. I hadn't heard them at the back of me! I helped them to get up, they took it in good sport and they laughed. I can't say a damn word in French, can't apologise. I said, "Factory", and they knew where this place was, so they walked back with me. They were trying to make me understand that they'd meet me there tomorrow night. I got it at finish. I had some glorious times with them two girls, all innocent, because they were two very nice girls. They were evacuated from Belgium when the war started, to Boulogne.

Eleven days I had there. Then they stuck a 20 franc note in my pocket, a parcel of cigarettes and sandwiches to get on the train with, and they bade me goodbye. I wrote to them for some time after and then we kept moving, different fronts, it sort of fell away.

Donald Berwick

used to have a break and we'd go behind the lines to the estaminets where you could get drinks. I wasn't a big drinker but you'd get to know the people. You'd go in one of the farms, nearly all had a stove with a long pipe into the room and if you put clothes there, they dried on the top. There was a bowl of coffee, they didn't bother cleaning it out, when it got empty they just poured more coffee and hot water in it. But it tasted quite good.

Being a nature man, I used to like going through some of the bits of coppices and woodlands which were just like they were at home, and there were a lot of wild birds and flowers I got interested in. In the front of Ypres at Hellfire Corner, there was an old church and cemetery that had been battered. Even in those terrible surroundings you got flowers growing and skylarks in the sky and I was reminded of home.

Edwin Bond was in C Company,

We were known as the 'Concert Battalion', due to Captain Davies who acted on films, and he brought films down, with himself playing the principal part, like 'The White Hope', the boxing film. There were concerts at the local cinema with 'The Bing Boys Are Here', brought down from London.

Jack Bouch recalls,

If the battalion was out of the line there would be sports and a lot of boxing. We had concerts and one night the battalion band was with us and it was a beautiful evening and it was just

Men in goatskins go to YMCA
(Mike Race)

The Knuts concert party, York man Billy
Pritchard on right in white hat and plait

(Mike Race)

Jack Bouch Hunstanton

(Rosemary Fox)

coming twilight. We had the usual three or four comedians who did a few ribald songs. Then a lad called Freddie Sinclair, a librarian, got up with the band. And if you can imagine this beautiful evening and Freddie, with a very good voice, sang, 'Somewhere a voice is calling'. And I bet there wasn't a man in those thousand men who hadn't got a lump in his throat. I shall never forget that night. Freddie got very badly wounded on the Somme.

Irving Camplin was born in 1896.

We only got a bob a day. If we went into a village we had to listen for hens cackling and pinch the bloody eggs before t'farmer come. And we'd go in t'fields and milk cows.

I played for the French army at soccer and the French knew nowt about soccer. They'd pester your life out to get a game and wherever the ball went, all the team used to run after it, there was only t'goalkeeper left there. And we flogged everything to them. I'd have flogged my horses if I hadn't to pay for them.

You got up to all sorts of tricks. We'd go fishing. We used a Mills bomb, we'd pull the pin out and throw it in the water and it would blow all the fish out. We'd get out half a dozen that were in one piece. And we'd see a hay cock [bundle of hay] and if we went past with a wagon we'd throw it in the wagon. But they all got paid did the French, our government paid them for everything.

We had the Crown and Anchor board [a gambling game with dice, which was illegal in the forces] but we never had any money. Once we were out for a rest, and I used to knock about with a lad from Sheffield and I was sat having a drink of vin blanc (you could get a bottle for a tanner) in a café, and a young tart got hold of my cap and run upstairs. I says, "You can bring it back, I have nowt". They were all on the game, but we'd had it driven into us about VD. So I never bothered with them. It was more officers than men because they had money.

At the end of the war, Irving had to take

civvies back to where they used to live. Some of them got in the wagon when they got sore feet. It were full of leather jerkins and blankets for the company. By the time I got to Bonn it were empty.

The nearest I got to being killed were after t'war when I were billeted just outside Brussels with a Belgian family. They had two daughters and the old fellow were a farmer. He caught me in t'stable with the youngest daughter. I'll never forget it, he chased me over t'field with a shotgun. Of course, I could run in them days. But I patched it up next day with a bag of oats and everything was alright.

Tres Bon sheet music
(Chris Poole)

Harry Christmas was in France in 1917.

One of these blokes I picked up in Le Havre, he'd been a sergeant major in the Guards and he'd been in trouble and got reduced in the ranks. He said, "How are we going on for a drop of wine for Christmas?" I said, "We shan't get none, we haven't the money". He said, "We'll go and see the cooks". The cooks had only got cans of bully beef and marmalade in flat round tins. We took the marmalade labels off and took them down to the nearest estaminet. We soon flogged them. That was all meat we told them. We had all the wine we could drink and took a couple of bottles for the cook.

Harry Cockerill on right and family
(Beryl Cockerill)

Harry Cockerill

got a respite about once a month. We'd go and have a look at the magazines, and they put a bath on for us. The Picture Post, there was plenty of those around. I was looking through it and I come across a picture marked 'Canadian artillery in action', and there I was, just at the side. And I thought, 'I'll send this home to my sister'. But I nearly got court martialled for it. Major Sissons sent for me and he said, "Young man, whatever you do don't write in that or send any literature". I had to apologise.

Arthur Deighton recalls,

This train came up from the base with everything on, and I saw this laddie pick something out of the gutter and chuck it in his wagon. He said, "I've found a case of rum." When we got to the stables and putting the horses away, I says, "What have you done with that rum?" "I've given it to the sergeant." And there was healthy pop all night.

I was running the officers' mess, and we went into a big mansion, the lady couldn't afford to live there, she lived in a cottage in the village. There was a game larder inside and big slabs for the game to be laid on. We went in the cellars and there were rows of wine, more than 18 inches deep from the floor. It was port, it hadn't been decanted. We'd cart one or two up and we buried a couple of dozen and then started on the stock again. And then the adjutant sent for me, "I hear you've found some wine. Leave it alone. The brigadier's got to know about it. If there's an enquiry, there's gonna be a hell of a row."

Ernest Doy had

been in 'His Majesty's Hotel' scores of times for different things what I done. I never had handcuffs on, only once down at Calais with an old sergeant major. I was coming on leave and I had a row with him and he sent me right back up to Wellington Camp for insubordination.

After 1916 I started the Crown and Anchor business. The military police, you'd got to square them! I was better off than them lieutenants. They'd come and borrow money off me afore they got paid again. I won £104 one night in a place near Mericourt.

(Ernest was often in trouble but despite all this he got the DCM).

Alfresco and impromptu concert in Amiens
(Mike Race)

Postcard from wartime
(Mike Race)

John Blakeway remembers

One of our chaps was running a Crown and Anchor board and making money out of the Australians. He dodged anything. But they found out he shouldn't have been in the trenches. He refused to run 'at the double' and they pulled him up and he got his ticket because he was far too old to be there.

Ernie Easton

used to go to see a lovely girl in the estaminet. I'd go and grind the coffee when I wasn't on duty and we'd have a game of draughts. She would clear me off the board in about two moves, I could never beat her. When I said, "I've got to go to hospital", she cried. She said, "Ernie, you depart for Angleterre, you're not returning". I could have married that girl.

Jim Gill

was in Fleurbaix, when we came out of the trenches. We used to go a house. There were two old ladies, and this pal of mine could speak a bit of French. And he said to this old lady, could she cook us some eggs and chips and bread and butter and coffee. And we had a real feed and when we asked her how much, it were very little. She said, "You can come again but don't tell anybody else". It were a home from home for me and this pal. And I was with him all the time until I was wounded.

Dinner attended by William Angus 1917

(Charles Angus)

While Jim and his friend delighted in their egg and chips, in June 1917 the Fourth Army Old Etonian dinner was held on the Western Front at Peronne, and 135 men, including Sir Douglas Haig and Sir Henry Rawlinson, attended. The banquet included Crème d'Italie Soup, Poisson à la Dieppe, Asperges d'Argenteuil en Belle Vue, Poulets de Mans Roti, Salade Japonais, Sorbèt à la Norbonne, Gateau Etonian, Fruit and coffee!

John Graham was in Calais when,

we were allowed out on an evening. And the shock to me was to see so many brothels just across the road from the old church, in nearly every door, and as many as a dozen men waiting outside. To me, as young as I was, it was disgusting.

We wandered about as we liked in Calais, there were hundreds of us, looking for an estaminet. Then there was a sign 'out of bounds', and it was a line of small prostitutes' houses. An old hag sat on the steps controlling the queues. This prostitute must have been having ten men an hour. I swear that most of these men were married.

There were three diseases, there was pox, shankers, and there was gonorrhoea. If you got one of those you had to report it, although in the latrines there were prophylactic treatments. You could treat yourself with liquid that you applied and you had a good chance of killing it. But if you went down the line to a hospital they treated you murderously. Yet they used to come back after three weeks and look for another woman.

There was one estaminet and a woman there had a terrible time, the Germans were there and she'd consorted with one and had a baby. She'd been ill-treated and abandoned and she was always drunk.

One time we unloaded a lot of stone jars of rum, real good stuff. We found one half empty, and we finished it between four of us. When we'd done that, we couldn't stand, so we were in this truck and somebody said, "Lean against the back, to keep ourselves up". The lieutenant came and looked at us and we must have looked all right, so we got away with that.

Jim Greenwood remembers going into estaminets.

We spent quite a lot of spare time playing cards, I actually learnt bridge. There were four of us, a corporal who was a fruit farmer in Kent, a Scot, he might have been a teacher, and a photographer from Biggleswade who was a Pioneer like me. We also played Brambles and Nap. I played a lot of bingo when we were near a Salvation Army or a YMCA. Bingo was the only thing that was technically allowed.

Advert for cigarettes - a far cry from the Woodbines in the trenches

(The Graphic 1915)

Claud Hey recalls how the men

got cigarette rations. Navy and Mayflower. Some people didn't smoke and they'd say, "You can have mine". But you couldn't get matches. In Ploegsteert Wood they had a little shop about 400 yards behind the line for cigarettes, matches and sweets. I used to have 100 Grey's tipped cigarettes sent every week. When you're in reserve, about a hundred yards behind the line, and nothing to do, we'd put sacks up at the window and play Brag and Crown and Anchor. But when you were three miles out at a village we used to get drinks and have concerts.

Richard Hopkinson

used to like the Australians. When I was just outside Arras, we'd get into estaminets with them and they would treat you. But these people charged them more than us. I was a battalion runner then and we nearly all liked a drop of vin blanc.

George Hutchinson was with the Friends Ambulance Unit. He recalls that

We played a great deal of football, and the French authorities approved of that because it helped morale. There were a lot of Americans coming. And one of the first black American regiments came to our division. They did a tremendous lot of jazz playing and it was all rather fun. We got Jimmy Europe [Lieutenant Jim Europe and his Hellfighters Band] *playing band day and night. We rather liked it.* [This would be the first introduction to jazz for the British soldiers].

Charlie Minett was at

a place called Flixecourt. We came out for six weeks on special training, before we went to the Somme. We were billeted in a great big place, more like a small hotel. She was a wonderful lady, Madame Shelley. We had a big room to hold concerts and we got up a concert party. Come Christmas time, Captain Rowe and

Lieutenant Hutchinson of the machine gun section, who came from big families in England, had turkeys sent out and plum puddings and we had a fine Christmas dinner.

Day at Chantilly races - French and British officers
(Daphne Dench)

Card sent by Claud Hey
(Robert Hey)

Reverse of 1917 card sent by Claud Hey
(Robert Hey)

When he was on rest, **Arthur Pierse**

had grooming to do, watering and feeding. There was a little bit of freedom but not much. We'd have a bit of sport and there was a concert party, the 'Very Lights'. There was the British Expeditionary Force canteen and when the Americans came, there was American canteens. They'd issue us with maybe a 20 franc note and we'd go and buy a tin of cafe au lait or a bar of chocolate. We got two packets of cigarettes a week when the rations came up and I gave my centre driver and the wheel driver one packet each. They were American cigarettes, Star, things like that.

Stan Robson remembers

one occasion when we had an enormous great marquee and it contained the whole battalion and we had one of these concert parties. It was a YMCA affair and these three chaps climbed onto the stage, to the applause of the whole battalion, carrying a small piano which he called 'Little Peter'. And just outside the marquee there was a 9.2 howitzer which kept on firing right throughout the performance.

Innes Ware

used to go into Armentieres and dine at Skindles. Burberry's had a shop there, and men used to go to the brewery for their baths in the big vats. I was too young to go and see 'Mademoiselle from Armentieres' at the Rue de Oakium.

On our horse line there was a place called Warloy. I used to see some of the officers going up the line and asked them to come into my very comfortable billets and on two nights we played poker. The sky was the limit and I lost two months' pay in two nights! Since then I've never played poker again.

There were often requests in local newspapers for books and magazines to be sent to the front as well as gramophones and records for officers. War Illustrated in December 1915 reported that there was a clamour for books which were not about war. Jane Austen's books became popular. In the Daily Telegraph of July 2013, Dr Paula Byrne explained that Austen's novels were often given to shell-shocked or wounded soldiers as they 'were able to give them a sense of security, providing comfort in a crazy world'.

Walter Greenhalgh

got back with some difficulty to Poperinghe on the Saturday night, and I spent the night at Talbot House. Then the morning after I went and found my battalion.

He took refuge in a house which had been opened in 1915 by army chaplains Neville Talbot and Philip 'Tubby' Clayton. It was named Talbot House (nicknamed Toc H) after Neville's brother Gilbert Talbot who was killed in July 1915. It was a place for rest and relaxation. There were rooms for reading and writing, a kitchen for refreshments, a lovely garden and a chapel on the top floor as well as a room to watch films and concerts. Above all it was a place to escape, and everyone who went there was treated as an equal. The sign on the door said, 'All rank abandon ye who enter here'.

Walter Greenhalgh
(Borthwick Institute)

After the war, Tubby Clayton returned to England and opened other Toc H houses in various places. But the original Talbot House remains a museum.

Grave of Gilbert Talbot
(Alan Milner)

CHAPTER SEVEN

SIGNALLERS

Joe Bircham was born in 1896 in Elsham in Norfolk.

If you worked at the colliery, you could be exempt if you wanted. They didn't take them from the pit. But I signed up. They tried to put me in the infantry. This didn't appeal to me, so they put me in the Royal Engineers Signal Company. Semaphore, Morse code, flags, buzzers.

Our job was to keep up communications. We got attached to brigade headquarters. At one place, they were doing a lot of mining underneath. They gave me a temporary stripe to go up to the battalion because they were going to have a special mining effort and they wanted to know all about it very quickly at headquarters.

Sometimes we'd go out laying lines and there'd be shelling coming over and smashing them up. You had this little black instrument on your back and you'd get hold of the line. You soon found out when it were broken because they'd want a message sending and you couldn't get through. So off you went until you'd come to wherever the break was. Then the trouble was finding the other end to join it up again. You carried a length of wire in case there was a gap. If both ends answered, the battalion and the brigade, you were all right. I've been out nearly all night on them jobs.

There were shells coming over most of the time. At first it wasn't too severe but the biggest difficulty was the cold and the mud. You'd to be careful of snipers, especially if you were sent out in daylight. If a communication was broken, you'd try and mend it. We went in all sorts of places on the Somme and I got one leave home in four years.

We came to a big quarry and the old brigadier set them to build him a latrine in the side of the quarry. We had a fella called Polly Perkins, he were just like a parrot. He were set on building this latrine. He must have gone into the general's quarters and found the rum jar. And next minute old Polly were absolutely blind drunk. The general come back and there were a hell of a row, but he got away with it somehow. I think the brigade staff had a soft spot for him. When Polly come out of the line he didn't bother about sleeping. His one ambition was to go to Bethune and find a house of easy virtue and he did every time. Poor old Polly, he got killed.

I had a friend, Seth Holloway, and we were out of the line and I were writing letters. I says, "Have you any letters to write, Seth?" "No I haven't". So I gave him my sister's address. And the first leave we had, they got engaged. And as soon as he come out of the army, they got married.

Grandcourt, a place near Cambrai, there was a blown down church. And underneath it were catacombs, and our staff selected that as a signal office and headquarters for brigade. They found some Germans in and they said that it were all wired for a blow up, it had got mined all over, they were frightened of being caught in it themselves. So they cleared that and used it as headquarters.

Signallers training
(York Oral History Society)

The Germans were shelling all the time in the wood. You'd to find a shell hole and look out for messages coming. And eventually at night it came, the first signal message with map references as to where they were, how far they'd got, and these continued to come all through the night. We were stuck in this hole and the shells *were all round. We had to read these signals, and another fella was writing it down on a pad. Each one, we immediately dispatched to the dugout where the staff were. What a rotten job that was, nowt to eat, nowt to drink, stuck in there for a long time. These intricate map references took some reading. After a day or two, the 62nd division relieved us. The brigade went in with 3000 men, they come out with a hundred.*

Signallers with Joe Blades
(Josephine Clampitt)

Tommy Oughton was with the

2nd Barnsleys in 1917. We were at Mailly-Maillet then taken into Basin Wood. My job was signaller and linesman. I had a small telephone over my shoulder, it used to swing like a woman with her handbag. I had to install this, and telephone back to headquarters that we'd got that certain position. We were told it had been shelled that much, there would be very little opposition. We were taken by surprise.

If a line was disconnected I'd got to get out. We'd perhaps a yard or four foot of cable and through that we'd have a safety pin. We were going to find where it was broke, stick your pins in and get in touch. That were a dangerous job. I did see German wire but I never got up to it, you could see bodies hung on it.

Two signallers had been blown up. That were my job to go up to headquarters during the night to take a telephone. We'd to crawl on our bellies. It were my nature as far as finding humour was concerned and I'm walking up this bit of trench and there's just a hand hanging out. I took hold of it and says, "All right old lad, we'll see thee coming back".

I'd been at Passchenhaele up to my knees in mud and the tanks went over, and they were absolutely useless, all that mud and slime and the tanks were held up. Then we were marched to Neuve Chapelle and I started with dysentery. I came back to England, I weighed just over six stone. And they didn't know me. I had a nervous breakdown after t'war. I were off four month. If I'd been sensible, I should have got a pension at that time but I hadn't the strength.

Tommy Oughton
(Alf Peacock Collection)

I had a brother and the two of us slept together. Things were that bad, he had to get out of bed on a night, I'd been bumping him. I woke up on a morning all the skin off my knuckles off with smashing the old fashioned iron bedstead. The doctor advised me to go away. My mother didn't want me to go.

I went to London to a YMCA hostel, then to St Ives in Cornwall. It was summertime and I were going from village to village along the coast. And I finished up in Deal in Kent. I was away about six weeks.

Wilf Braithwaite

was born 1895 and I joined up in early May 1915. 4th Battalion Territorial Regiment Green Howards. Then I went in for a course in signalling. We had semaphore, flag signalling, Morse, using the sun, what they call heliography and lights for night signalling. Then we went from Southampton on a ship called the Viper.

One of the advantages was that if there was a shelter you had to have it for the telephones. I had one segment with tons of sand bags. It had a gas proof blanket and a wooden framework. Originally Siemens used to make all the telephones for the British army, and they had a plate bottom, and all the messages that went through that telephone, the Germans could read it. So they decided to use metallic returns, that's two wires.

The Germans were always methodical, they'd start at one o'clock, give you half an hour of hell with minnies, [minenwerfer] trench mortars. These minnies were like an oil drum, filled with everything, metal and nails and oil. They used to shoot up till they'd lost momentum, and turn on their sides and roar.

I was in a communication trench that was about three quarter of a mile long. We were huddled up with the telephone, the lines had gone, they'd levelled our communication trench, and we were just sat in this little place and we heard these damn minnies howling and dropping. One of them blew the blanket and the grass roof and the wooden frame in among us. One dropped in the trench behind us. We just sat there wondering where the next one was going to come, it was hell.

We entrained again when we were relieved at Ypres. We were in bivouacs. It was a sunny day, and one of our lads had a pair of riding breeches and laid them out in the sun. I thought the blooming lice were going to carry them trousers away. They breed faster on some people than others. I'd never seen such a heaving mass.

We got our positions secured, between High Wood and Martinpuich. We were on the high ground. We lost 500 in three days. They had no idea, it was just mass slaughter, sending blooming men loaded with barbed wire and such like, as well as their equipment. They were jiggered before they got to the German trenches. Then one of the tanks broke down just behind our forward position. The Germans had observation balloons up, wanted to destroy this tank you see. There were six or eight inch howitzers sent across. One poor lad who was just conscious, he joined up the same day as I did, I gave him a drink of water and helped him as much as I could, and the stretcher bearers came and took him away, but I don't think he'd live.

All the ammunition for the front line went through the caves of Arras for the offensive. There was a mile of these caverns. It was a bright Sunday morning when we marched in and we were in there for a week to a fortnight. It was a slimy job. All the moisture from your breath and all the chalk rock above. Arras had been a lovely town. We once went to one of these theatrical groups that used to travel for the troops. One end of the theatre had been blown out but it was very good.

The caves became a network of tunnels, which sheltered 20,000 British and Commonwealth troops before the Battle of Arras in 1917. Rediscovered in 1990, they now house a museum to commemorate those soldiers.

This useless officer sent three of us up to establish a flag signalling. We were there in this captured German trench in a very prominent position. After ten minutes one of our officers came with an urgent message. We hadn't been ten yards out when I heard this howitzer coming. I said, "Get down". One lad was injured in the shoulder but the lad who was carrying the message had half his calf blown off. I put the whole wad [field dressing] inside to replace his flesh, and wrapped him up, and I was having to shield him from mud and soil that was dropping down on us, and shell fire. I got back to headquarters with the message. But a shell came over and I got hit. I managed to walk two kilometres back. All wounded that could walk had to go to a dressing station. They roughly bandaged me up, then there were military ambulances come in. They got me alongside the driver, because the other bad cases were at the back. We hadn't gone half a mile, when we met Sir Douglas Haig with his thigh top boots, and about thirty of his Bengal Lancers escort. I was saluted by Sir Douglas Haig that day.

I was marked for an operation but they couldn't do it because there was that excess of wounded. That night my temperature went up to 104 so they made me a case for the next day. Before I went in, an orderly came round with some rice pudding with currants in that looked appetising. I had the operation about half past three, by half past four I was stuck into that rice pudding. I was six weeks there then we got on board a ship. I never had such a lovely journey in my life. There was four of us with crutches, we had a cabin on the top deck. This was in May, everything was in full flower, almonds, cherries, apples and pears. We travelled to Le Havre that night and joined the convoy, 20 vessels going across.

I think the war was a tragedy. I think they were right, 'lions led by donkeys'.

Harry Christmas was a signaller.

The messages were all in code. It would be in a block of five letters and the COs knew the code. I'd put the letter down that the signal represented and then they'd work the code out. I nearly always knew them but I wasn't supposed to and they didn't pay me to.

John Yates was born in 1897 in York.

I wasn't in the front line very long. I was in an officers' dugout maintaining the telephone. I remember going over in no man's land once with the telephone line and bullets were flying all round. We'd have to lay a line and then took turns as signallers to man the telephone.

It was flooded and battered about, the traverses were all broken, but the conditions were worse in Flanders. The great thing of being a signaller, you were more or less on your own, you weren't regimented so much. I could get a bike and go and see my friends if I was out in the rear. I met quite a few of our Methodist friends over there. I had a cousin in the air force and I cycled out to see him. And another member of our church, Centenary in York.

Gerald Dennis had

the Mark D3 telephone. We were linked up with the battalion on the left, the battalion on the right, the reserve battalion, and they were linked up with brigade. And we were also linked direct to the 18 pound battery. You were a rifleman as well as a signaller.

There was a lad of 16¾, a lad of 17, a lad of 18, myself 19, another 19, and an old man of 26. That was the left sector of Ploegsteert Wood. Everything's calm and quiet one Wednesday afternoon, beautiful sunshine, tea was up. You'd go with your dixie, and get your half pint of tea, and left two signallers in the dugout. I came round the bay, to sit on the firing step, and enjoy the sunshine. And I'm just walking into the bay, and the 18 year-old is stood there, and his blood spurts out and he just sinks down and dies. I think it was a sniper. It upset me very much.

So many troops went every night up to the front line, carrying A-frames, sandbags, tools, equipment for the REs, barbed wire. So there was always too many men in the front line. The officers would have mess, finish about half past eight, and at the colonel's instigation, one officer says, "I'll go prowling in no man's land tonight," and he'd take a man with him to go across and bag a Hun. But nobody ever succeeded because the Hun would have a sentry in his front line, a hidden machine-gunner, and a man with a Very pistol just firing off. They really looked after their men better. Old Tockey Turner, our signal officer, decided to go over one night and he took Signaller Bell, and Bell got a bullet through his foot.

You put your haversack onto your back with your enamel mug, or a plate and knife and fork, and little possessions, your iron rations, an extra bandolier over each shoulder, that's 200 rounds, a bomb in each trouser pocket and a flare in each tunic pocket. And a spade stuck down me back, a flag and a telephone, and my rifle. It's farcical when you look back. You went over to gain ground at a cost, you didn't engage the enemy.

When we came to the edge of Delville Wood, that was in a pitiful state, and it was dusk. You could see trees broken down, bodies lying about. We waited there and we heard the chug-chug-chug of some mysterious machine. The officer had allocated six men of a section to guard a 'landship'. It was a tank. They all were killed.

We were to the right of Flers. The colonel's a bit anxious, because the final objective should have been Guedencourt and he just hasn't enough troops. And they send word back, but no message comes through to tell them to stop. So the colonel starts waving this flag, "Come on men", and they go on. They run into terrific machine-gun fire along a cornfield. The colonel got shot straight through the forehead as he'd knelt on one knee to look through his glasses to see what was ahead. He was a very brave man.

Gerald was in the same unit as Anthony Eden, British Prime Minister in the 1950s, and he was asked to check some of the details in his autobiography.

I was vetting Eden's 'Another World'. I wrote to the War Office and got the official figures, and I was 16 out in my estimate. I was orderly corporal that day, I had to be present when all the roll calls were called out, and we lost 394 out of 660. We lost the colonel, the adjutant, all the officers but one. The junior officers just got killed off. The Germans were clever. [They would look for the officer's Sam Browne belt]. *Sometimes the officers went over dressed as Tommies.*

Many a man never got leave in 20, 22 months, the Tommies in the line. But the man at brigade headquarters, he was having his third leave. I went home on leave and it was another world. Nobody's in your world, nobody understands anything. I'd sit with mother, she was a widow. I'd get up and go for a walk, come back, sit with mother. You couldn't tell them what it was like, you had the feeling they'd never believe you.

CHAPTER EIGHT

ROYAL ARMY MEDICAL CORPS

The Royal Army Medical Corps was the non-combatant arm of the British army. Its role in the First World War was a crucial one. Casualties in the battles were taken by stretcher bearers to a dressing station, (often a dugout), from there to a casualty clearing station which was often a few tents behind the lines or a building if one were available, and to a base hospital. Men were returned to the front line as soon as possible, but for more serious cases, for a wound known as a 'Blighty', they went by ambulance train and boat and returned to England.

George Harbard was born in Slough in 1895 and was

George Harbard with father George, mother Anne, sister Louise 1914

(Martin Roberts)

in the 44th Field Ambulance. We did months and months of training. We went up to St Omer. And then from there we marched up to Poperinghe and operated right up to Ypres with the horse wagons, the ambulances.

We were collecting casualties from the Cloth Hall in Ypres. They were brought there from the Menin Road. The Medical Corps had no rifles, only first aid dressing bags. We were divided up into areas. The stretcher bearers went into the line itself, the first aid men brought casualties to a clearing station and our people patched them up. The Friends Ambulance Unit operated from the final clearing station behind the lines and there were a lot of women taking you back.

One morning, the Germans were shelling and there was a platoon of our infantry in one of the cellars in Arras. A shell dropped on the wall and blew the gas into where these chaps were sleeping. They came into our dressing station and by midday they were all dead. The whole platoon. One of my pals was sent crackers and he had to be evacuated and sent home. He was one of the stretcher bearers and he went absolutely nuts.

There was a German tunnel running under Menin Road and I know because I've slipped in it. It was only discovered when we went forward. But they were clever.

Behind Delville Wood the Germans had dugouts down as tall as a house. They had passages all filled up with bunkers. So when the Germans had a rest they had a real rest. They brought them in there and they were fed down there.

George Harbard 1916 with 44th Field Ambulance RAMC, on right at back
(Martin Roberts)

They were too strong and we weren't equipped like they were with the variety of machine guns.

It was a war without proper direction. The men were asked to do things they should never have been asked to do.

George Harbard training
(Martin Roberts)

Arthur Devereux was a member of the RAMC.

There was 50 ambulances. There'd be five probably laid up for repairs, leaving 45 in commission. Then there was the store wagon, the workshop which had lathes and drilling machines and a blacksmith's shop. Then a supply wagon, two staff cars, two dispatch drivers.

It was the last day of June, a Friday. I was up a little way behind the line and parked in what had been a village. Alongside was an old farm building. Outside were all these men lined up handing in any surplus kit, which appeared to be mainly great coats. When I saw these young fellas, I knew that within a few hours many of them would be seriously wounded or killed. It made me wonder, where was our civilisation?

The attack [on the Somme] took place at 7.30. By 8 o'clock we were picking up casualties. This went on all day and the traffic was somewhat heavy, both mechanical and horses. Several weeks after, our company orders stated that our unit alone had moved 1500 stretcher cases during the first 24 hours. There were continual trench raids which meant unnecessary casualties because there was nothing gained. The price paid was not worth it. One night I went to the dressing station and there was a young man in the Royal Engineers and he had a severe dose of gas. When they were carrying him out, one of the medical staff said, "Twenty minutes". It was impossible to get down to the casualty station in twenty minutes. I had with me a medical orderly, he got in the back of the ambulance but he couldn't do anything to help except keep clearing the discharge coming from his mouth due to severe lung damage. He just opened the window and said, "He's worse". We left him at the casualty clearing station.

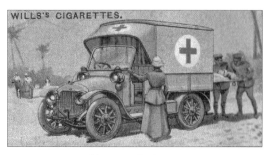

Motor ambulance
(Mike Race)

In one point on the Somme they had a miniature railway line and a crude truck with two tiers and they slid the casualty onto these, and would probably get about half a dozen on, and they'd just push them down the line to a point where we would pick up at the bottom of the ridge. During that vile weather, many of the casualties were caused by frost bite and gangrene.

At Messines Ridge when that was blown, the explosion was reckoned to be heard in London, but I never heard it. Must have been accustomed to it. Australian troops were involved there and we had to pick up the casualties and take them to a chateau. We went round the back and there was a kitchen garden, and there would be about thirty stretchers with the bodies of these lads, rolled up in blankets and labelled ready for burial.

Motor Ambulance Kitchen
(The Graphic)

The casualties were transported over bad road conditions. Those with head wounds would be put on the lower rack in the ambulance. Two small sandbags, one each side of the head, would be placed to prevent as much roll as possible. Those with a serious leg injury would again be on the bottom rack but a sling of bandage or other material would be used to place under his leg which would then be tied to the framework of the top ambulance rack. I remember on one occasion up near Albert, it was a fearful morning, and I had a mixed load. There was one German boy prisoner and he had a bad leg injury. He was on the bottom rack and his leg was slung to the top. I had this corporal with me who was very much disliked. This German boy screamed out and the corporal said, "Take no notice of the so and so, carry on". I decided to pull up. And this boy's leg, the sling had collapsed and his leg was lying on the stretcher. Every movement of that vehicle must have been agonising.

You'd only have a medical orderly occasionally. You were on your own more or less. One night I was down at a transport farm loading and there was a horse limber at the top of the road and a Jerry balloon came up over the ridge. This limber driver must have seen it and he put his horse into a hell of a gallop which attracted this observer in his balloon. So he decided to put a shell over. Fortunately the ground was very soft and muddy and the shell buried itself. I'd ducked automatically and all I received were a shower of muck. But the orderly in the back, when he heard the scream of the shell he took one dive out. I got up and went to the back of the ambulance and jumped in, just in time to see one lad getting off the top. Fright! So I pushed him back and said, "Cool off".

At night, leaving the Menin Road to come down to Ypres, if it happened to be a moonlit night, it was eerie. You'd be picking your way through the rubble and you would probably hear just an odd crack of a gun and the whine of a shell. It gave you the creeps. One Sunday, I'd been up on the Menin Road all night and early morning it was immensely quiet, I picked four casualties up and we went down to near Poperinghe. We made our way back and as I was a mile away from Ypres, I looked over the German line and there was a string of balloons. As we entered Ypres, I'd hardly got into second gear before there was a hell of an explosion. I could hardly see with the dust, I was rubbing my eyes and smoke went in them. I tried to clear the muck out of my sight which I couldn't very well. I was in hospital about seven months.

RAMC Ambulances

(Mike Race)

But some used various practices to injure themselves. One was putting their foot under a transport wheel. I heard of one poor devil, he must have been mentally disturbed, he took his boot off, shot himself through the foot, put his boot back on. There was a special hospital for the self-inflicted. Then they were up for court martial.

William 'Bill' Newby joined the RAMC in 1914. His son Ted tells his story.

He joined the Red Cross and went to classes and learnt about first aid. He was 21 when war broke out. He went to France in 1915. He was once wandering along looking for anybody injured and he was in a trench and there was a German officer standing there. They just looked at each other and the officer saw he had the Red Cross and just beckoned him to clear off. He realised he was in German lines and got himself back as quick as he could. He was lucky it was a German officer, if it had been somebody else he could have shot him.

They were tending wounded all the time and he went to one man, a French soldier. He was lying there, clearly not going to live, and he pulled out a picture, (he assumed it was of his wife), and the Frenchman said, "Quelle dommage", it meant, "What a pity", and just died. That must have struck home, it stuck in his mind, that poor man.

He was wounded twice. The first one, he was hit with shrapnel in his legs, brought back to England. To his dying day he had one piece of shrapnel in his calf. As a kid he let me feel this jagged bit. It was stuck in the fleshy part, one bit they never bothered removing. Then near the end of the war he got shot and had a bullet in his elbow. But each time you're wounded, you're sent back again.

After the war, because he'd been in the RAMC, in the streets round us he was the man who bandaged people. We're talking about the '20s, '30s. When somebody had an accident, he had a good store of bandages and lint and iodine. People would knock on the door and father would go and bandage them up. He would never refuse. He still had the iodine, which wasn't very pleasant on cuts. That really stung.

William Newby at front in RAMC
(Ted Newby)

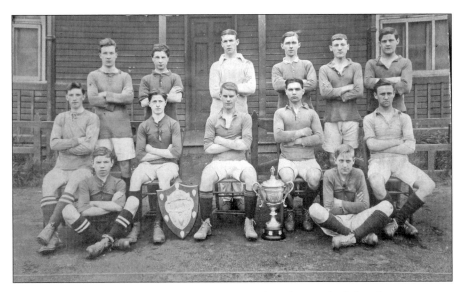

William Newby in football team just before the war, far left at front
(Ted Newby)

He got the Distinguished Conduct Medal and the Military Medal. He got a piece in the Press, but he was an unwilling hero. The Lord Mayor of York said that the one who comes back from the war the most decorated soldier would receive the Freedom of the City of York, and he wouldn't apply. He said, "They can find out, I'm not going begging". In fact the man who was given it had two MMs, so my father would have got the Freedom.

The Yorkshire Evening Press reported in 1917, 'Private William Newby, 24 years of age, serving with a Field Ambulance of the Royal Army Medical Corps has been awarded the Military Medal for conspicuous gallantry and devotion to duty. Previously at Messrs Rowntree's, before the war he was a keen member of the youth ambulance class at the works, and gained the medallion of the St John Ambulance Association'.

Bill Newby was awarded the DCM 'for conspicuous gallantry and devotion to duty bringing many wounded from shell holes. He made two journeys into an area swept by machine gun fire and brought back nine cases'.

(See chapter on York in World War One for details of the York men awarded the VC).

Frank Wood

went out with the personnel for 56th General, and that was the hospital unit. We had to take all the equipment across from Southampton, it had to be unloaded at Cherbourg, and then we got on a train to an unknown destination. Eventually we arrived at Etaples.

Motorised soup kitchen

(Mike Race)

I was kept on a ward and we had to work the night, take on the patients coming in, assist in dressings and generally keep the ward tidy, all the wants and whereabouts for the patients. I was in the operating theatre for a time. We'd give them anaesthetics. It used to be a bit of a sight, amputations in them days, used to clip the pieces together *instead of sewing them. We had an incinerator and if you got amputations you'd take these down and throw them in.*

There was a terrible epidemic of pneumonia and influenza. We had men carrying corpses down for burial. We got that many that they used to bury 'em in sacks inside the coffins. The Etaples cemetery, a lot of chaps are buried in there that I knew.

Lewis Wyrill was in the Medical Corps.

Once in early 1915 a shell dropped into the wagon lines and killed three horses and I had to bandage a wounded horse up. It was a change from bandaging a man.

On the Somme, I don't know how many hundred guns all went off together, it was terrific was the noise. But it was a beautiful summer day. I spent quite a time giving drinks to the wounded. One incident in Aveluy Wood, the shell burst as it left the muzzle and it killed one gunner and injured another. It had taken all the back off his head off. We got this man on a stretcher and we'd half a mile to walk to the dressing station. That poor chap died and then we had to bury him.

I had to start going to Albert to fill my water cart. I came across a bed of strawberries of all things and had strawberries for tea that day.

I had various jobs. I was in charge of a machine that was stoving blankets just outside Ypres. Each unit had to send a party of six men and I superintended putting blankets into the stove and timing it and getting them out again. I had 2,000 clean

Royal Army Medical Corps
(The Graphic 1915)

blankets. On three occasions, I was in charge of the divisional baths. I had to superintend heating of the water and the dishing out of the clean clothing.

There were four of us stretcher bearers, and a doctor in charge. I recall a creeping barrage, a line of bursting shells coming fifty yards. Our dressing station was in the cellar and the piles of rubbish on the top was our safety. But looking out

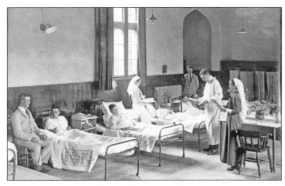

St John's VAD hospital, York 1917

(Hugh Murray Collection)

of the barn window we were watching this barrage getting nearer and nearer, it was a nerve wracking experience. We were out in the open taking the wounded to the relay post and Jerry was throwing gas shells over. The result was that we four all got gassed. The unit pulled out and we had to return to the Field Ambulance. Next morning the four of us woke up, we could neither see or talk. We were packed up into an ambulance. We finished up at the hospital in Etaples for a week. Fortunately my eyesight came back but I couldn't talk for a few days.

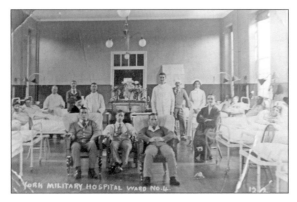

York Military Hospital ward 4

(Hugh Murray Collection)

St. Edmund's Hall, Roundhay, Leeds

(Mike Race)

CHAPTER NINE

THE ARTILLERY

If an infantryman showed particular promise in marksmanship during his training, he would be suggested for a gun team. This would earn him more money. He might join the Royal Field Artillery or the Royal Garrison Artillery, join a Lewis machine gun team, become a sniper or later on, join the Machine Gun Corps. Whilst this was less dangerous than 'going over the top', if he were captured it was more than likely that he would not be taken prisoner.

Arthur Abel

joined the Garrison Artillery, we were on an old South African gun called a 4.7. We ultimately settled in the Field Artillery on the 60 pounder gun. In the training in Tadcaster at John Smith's brewery, the guns were hopelessly out of date, you'd never dream of firing them, but it enabled you to know what a gun was all about. I was imbued with the idea of fighting for Britain. You really hadn't a clue. We hadn't had a real war. You were encouraged to hate the Germans and it was enough to make you do so.

In Tadcaster I was a bombardier in charge of some men. The authorities seconded a man from the Coldstream Guards, a sergeant known as Spikey because of his spiked moustache. He obviously knew nothing about horses, but he did smarten us up. All the guns in those days were pulled by horses, and they're not easy to manoeuvre, you require a lot of training. We received an order from him to give the horses a bran mash which is bran soaked in warm water and you can add linseed. Every horse has a bucket, out of which it both eats and drinks. These buckets were about three quarters full of dry bran. The poor horses snuffed it up, it was in their mouth, nose and eyes. It nearly finished the sergeant off.

We went to Borden near Aldershot for more realistic training in gunnery. You've got to discover why guns fire and where the shells go, and the time came when we had to go to Lark Hill on Salisbury Plain to fire. The 60 pounder is the gun that I remained on to the end of the war. It fires a three inch shell, weighing 60 pounds, it can be quite lethal. On the way we stopped at Stockbridge. The River Test is probably the most famous trout river in the country. We were allowed to bathe. I liked to swim underneath the water, I remember seeing the most magnificent trout. And 30 years after, I took my children there.

There's eight in the gun team. I was number two. The team can't be on duty day and night, they've got to sleep, so the gun team is split. While number one and his half are resting, number two and his half are actually firing.

We were ready to go overseas, and suddenly discovered that we were destined for Mesopotamia, and you require sand rims. Our sister battery had the guns with the sand wheels, so we were switched to France. We got to Le Havre. I was leading the number one gun and riding on a horse, and there was a little Frenchman going to work in a bowler hat. To my amazement he went into a pissoir in the middle of the street and whilst he was firing away, he raised his hat to a lady on the other side who bowed, and I thought my gun team would fall off their horses!

We went to Vimy Ridge. We were being broken in to the sound of machine gun bullets and rifle bullets and shells and given some experience. The train journey was notable because it took two days to do what the average train nowadays would do in a couple of hours. Carriages were reserved for officers and other troops who had some standing. I soon discovered that the best place to travel on a French train was in a horse box. There you could stretch your legs and lie down.

We were on a quiet front, amongst fields. We discovered French peasants harvesting oats and I was induced to use my French to move them. The French farmer was cursing but he moved his stacks or we'd have moved them for him. After battle began on July the 1st 1916, we were in reserve. There was an unbelievable quantity of troops. You heard the barrage, a vast number of guns on both sides. We're dealing with millions of men, supported by equal numbers of artillery of all calibres. The wounded started coming back within 24 hours. It was soon clear that there'd been awful carnage.

At Contalmaison, the Germans had blown up the centre of the road, so the guns had to skirt round. My lead pair of horses pulled in a bit too sharp and down the shell hole we went, which took an awful lot of getting out. It was the only place *where we could get our guns below a slight crest, otherwise you'd be blown up in a matter of minutes. You must go in the dusk, and get them in a position so they're heavily camouflaged. You dig little pits.*

We went up a communication trench carrying equipment. In the half light of the dawn, the infantry moved forward and, suddenly, machine guns opened up and they vanished into the ground. They were a Durham Battalion. It was a shock to see these well trained troops just vanish into the mud in a matter of minutes.

105 mm Heavy gun firing
(Daphne Dench)

At Bazentin le Grand to my astonishment I saw what must be 20 or 30 thousand cavalry. But I never saw any get through. It was one of the saddest days of the war. I saw a South African division go in on the Somme, about the finest set of men I've ever seen. Well equipped, physically in first class condition, about 20 thousand. It took all afternoon and evening to get them into the line, but next night you could have brought them out on a spoon.

To fire a gun, you use friction T2, it ignites the cartridge and the cartridge blows out the shell, and it's clipped into the bridge every time you fire. It would probably weigh a couple of ounces and the socket in which it fits had become warm, and it tended to fly out backwards. It was quite lethal, we killed one CO with it but he'd been warned not to stand where he was.

We were in the middle of action. One of the gun crew who handled the cartridge was smoking and he'd been warned seriously about this. The cartridge is cordite in a silk sheath. It doesn't explode, just this terrific ignition. It burns fiercely and quickly and the last time I saw the man, his face was like cornflakes, and he dived into a big shell hole, because he was in agony. Most of the gun crew were out of action and I got blood poisoning in my thumb.

Having in effect given the declaration that I'd endowed the state with my body, I didn't realise the full extent of that until I was in a hospital in Rouen. A doctor stood by my bedside and said, "We'll take his arm off this afternoon". Which frightened me to death! I had a sack under my arm as big as a football. I was being injected every half hour for tetanus. Anyway it burst and I've still got my arm. They sent me straight down to Etaples to a Canadian hospital. I was there for six weeks, then straight back in line again, onto the Somme.

In 1918 the Hindenburg Line was strong, but it was very lightly held at the front. We were just north of St Quentin and I was sent on horseback to a place called Levergies. I went round the corner of a battered church on horseback, and the Germans were all looking at me, manning machine guns and I was sitting on top of a horse. I got undercover quickly, and then I inspected this position the CO had sent me to. The outcome was we put sacks on the feet of the horses, and sacks round the rims of the guns, and moved up just within yards of our frontline trench, and some diversionary shelling was happening a short distance away, and then we opened up with direct fire straight into this German trench and blew the trench to pieces with high explosives.

At St Quentin we were preparing reserve positions. We had a man in charge of the stores and ammunition. He got hit with something, and I was sent down to take charge, occupying the same bit of ground as the reserve lines of the Gordon Highlanders, the Black Watch. They'd got their band there, with their bagpipes, and for about 72 hours, they nearly drove us frantic with the skirls and *the bagpipes. There was a code word that all the British army had got, Battle Commenced. That meant the German attack had started. They smothered us with gas and smoke, and high explosive. The band of the Black Watch were at the field kitchen having hot soup at half past five in the morning, and the Germans landed a shell. Not only did shell splinters kill and wound the Gordon Highlanders but the hot soup was flung all over them.*

155m heavy gun and preparation for field military service
(Daphne Dench)

Arthur Britton

was trained as a rifleman. We had three units and each platoon had a Lewis gun, but machine guns were under the Machine Gun Corps.

I had a Lewis gunner with me, he were a grand little fella. We were in one of these shell holes and he were rat a tatting away with this Lewis gun. We found out there were only two of us, and we were fighting the whole German army. I said,

"Let's get the proper side of the canal". So this little fella went one way, I went to this little stream, there was a plank across. I got on this and of course they'd just been waiting for somebody because they dropped a trench mortar and blew me and the blinking plank up in the air. I came down and blood were running off my chin end. I ran my fingers round my head and my head was still on. I picked myself up and the canal had got a lot of trench boards lashed together. So I set to and crawled across. And then I must have passed out. When I came to, I was in a field hospital. And they said, "You were lucky. We just grabbed you, threw you in the ambulance".

Harry Cockerill was

a gun layer. The gun coils up and pulls back again and on each gun there's a sergeant in charge. When I went in I was only a lad. I couldn't help with lifting a shell. I hadn't the strength. But I had to persevere and I got it eventually. In 1917, on Easter Tuesday, we started firing and we were getting a lot of hits. We brought down most of the balloons. Our aeroplanes went round and brought them all down. It was marvellous.

In Ypres they put us in an old convent underneath the ground. You couldn't lay on blankets, they were all wet. They moved us after a day or so. I saw an army of rats escaping from Ypres near the river with a big white one leading them. They were all as blind as a bat. They'd been gassed.

I was always on the guns. It got really monotonous towards the end. If you're firing a gun there's nothing else on your mind. We'd be firing four or five hundred rounds a day. We didn't take our clothes off. You were lousy, in a mess really, right till the last day when I got demobbed. On Vimy Ridge, I heard that my brother was in Arras. They let me go. I had to walk across strange country, I did eight miles, and I met the poor little beggar. He had frostbitten legs and was in a bad state. I spent a pleasant two or three hours with him, took him up to the canteen and fed him.

Ernest Deighton was born in 1894 in York. At the age of 87 he took a tour of the battlefields.

I joined up at Fulford Barracks [Imphal] and went to Pontefract. I'd been there four days and they put me into hospital. I had pneumonia and measles and was in an isolation ward. Then they put me in as an ordinary runner doing all the letters down to Pontefract, I was there for six weeks.

The first night in the trenches was terrible. I were all nerves I can tell you, like a lot of them. We didn't know what we was going into. The first night, about 20 of us were helping cut from one shell hole to another. I'm sorry to say that our mortars didn't smash the barbed wire up for us to get through. It was only cut in places. I got hit and had five wounds. Finger ends, shoulders, piece missing from my big toe. I still have shrapnel in my thumb. I managed to get into a shell hole and there were five of us. I was the only one that lived.

Ernest Deighton July 1986,
70th anniversary Battle of Somme
(Mary Sylvester)

There was shell fire and smoke and my tongue was as big as two. I started to go, I didn't know whether I was going to the German line, but I dropped not far off our first line and I heard a voice, "Halt, who goes there?" I just shouted, "Orange" and he says, "Pass". Wasn't I thankful? Out of that division of 997, only 87 came back. They sent me straight down to Etaples hospital.

After recovering, Ernest trained as a Lewis gunner. He went to Thiepval.

Imphal Barracks. York 1916
(Mike Race)

We were there one night and a shell came over and we hadn't had owt to eat, and it up-earthed potatoes in a garden and the lot of us grabbed these potatoes. And we crawled through two fields of corn and all kinds of stuff.

As a Lewis gunner, I was number 1, I had the gun. On Sunday, October 1st the order came, my objective was an old farmhouse. But they dropped

Ernest Deighton presented to Queen Mother, 1988 Nostell Priory, presentation of colours to 8th Battalion Light Infantry

(Mary Sylvester)

a shell not far off me. All I saw when I came round, was part of my gun, at the side of my face, in the shell hole. The leg was partly turned around. A piece of shell was still in my leg. And shell burns. I put my puttee and string round it, and my entrenching tool in to tie it, because I was bleeding. I started to crawl back, I fell in another trench and the stretcher bearers picked me up and carried me back to Contalmaison. And there were rows and rows of us laid out badly wounded.

Bill Harrison

was in the Lewis gun section carrying panniers, with magazines and ammunition. I'd put an army coal shovel down my braces. Then they counter attacked, swooping the trenches in a biplane. My number 2 were shot in the head and I took over. I fired till we had nothing to fire. We got into a sunken road and reinforcements were later coming up.

There were 120 of us in our company and 110 were either killed or wounded!

Herbert Cussons was born in 1890 in York.

I was in the 1ˢᵗ West Riding Royal Garrison Artillery. We went to Armentieres. The infantry had such smiling faces when they saw us with guns. I was in charge of a black horse called Nettle. He did everything, even plough. I was an outrider. It was a quiet part of the front.

We went in training for ammunition, and we bombarded. Then we went to Festubert. Lloyd George said, "Give us the guns and the ammunition", and we did. I was a mounted orderly, going up to the guns headquarters. We were near the crossroads at Ypres and shelling all round. We'd been on the run for five days. I was glad to get the riding breeches off. I dashed in there, in my shirt. They said, "Go on foot. If a shell bursts, it'll just hit your shoulders". I went back. There were thousands of troops. We realised something was to happen.

Arras was bad too, there was a big ammunition dump and it went up. I got on a horse bareback and got out of it, we were very near, shells was dropping. It was such an inferno. All ammunition, 60 pounders, all going west. This was worse than Sodom and Gomorrah in the Bible. Then gas came, tear shells. The general says, "If you've got your goggles, put them on. Because it's gas shells".

We were in the salient for 11 months. We had truckloads of the wounded. The firing nearly knocked me off my horse. Then we went back to Armentieres. We were there while the finish.

But I'd have sacrificed a limb to be home.

Ted Hartley

arrived at the German barbed wire and luckily the tanks rolled it all flat. It was easy for us to get into the trench.

Herbert Cussons

(Eileen Tutill)

They asked who could use a German machine gun. I said, "I can". "How do you know you can?" He was a bit sarcastic. "Because I was trained on one, on a Maxim gun". So he said, "I'll give you two men, as a crew". The Germans had dumped this machine gun, and we picked it up and carried it back. I mounted this gun and fired a burst with it and it seemed to cheer everybody up.

He asked me if I could knock a German sniper out of a building. "One or two of our chaps have been sniped out of there". It was built of bricks and 9.2 inch shells were blowing the place to bits, there was brick dust flying all over. I didn't see this man again until the Second World War, when he was colonel of the Home Guard Battalion I was in!

I had a job finding ammunition. I had to go along the German fire step and find bandoliers that the Germans had left about, and load the belt up. In the meantime the Germans made an attack. Three of us stood on the fire step and fired at these German helmets. We couldn't see the faces. But my rifle bolt jammed. I saw another gun that had been dumped, so I picked that up and it was a good rifle. As I was walking down the trench, looking for ammunition, a shot rang out behind me. I whipped round instantly and fired from the hip. Unlucky for this German, the

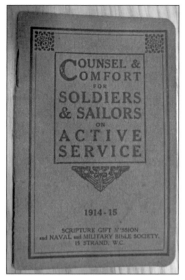

Counsel and Comfort for troops
(Borthwick Institute)

bullet hit him in the shoulder. He was going to pick this rifle up that I discarded but he panicked and I hit him. He didn't half yelp. But I told a stretcher bearer to go and look and he bandaged him up.

The day was going on and it might have been six o'clock, and the Germans made another attack with bombs, and there were movement in some bushes which I thought was an enemy lurking there. I give a burst of it with machine gun, and next thing a trench mortar bomb burst just beyond me. A piece of this bomb had struck the machine gun. It cut the belt in two right against the feed block and it broke a piece off. I bet that piece of bronze is still there, and somebody with a metal detector could find it.

There was some rejoicing in our company. The sergeant major said, "Here, Hartley boy," and he gave me half a mug full of rum.

Claud Hey

was a corporal in the Lewis gunners. When we got to Aldershot, we were able to specialise. Signal unit, cookery, machine gun service, sanitary squad, snipers. I liked the Lewis gun because it was light and you could fire it from the hip. We were trained every day how to assemble and take down and there were drums to put the bullets in. They'd fire 60 a second.

Our baptism of fire was in Ploegsteert Wood. It was like a forest with huts in. No sandbags and it was only 200 yards from the line, bullets used to whistle through the huts at night. There was a farmhouse just behind the wood and every time troops were changing over, the windmill sails would go round. We spotted that, it was a signal to the Germans that they were changing over. He was a spy so he was put down.

We hadn't been in the wood an hour before the heavy bombardment. About six killed straight away. The first to be killed in our battalions was Goldberg, a Leeds College lad. His parents were very sorry he joined up, they didn't want him to. He was a splendid chap too.

We made a petition to the colonel that if we were going to be in these huts at night, we'd better get some sandbags. One man was killed by a bullet which went through the woodwork of the hut, hit his equipment hanging on a hook, hit the scabbard of his bayonet and ricocheted down into him and killed him in the hut.

The Germans had a special gun, better than our 18 pounder and that was a good gun. We called it a whizz bang, it had a very low trajectory, 'whizz' was when it was fired and 'bang' was when it dropped into the trench. One day a German big shell fetched the top off a tree and the authorities in our brigade thought they'd dig that tree up and put a steel tree in with a little loophole and there was an observer and they could see right across to the German trenches. Do you know that steel tree wasn't up two days before it was knocked down? We had a water tank on stilts, they put a shell through that, we had no water for two days.

Arthur Pierse

was lead driver of the firing battery. You had six horses and a gun, and ammunition carriers to feed your guns. We had 18 pounders. You were feeding guns, going back for more ammunition, it was no way to live, you just lived like rats. There were no tents. All the trees blown to pieces, Ypres was all blazing.

The gunners would say, "Are you going by Hellfire Corner?" "Yes". "Well put some of these in", and they'd throw a lot of our dead boys in, for us to lay them down in this big graveyard.

Our wagon was a limber. You dropped the back down and there were 18 pounds in each pocket. We also used pack horses, with just the saddle and the packs on. We put four shells in each side and two on top. We'd go round the shell holes and tip them off and get another load. Sometimes it seemed very quiet and you just toddled along, but many a time if they were doing a bit of strafing, we'd have to gallop. If we lost a lot of horses and men, we'd go down to the reclamation place and there were proper broncos from Australia and Canada. The horses had to stand up to their bellies in mud. There were some craters you could put a church in. And there was dead laid in them. I had two horses blown up and I was left for dead. I was woken up on a road, but eventually I got to my division.

There were gas masks for horses. It was in a bag, you opened the horse's mouth and put your hand in and pulled its tongue out and you put a clip on its tongue, and then let go. It went like a pocket right over its mouth and we had to do that regular.

James Walton, who was Mayor of Barnsley in his later years, was born there in 1890.

I'd always had an inkling for big guns and I may have thought a big gun will be further away from the front. I joined the Royal Garrison Artillery and went to Fort Burgoyne at Dover Castle.

They'd train officers on the same parade ground and that's where I learned the difference between officers and rank and filers, because they used to say, "Officers and gentlemen dismiss", and to us, "Parade fall out".

We were trained on ordinary field guns and transferred to the Pier Turret Battery in Dover. Then we went to France, where they said, "Sorry, there are no heavy guns available so you are now going on to trench mortars". It was a frontline job so it meant eight days of intensive infantry training including bayonet fighting and the old routine of, "Present arms, shoulder arms".

The mortars were long sticks with a great big sixty pounder at the end. But it's amazing how many men were lost through our faulty ammunition, with premature explosions. They were supposed to last so long but sometimes they only lasted one second. A trench mortar battery consisted of four guns. Twenty men plus an officer, a sergeant and a corporal.

At Rouen I met a chaplain who asked if there was anything he could do for us. "Yes sir, I'd like you to write to my wife if you will". "Certainly I will". It wasn't till I got a letter from my wife that I got to know the chaplain was Studdert Kennedy, affectionately known as 'Woodbine Willie'. He'd come in the front line and there was a packet of Woodbines for them that wanted them. So I had the privilege and pleasure of meeting 'Woodbine Willie'.

We spent quite a bit of our time filling sandbags. We kept hearing a sniper rattling away. I was lifting the shovel, with soil and water, to put in to a sandbag. And my pal's stood here holding it. I just turned round and down he went. I lifted his cap off and the top of his head had gone.

The infantry used to say, "You fellows are a damned nuisance because you provoke retaliation". And we did.

James got the Meritorious Service Medal in 1918 for rescuing a wounded officer while he was wounded himself.

Hugh Whitehead

joined the Royal Field Artillery in 1915. We had to learn all the parts of the guns, to take an 18 pounder gun apart, and replace it. We had a man at one side arming the shells to track up into the nozzle of the gun. We went to Salisbury Plain and were taught to fire live ammunition and use rifles on the range.

There were four guns to a battery, and six of us on each gun. We got our range from the officer in the front line. We went to Southampton and onto a four storey cattle boat. Iron boats with guns and ammunition in the bottom, all the fighting equipment. All the animals were on the first storey. I happened to get in a flying column taking ammunition, that's what I did for most of the war. I had my 21st birthday there. I got a parcel from home, and there were meat pies and it were all broken up. We emptied it out on a sheet and just got stuck in with our hands.

Hugh Whitehead officer training

(Ann Firth)

Hugh Whitehead (seated) at Amiens

(Ann Firth)

Hugh Whitehead 2nd right, 2nd row up from front
(Ann Firth)

On the Somme all the artillery were lined up, in sections of their calibre. The 18 pounders, then the howitzers, the 16 pounders. It must have gone on two days, all the bombardment.

Hugh and May Whitehead 1950s
(Ann Firth)

We were in mud. But the mules were marvellous, they could walk round the shallows. We usually got the orders the night before, where we were going. We had to make the route, do the map reading.

After the Somme battle itself, there were chaps on the roadside, some of them without legs. We weren't allowed to touch them. [When the Germans broke through in 1918] we were at Metz. We walked from Metz to Cambrai, and they shelled us out of our positions. It was chaos. There were mules with half of their backsides off. Somebody would shoot them eventually. We had the best captain that ever went to France, Captain Edmondson and through it all he stood there calm as a cucumber. And they were shelling us, and all the mules were tied up on ropes. And where the rope broke of course the mules were off. There were light horses commandeered from farmers and we were burying them every day. We had a big mule, it were built like elephant. We called it Jungle, and you could fasten a harness around it to the gun. Marvellous how strong it was.

I used to think the infantry were worse off than me once they got into trenches. We did get a bit of respite when we come down the line because there was a damn good cook, and they'd have something hot waiting for us. We had some young Indian lads. And it were that cold, on a morning if you'd been on picket, they'd say, "Chapatti, corporal?" The winter were the coldest for 55 years there. And we had to break ice and crush it for the mules to drink and you had to drink it before it froze.

After the Battle of Arras I got recommended for a commission, I come home and I met General Haig. But the war finished and we got sent back to our respective units and I finished up at Woolwich Arsenal.

Harry Shaw

was in the King's Royal Rifle Corps. When we were going up in the train there were some prisoners coming down and they were great big Germans. And I thought "We haven't much chance against these". We were billeted in Ploegsteert and there was a wood, all done out in paths with the name of the streets of London and London Bridge over the little stream. We were there two or three months. We'd go over the barbed wire about 20 or 30 yards in front into a cellar, a listening post, with wire cutters and bring some German wire back. They were shooting Very lights up often. We were in Dickebusch all the winter of 1916 and '17, it was very very cold. They gave us a spoonful of rum and we laid down in our bivouac and next morning your clothes had dried on you.

Harry Shaw
(Janet and John Hayton)

Harry Shaw and grandson
(Janet and John Hayton)

On 5th September we went over the top. And the first tanks that were ever made went over with us then. We had a lot of casualties and our colonel was killed that day in front of Flers. The artillery barrage was on for about 20 minutes and then we had to go forward, stay down until they lifted and go forward again. We took more ground that day than any other battalion. We hadn't to get too near the tanks. You could follow at the side of them or behind them very slowly.

Some mortar men came up and they'd evacuate the front line except for us Lewis gunners. They'd send the mortars over us. While I was there my revolver fell out of my holder and one of the lads picked it up, I was just putting it in when something came and knocked my elbow and a piece went in my leg. The ground was all marked with white tape, which way you had to go to dressing stations. I went down to Le Havre to 56 General Canadian hospital tent. It was a marquee. And I was there a week. One morning the doctor came round and the sister said, "He has to go to surgery to have his dressing done". And the doctor said, "Well he can't go because he's going to Blighty at eleven o clock". She said, "I'll hold him while you take it out". And there was yards and yards of this dressing stuck in me arm and the sister packed it up with fresh.

Field gun emplacement
(Daphne Dench)

Harry won the Military Medal,

'for duty on 31 July 1917 near Klein Zillebeke when you ably assisted to beat off a heavy enemy counter attack by skilfully engaging enemy machine guns with your Lewis gun from an advance shell hole. Your work throughout the attack was of great value'. Signed by Sidney Lawford, Major General commanding the 41st division.

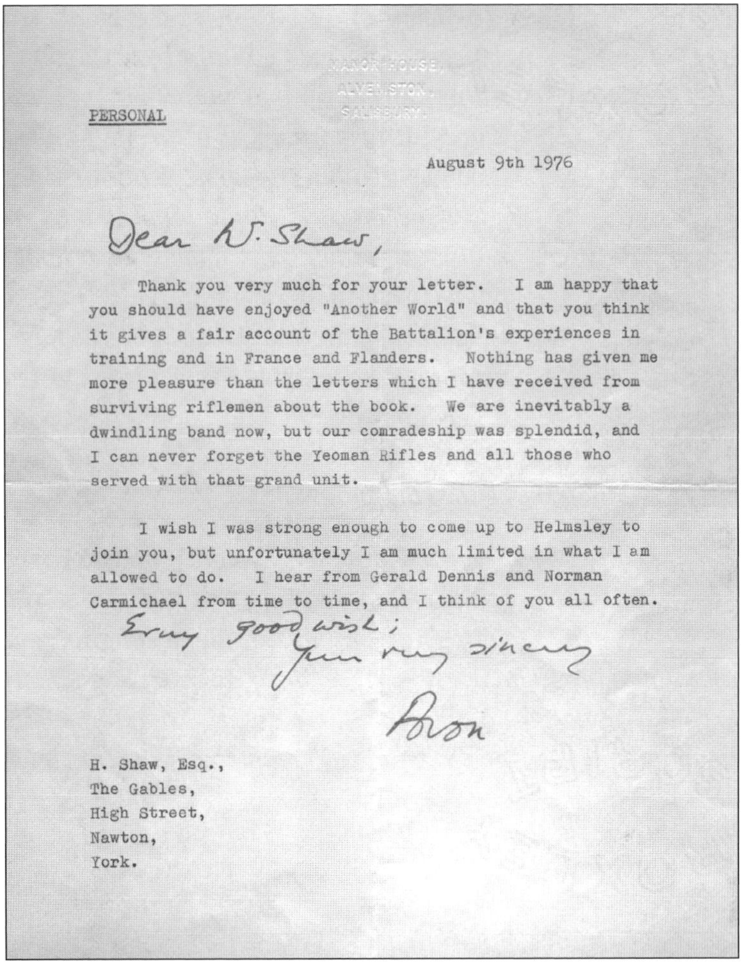

MANOR HOUSE,
ALVERSTON,
SALISBURY.

August 9th 1976

Dear W. Shaw,

Thank you very much for your letter. I am happy that
you should have enjoyed "Another World" and that you think
it gives a fair account of the Battalion's experiences in
training and in France and Flanders. Nothing has given me
more pleasure than the letters which I have received from
surviving riflemen about the book. We are inevitably a
dwindling band now, but our comradeship was splendid, and
I can never forget the Yeoman Rifles and all those who
served with that grand unit.

I wish I was strong enough to come up to Helmsley to
join you, but unfortunately I am much limited in what I am
allowed to do. I hear from Gerald Dennis and Norman
Carmichael from time to time, and I think of you all often.

Every good wish;
your very sincerely

Eden

H. Shaw, Esq.,
The Gables,
High Street,
Nawton,
York.

Letter to Harry Shaw from Anthony Eden
(Janet and John Hayton)

John 'Algy' Lawson

was a gun layer right till it finished. We got threepence a day extra. Up at Nieuwpoort it was bad, we were all wet through. There was plenty of chalk issued to us, to write down the distance where our fellas are. Say they're 2,000 yards, and they gave me a range to fire at 1,900 I won't do it because it would hit my own men. You've got to make other judgements as well. You have two sticks out in front, one's about 100 yards out and the other's another 100 yards out, you've got to get the gun lined up on the two. If there happens to be a building, you say,

John George Lawson 1919
in Germany

(Peter Lawson)

"Target so and so from aiming point." You want 50 degrees right at the aiming point, so you put your sights on the aiming point, but you mark 50 on. You're dead on then, if it goes all right. But when it comes to night time you've got to put a little light on, a special candle onto an old lamp. And you put it on that aiming post which has a hook on. It was my job to see that the aiming posts are all right, and the sights on the gun. You've got two lots of sights on the guns, and you had to start taking them out when it fired, because they were shaking them and going wrong and people at the back that mended them, couldn't keep up with it.

The cartridges were made with cotton wool holding sticks of cordite. They had a little red thing at each end, so if you put it in the wrong way, it fired that way. There was gunpowder in it, and that set fire to the cartridge. You don't want lights to surround your gun, giving the game away. A wagon comes up every night and you might need some of them firing pins, they used 303 bullet pins.

You stayed with the battery. One place we went to, we had to go every night at 11 o'clock, march or scrounge a ride on spare horses, about seven miles up the road. You'd put your guns out and give 'em a bit of a good doing, fire like hell, about 100 or 120 rounds and then you'd sling your hook. And then the shells would come all over where you had been, they're trying to find you.

Motorised AA gun, France

(Daphne Dench)

The officers would come along behind, come and ask me different questions. They'd tell you something but they don't tell you enough. They'd say, "We're going up tonight. There's a battery wants annihilating, they're causing a lot of trouble". As soon as it goes dark, you pull the guns out of the gun emplacement onto the road.

Christmas dinner 1918 Germany -
biscuit and bully beef

(Peter Lawson)

RGA postcard

(Mike Race)

I was up at Nieuwpoort a good bit, at a farmhouse at the back, broken down, had been hit two or three times, but it's still better than nothing. And that's your headquarters where the cookhouse is. You went separate ways round. You didn't go marching to it, because there's too many spies up above in aeroplanes. And we slept in clothes because you had to be out like lightning to fire off guns.

There was hardly any bread, all you got was biscuits, and your mouth gets really sore with them. When we went into Germany [at the end of the war], *we still got bloody bully beef and biscuits. I said, "It wants a photograph taking". I got the blackboard and wrote on, 'My Christmas dinner in Germany'.*

Innes Ware was with the Royal Garrison Artillery.

We were armed with a 4.7 gun, a dead accurate gun, and the only other heavy guns were naval guns. We hadn't reached the stage of the 15" howitzer. Then you had the Royal Field Artillery who were armed in brigades of three batteries of 18 pounders and one battery of howitzers, and the Royal Horse Artillery, which was very limited in number, with their fifteen pounders. The Germans had very good artillery weapons. They were 5.9 which they never altered, but we improved our guns throughout the war.

Innes Ware 1915
(Jeremy Ware)

We were counter battery, shooting at the German batteries on the other side. We were told what our targets were, when to shoot and it was the most complicated affair when there were barrages. I'd go and sit in the roof of a farm house where most of the tiles had been blown off at night, and try and get Hun battery flashes and mark it out on a board. We could practically see each other, the plains were so flat up near Armentieres.

The 2nd Leinsters were actually underneath me. You took a very simple board with a map on it at night and as the Hun gun flashed, you took a line to it. And you hoped that somebody else on another OP [observation post] was doing the same so that you could get a cross section. It was a very crude and early method of counter battery work, nothing like we got to in the end. The Observation Officer saw everything. He was up in the front line, at a safety observation post. He telephoned the communication. Your line would get cut by a shell fire and the signallers would go and link it up again, they're a jolly brave lot.

We could shoot up to about ten miles into the back areas. We fired Liddite high explosive and shrapnel. As the war went on, an awful lot of ammunition was wasted and lots of fuses would have a different error. You took the temperature of your charge because the varying temperatures of the air would alter the strength, and you've the wind to allow for. Having decided what our object was from the OP, the officer who'd been sent up would say, "I can see the target", and we'd work it out.

We moved to a little place called Warloy where we set up the horse lines. We settled down with a battery in behind Martinsart Wood which was opposite Thiepval. We started then to co-operate with the Royal Flying Corps Number 6 Squadron and we were one of the earliest batteries to have a wireless communication between aeroplane and battery. We were interfering with the enemy communications. The aeroplanes would see somebody at a Hun battery firing, target X7. We would look up X7 and lay it out on the map and order to fire.

Gunners at Somme
(Borthwick Institute)

At our post I would have a wire bed and I'd take my boots off and put them on a petrol can to float about. I was on night duty in the command post and I wore pince-nez. I'd put them in my gumboots and then kipped down. Quite early on in the morning a plane call came through. I leapt out, but could not find the pince-nez. I ruled out X7 or whatever it was and gave them the orders. Having found my spectacles I ruled it off again and found out I'd ruled it onto another battery altogether. Then just to show you the chances of war, he'd given me the wrong battery and I'd ruled it off to the wrong battery and we'd hit something that he wanted to stop shooting into. We were also sent out at night to help with laying cables in front of Thiepval. That wasn't my metier at all, wandering about in the middle of the night.

We moved down to Bois de Bray, and that was the first time I met that very unpleasant creature, the louse. Our adjutant was most fastidious, he had silk underclothing. And there was a funeral pyre of his clothing after that night in Bray.

At the mature age of 20, I was looking after 250 horses. My duties then were horse management and man management and bringing up the rations. We went to Avaluy and were a considerable nuisance because we were firing gas shells for the first time. They got definitely angry with us and put up an aeroplane and an eight inch railway gun started shelling us. The shells all fell over the back of the battery about 500 yards, there was a dip behind and the only casualty was the battery tailor. I had to put him in his old blanket and bury him, which was the first time I'd met death in any serious form. When the Hun had really got his range on us, he knocked our four guns out. That was very unpleasant. I got into the dugout and I had a man blown all over me, and I suffered from shell shock after that. I had dreadful insomnia for years afterwards which always started as a nightmare.

Our battery moved on from battle to battle. Ypres, the Somme, Messines, then we were in Passchendaele. We marched, pulled the guns out, spent a day at the horse lines cleaning up and then moved on. The winter of 1916 was so cold, we sent a wagon to Amiens to collect two barrels of beer for the men for Christmas, and the silly asses didn't cover it up properly and it froze solid. The battery moved out of a long valley, crowded with artillery, further towards the front line. We were able to break up a counter attack with our shrapnel with the 51st Highland Division in front of us. Unfortunately you don't get any honours for that because a fighting battery moves on. We were re-armed with 60 pounders. But our guns were completely knocked out, destroyed by fire.

We went to a place called Dickebusch. I was in command of the battery then, at the age of 21, my major had been badly wounded. We'd get bombed by day and shelled by night. When we had an inspection, I got into trouble because the spokes in my limbers were not all in line! I think everything else was in order, plus the two match sticks left at the entrance for him to bite his teeth on.

One great difficulty was to keep the horses clean. As long as you had clean food and water, they were absolutely splendid. But they used to get a kind of ulcer that came up through the leg.

At Christmas 1917 we went into Bethune to celebrate. On the way back, getting into the lorries, I told Mr Ruddock that he had to get in the back but he didn't want to, and a rather heavy hand came out and both my front teeth went. I remember going down the line to an old dentist. He just sawed them off and I went through the rest of the war with my two front teeth plugged.

We went through a nice little town, completely empty, all of the civilians had gone and we acquired a cow. It used to travel round with us everywhere and supply the officers with milk. And there were hens and eggs galore from farms where people *had gone away. But I found out later one of my gunners had flogged Susie the cow for 3,000 francs. So our milk supply stopped.*

One's courage ebbed after a time, it was hell. If you had any imagination, after three years of war and you'd been blown up and had a slight wound, you lived from day to day and your mind wasn't focused on what was going to happen or who was deciding where you were going to go.

We had a brigade commander, he didn't last very long, who insisted on every section commander visiting the OC of the battalion in the line in front of him. We lost about twelve or fourteen officers in about ten days and quite a lot of horses. A lot were destroyed in one night in the square at Ypres coming through. I was blown up on the Somme. There was no man mastership, they were asking a young man of 21 to carry on in command of six guns and living through that hell.

CHAPTER TEN

SPECIAL DUTIES

Dick Smith was born in 1894 in York. He joined the Special Brigade, Royal Engineers.

The Germans started the gas business in mid-1915, and our people wanted to retaliate so they formed a company composed of anyone that had a knowledge of chemistry. Science masters, chemists, people like that. They had a gas attack at Loos and it was a success so they turned it into a brigade to cover more of the line, and that's when they called such as me from different regiments. In an ordinary battalion you have four platoons to a company, four companies to a battalion, but ours was six and they called them sections, with 24 or 25 in each. Some companies were trench mortars filled with gas, and other companies, like mine, were shell gas cylinders.

We'd no idea what the trenches were like. Our practice trenches were just a little affair. Everything had to be carried down the communication trenches, about a mile to the actual front line. We'd travel as far as we could with the lorry, then walk about a mile to the ammunition dump. We picked up the acetylene cylinders. They had two collapsible folding handles, we'd shove a pole through and carry them on our shoulders, one in front and one behind. We were just told how to dig the stuff in and how to cut up pipes and wire them. The trenches were like a zigzag, a bay and a traverse. Each bay had a fire step where the sentry used to stand on and look over the top. We'd dig 20 cylinders in each bay underneath the fire step, and bury them and sandbag them up. They connected up in fours, a pipe leading from each, and the metal one over the top, and we'd pin it down with a big staple so it was pretty stable, to keep it from being blown back, or losing direction.

Other regiments used to fatigue for us, any that happened to be knocking about at the time. They didn't like that, they looked down on us. At first they sent four men with each cylinder, but they must have thought that was a waste of manpower and they gradually got down to three, then two, then in the end we had to carry one cylinder, one man. These things were full of liquid and weighed about a hundredweight. Shaking about and walking on uneven duckboards, sometimes knee deep in water, was no joke. Everything was done at night. We went up in the evening, and came back at dawn.

Dick Smith Unit Register Card
(Borthwick Institute)

British trench
(The Graphic 1915)

We started on the Loos front, we couldn't be where there was a lot of action in case Jerry came over and discovered it, and it would give the game away. Everything had to be secret. We had no protection, except your gas helmet. We were told if anything did leak, to clap soft mud onto the leak and the expanding gas would freeze over and seal it, but that's all the precautions we had.

We got to a place called Helfaut, about six miles from Bethune, that was our company's headquarters and we started training with poison gas, digging trenches and training with masks. They were only a flannel bag with two eyepieces and a sort of squeaker business to breathe out. You breathed in through the flannel, put it over your head and tucked it inside your tunic. Getting used to the gas, we'd walk through clouds of it, it was chlorine in the first place.

While we were in the front line working, the infantrymen were drawn to the second line because we couldn't do our job while they were there. We were knee-deep in mud, carrying these cylinders up. If it were a nice summer evening, you'd go along and over the top of the communication trenches there were flowers growing and nightingales singing.

Gas masks
(Mike Race)

Once we got the cylinders dug in, perhaps 2000 along the line, we very seldom met another company. It would take us a few weeks to get arranged and pipes cut up and measured. A spanner had two prongs to fit in the wheel of the cylinder to turn it on. We had to wait for ideal weather conditions. The wind had to be four or five miles an hour. If it happened to be too strong, it dispersed it, and if it was too slow there was always the fear of it catching our own people. Everything had to be more or less perfect. We got meteorological office reports every half hour.

We went up night after night, standing by and they'd usually be let off about midnight or one o'clock. Many a night, just at the last minute, it would be cancelled. You'd disconnect all your pipes, take them back to the second line dugout, store them there and back to your billets.

When we got the order to go, a man in each bay had a watch, everything was synchronised to the second and we'd be standing by with an NCO telling us whether it was on or not. And when it came to the very moment we just turned everything on, all going full speed and it all drifted over.

We had orders to stay with the cylinders for half an hour until they were absolutely empty and the first thing I saw was green and red rockets up. That meant the artillery was going to open up and they blasted like hell, it was my first experience of any shelling of any description. The Germans thought there was *going to be an infantry attack following the gas. It was hellish. As soon as the artillery stopped, we released our pipes, sandbagged the cylinders up again and took our pipes back to some dugout for storage and made our way to where the lorries were. We straggled back in ones and twos, never marching back. We got reports of observations the next day, ambulances streaming up and down behind the German lines carrying the gassed people away. It was heavier than air and it just went across and poured into the trench, and then the dugouts, and onto to the next trench. We used to stand on the fire step and watch it for a while until the artillery started up.*

They were real stout first-class rubber pipes from the cylinders, and after they'd been used once you can snap them very easily. It rotted them. What it did to your inside, I couldn't say. But if you got a good dose you were done for. The infantry came back after we'd finished, when we were preparing for an attack, and they didn't know there was anything underneath them. They just thought we'd been repairing the trenches. We were told not to talk too much about it. And we weren't allowed to let our people know at home. We went onto phosgene later on, and that was more deadly still.

The Germans used shell gas now and again and they used to put it well back over our line and I got a touch of that one time, mustard gas. Coming out early one morning, Jerry started lobbing a few gas shells over. They didn't burst like fragmented shells with shrapnel. There were just a loud explosion, just sufficient to burst the shell case and release the gas. I thought they sounded a bit light, and the next minute I got a sniff of the gas and I was on with my helmet. But, even then, I lost my voice for a fortnight. My eyes had to be bathed for quite a long time.

Then came Livens projectors. They were metal cylinders, with an open top the shape of a test tube, and the same size as the cylinders, about three foot six. In the base was a charge of powder, like a cake tin, with sections in. They were placed in the bottom of this projector, they had two wires and a detonator, and then they'd lead to another projector, and we'd have 20 of those, dug in on top between the first and second line. As soon as the officer fired his shot, everything went up at once. You didn't know whether you were on your head or your heels, and flames shooting up into the sky.

Then another refinement, that was only tried once. 21 cylinders, in tiers, they sloped down to the front edge, seven in a row. There were two petrol engines, one at the front and one at the back. Everything had to be camouflaged because the ground was chalky, and everything where we dug it up was white. It was the only attack that I know of with trucks. They were level with the trenches and there might have been 20 or more but both engines were red hot at the sides by the time we got there because it was such a weight to pull. Our officers arranged a small track railway, with short trucks. The nozzles of the cylinders were sealed, with a detonator inside. One lever, and it blew all the nozzles open. We turned the gas on beforehand, but nothing came out until the detonators were burst.

They gave me a Vermorel spray to spray the trucks after we'd finished, to kill the gas that remained. I had a tank strapped onto my back and a tube running through and you pumped it with a handle. Phosgene corroded everything, our revolvers were bright and sparkling and they'd rust in five minutes. We had brass buttons on our tunics and they went green in five minutes, and I think Jerry found out that this phosgene clogged the artillery up so we didn't get so much retaliation.

There was one time while we were on the Loos front and the Yanks were attached to us for training. The first night they went up with us, a sergeant and three or four men, all they had to do was watch us dig them in. We got to the dump and it was a quiet night and there was the odd shell and machine gun burst, an odd trench mortar. And their sergeant came into our office and said, "We're not facing that", and they all went back. They left us. All they could think about was, "You wouldn't have won the war if we hadn't have come in". The Americans were all wind and water. Back at the billets they were swanking about with their automatic rifles and up to date affairs, but when they got up there, they were ignorant. Everything was better than we had. Their iron rations consisted of cream crackers and tins of fruit and ours was dog biscuits and bully.

There was a group of men in Dick's company who put false bottoms into their water bottles and took rolls of film into the trenches, which was illegal, but the film survived and was able to give future generations a glimpse into their experiences.

When we'd got the gas installed we used to leave two chaps up there as a guard in case anything got upset. They'd stay up four days and that was the longest any of us had been in the line at a time. One time there was some Portuguese troops knocking about, and we were on the march and there was a Portuguese officer passing, all dolled up like he was on the ceremonial parade. His hat was on one side, and a sword dangling. Clatter, clatter, bang as he walked along. Of course, our fellas struck up 'Any Old Iron'.

Alex Thomson

was born in 1897. In 1915 I took my London Inter [exams] and in that September we were notified that chemists were wanted. This struck me as an admirable opportunity of getting practical experience. I went up to Whitehall and made enquiries and I was sworn in. I was only seventeen but we were taken to the station with railway warrants and sent down to Chatham. We entrained twelve days later and were shipped across to Le Havre. We were handsomely treated, paid the amazing sum of three shillings a day. Privates got a shilling a day but we were full corporals.

We had little revolvers with us. I didn't know which end of the revolver the bullet came out of, never mind anything else. We went up to Rouen, all the chateaux amongst the hills as the river curved about, with the hills first one side and then the other, a marvellous journey.

The train ambled along very gently and at times we passed where there had been an accident or something had broken down and they were just pushed over the side of the embankment. People went along the tops of the trains, dropped off, robbed the orchards and caught the back of the train. The engine drivers were very cooperative, they would supply you with hot water out of the engine to make tea. We got to St Omer, headquarters of the British Army and Douglas Haig and all the rest were there. Then they told us, "If you don't want to do this we're not going to force you, you can join the infantry but you cannot go back to England".

St Omer

(Tina Milson)

The privates stared in amazement to see a troop of corporals marching along the road and doing ordinary fatigues. The idea was that when the gas was sent from the trenches you were in charge and you could order the infantry to get out or do whatever was necessary. We had a special armband, green, white and red. And that was a pass out, so that after the gas had been sent off we could come out of the trenches when the infantry could not. They would have been shot if they had attempted to get out. When the gas went off, all hell was let loose. They threw everything they'd got at us, things exploding away right, left and centre. All you could do was sit there and hope that none came your way.

Once we had 90 tons of gas went over. Nothing would fire on the German side at that time. They had to shell from a long distance away with quite hefty guns. The gas corroded the rifles. We were 25 miles behind the line and the horses were affected so far back and the concentration of gas would be so enormous that nothing could possibly have existed in the actual trenches.

About the middle of 1917, quite a number of people reported sick and were sent to hospital. I think it was strain, overwork. I said to the sergeant, "Feel my heart". They couldn't put a stethoscope on it, it was just simply belting along. And while I was in the hospital, the Germans started shelling the village and they wouldn't even let me walk downstairs to the cellars, they carried me on a stretcher and then whipped me back to a heart hospital at Cayeux. It had to be eight weeks, we started with doing nothing and then very slowly increasing what you did day after day.

In the middle of this the Germans used mustard gas for the first time and they wanted all the hospitals they could, so they kicked us all out and I was sent back to Rouen. Then they packed me off back home to Devonport as gas instructor.

They experimented with different types of gases, lachromatry gases, sneezing gases. They even tried prussic acid gas, but it was far too volatile, you couldn't get sufficient, it just simply disappeared in the air in no time. The most poisonous gas was hydrogen sulphide. It smells of rotten eggs. Phosgene had a delayed action which they didn't realise at first. People didn't feel too bad and started walking back and then they would collapse and maybe die, when, if they had not walked, they might have survived.

It would be the middle of 1917 and we were coming out of the line. A German whizz bang came along and it landed almost in the trench, just at the edge. The trench was filled with smoke and so our number two was killed. He was the same age as I was and it hit me hard. And it brought it up suddenly, that fellow was only nineteen and his father was a policeman in Glasgow and he and his mother scrimped and scraped to give him a good education and that's how he finished up.

Sometimes I would be told to meet a company of infantry, report to the officer and then guide them up and guide them back. I was thrilled when one officer said, "Thank you very much corporal, you've done marvellously, everything's gone swimmingly". It made all the difference in the world.

George Sutcliffe was in M Company of the Special Brigade.

When the war broke out in 1914, I'd started teaching. I offered for service but I was turned down on the grounds of caved-in feet. Early in 1916 there was a request for people interested in chemistry to join this special brigade. I was intending taking a degree in chemistry. I was accepted, and after a few weeks training, I was sent to France.

Our job was to receive cylinders of gas and test them for efficiency then transport them to the front line. It was difficult to walk because of my feet. The trenches were lined with duckboards. The men who joined at first were corporals but we who joined later were pioneers. They were a mixed lot, fundamentally good fellows, ready to help in time of need. I developed a lot of boils, I was doing a dirty job. I applied for a lieutenancy in the infantry, that meant a medical examination. The doctor said, "You're not fit for this, let alone the infantry. I'm sending you down to the base". So I applied for the meteorological section when vacancies arose.

I was fortunate to escape the worst features of war. Our job was to take the wind observation and we had cloud observation. We had to send up a balloon filled with hydrogen that was weighted to rise at a certain speed. One man followed the flight of this on a theodolite and gave the readings and another man took it back. We sometimes followed up to 30,000 feet but that took a long time so we didn't generally pursue it. The results were telephoned in. We were required by the artillery to correct the flight of shells.

I was on guard one night and I'd developed a very severe cold, turned out to be a slight touch of pneumonia and I sat down in a farmer's cart. There was a gramophone playing, "If You were the Only Girl in the World". Queer how little incidents like that linger.

Jim Greenwood

was 19 on the 2ⁿᵈ October 1915 and I joined Fitzwilliam's Royal Artillery Battery.

Later I joined the Royal Engineers. We were supposed to be a secret corps. One of the officers told me that if they didn't make their way back behind the line, they'd shoot them, they had not to be taken prisoners under any circumstances.

When we first went out, we were issued with flannelette hoods with eyepieces and the mouthpiece. It wasn't very long before they brought out the box respirator, a canister in a sash, that had a valve in the bottom through which air could go. It covered all your face and strapped round your head.

Being gassed was classed as a gunshot wound so I got a wound, and a good conduct stripe after two years in the army.

Percy Roantree

was born in 1895 in Holme on Spalding Moor. I joined the East Yorkshires. Then transferred to the Royal Engineers Special Brigade. We had the old gas masks, like a bit of shirting and the thing to breathe in and out. We trained at St Omer. They let us play football to get used to the gas masks.

Percy Roantree in condensing unit at Northern Dairies

(Peter Roantree)

We filled these cylinders with gas and learned how to put them into the line. It depended on which way the wind was, as to the effects of it. It was dark coloured, like a fog, and we had to stay with them in case Jerry come over. On the first day the wind changed and so we'd to shut it off. We hadn't any other duties, we released the gas and they'd advance. We was doing a risky job. If the wind was wrong, it'd catch your own men.

We helped to take the wounded too and I was company runner once, you just had to go through it. The worst sight was seeing those that had been buried, old mules and horses stirred up again with shelling, and the stench! It was hell on earth.

Percy Roantree medal
(Peter Roantree)

I had my first leave from the Somme, after 18 months. And during the time I'd been out, the Germans had counter-attacked and took some villages back. My company was lost somewhere, I got to the Ypres sector with the Royal Engineers again. I was digging and repairing the trenches, repairing the dumps. Then they transferred me to the light railway. We were stationed at Poperinghe, I was taking people up to the line in a camel truck, driving the engine. I was demobbed in 1919.

CHAPTER ELEVEN

ROYAL FLYING CORPS

The Royal Flying Corps was founded in 1912. In 1918 it merged with the Royal Naval Air Service to form the Royal Air Force. At the beginning of the First World War, it had just over 2000 personnel, but by 1919 the RAF had 114,000 personnel in 150 squadrons, and 4,000 aircraft. The average age for a pilot in the RFC was some six weeks, as the aircraft was still primitive, with an open cockpit and no parachute.

Cecil Lewis in his excellent autobiography 'Sagittarius Rising' describes the experience of an RFC pilot. 'We were always at the mercy of the fragility of the machine and the unreliability of the engine. One chance bullet from the ground might cut the thin wire, put the machine out of control and send us plunging to a crash we were powerless to prevent. We had to win victories for ourselves long before we won any over the enemy. But we were never under fire for more than six hours a day. We had a bed, a bath, a mess with good food. We could get to neighbouring squadrons and towns. We were never under any bodily fatigue, never filthy or verminous, or exposed to the long disgusting drudgery of trench warfare. Courage takes various forms. With us it lay with audacity rather than tenacity. The infantry admired our nerve, we admired their phlegm'.

Arthur Watts was born in 1891 in Beverley. He decided to join the Royal Flying Corps.

I had learnt to handle a horse and tie it up and everything from about three year old. (I rode a horse until I was 86). When the war broke out, by that time father had three or four men on the farm, but they had to join up and then they commandeered some of our horses. They wanted the blooming lot and of course father played holy war. I had a nice hunter which I'd bred and broke in and used him to run the parcel cart sometimes and I rode it to Hull, what was then the Lucky Stables. And that was the last time for a long period I rode a horse.

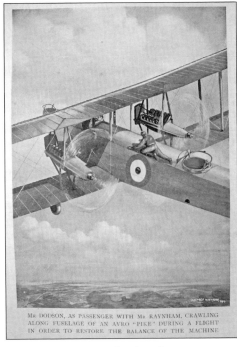

MR. DODSON, AS PASSENGER WITH MR. RAYNHAM, CRAWLING
ALONG FUSELAGE OF AN AVRO "PIKE" DURING A FLIGHT
IN ORDER TO RESTORE THE BALANCE OF THE MACHINE

Avro pike aircraft

THE BRITISH EXPEDITIONARY FORCE CROSSING
THE CHANNEL.

British aircraft cross the Channel

I didn't rush into it, to try and please everybody and find a compromise, which got me into the Royal Flying Corps. I thought I should learn a lot about mechanics, as well as serving my country. This was early 1917. I walked from King's Cross to Waterloo and got on the train to South Farnborough. The place was absolutely crowded. I began to wonder whether I'd done the right thing. By 11 o'clock at night there was a place where we could sleep. There was a concert going on in the hall, and we had to wait until it was over. Then we had to clear the hall and put our palliasses down, and the sergeant in charge says, "When Reveille goes at five in the morning I want to see every man."

Cigarettes advert
(The Graphic)

Morse key of Joseph Blades
(Josephine Clampitt)

Eventually we got a uniform. I remember my first attempt to put a puttee on, it seemed about three times over long and when you eventually got the master of it, it was over short. I expected to graduate as a fitter, or a driver. I passed my test and I was what you called a Second AM at two bob a day, when the infantry had a shilling. You was really the goods when they had finished with you. You had to shave twice a day. Then they started to put you into squadrons. There was a rumour that me and a pal of mine was to be posted to yon side of Tadcaster.

Next morning I was sent down to Wimbledon to join the Infantry Training Corps. The good thing was that they couldn't reduce our pay but when we got to Wimbledon the atmosphere was different altogether.

Arthur was then moved into the Machine Gun Corps!

Joe Blades was born in York in 1900. He joined up in July 1918.

We went to Port Said, half way down the Suez Canal to a place called Ismailia. We disembarked and went up into Palestine to Lud, ten miles off Jaffa. Our camp was 10 miles off. We used to swim off Tel Aviv, it's quite warm in the Mediterranean.

The Flying Corps had two or three hangars there and a short runway which was just in bare desert. They had this training place where they banged Morse code at you. You tried to learn how the wireless worked, a cat's whisker, a carborundum crystal. When we'd done about a week's training, they said, "You've got to go up in the aeroplane and receive a message". There was only half a dozen of us, we went up one at a time

Joseph Blades
(Josephine Clampitt)

with a pilot. They give me a receiver, a crystal set and headphones. I saw the transmitter on the ground, it was two posts and a wire. This instrument on the floor, we had a battery and it created a spark between two points when you pressed the buzzer, the Morse key. It radiated waves, to about five miles at the most. And you received it as a buzz through the earphones. Then, "We want you to fire this Very light". It was like a pistol. So I fired this, and whoosh, the Very light went up. We had a fly around, and I could see the Bitter Lakes on the Suez Canal. One chap wouldn't go, he got the wind up. Flying an aeroplane was something new and dangerous. So I went up again. I liked it.

Joseph Blades on left
(Josephine Clampitt)

The officers got the information [in Morse]. We'd go up to a high point, a little mountain or something, we could see the target. It was my job to send orders down to the battery, to tell what angle to put on the dial sights which would, when fired, hit this target.

Stanley Lattin was born in 1896.

In 1915 I joined the Royal Flying Corps. They'd advertised for young men of reasonable education to join as wireless operators. I had to be examined by the local doctor and passed as fit and then I travelled down to Farnborough.

We were there six weeks, being initiated into army discipline and were all rigorously drilled by guards. In London we were learning Morse code, we had to pass out at least twenty words a minute and we were given receivers. We had to learn right from the very bottom. Every nut, nail and screw. We then went for a fortnight's field course at Brooklands race course and from there to France with 52 Squadron. That was right on the Somme, near Guillemont. [The squadron moved to France in November 1916].

After I'd been about three days there I had a splinter in my arm. And that was the only thing that ever struck me all through the war. And I was in plenty of hot spots. We were concerned with our own battery firing on other enemy batteries to *put them out of action. There would be a pilot and observer. We received messages from aircraft above, they'd give you a map reference on which the battery major set his guns. He'd calculate the range and elevation and the plane would fly in a roughly oval circuit. As he flew back he gave the order to fire and when we fired, he was flying forward so he got to the front of this ditch and he could see the shots falling. The observer would see where the shot landed and report this on his way back to the battery.*

Normally you were on from daylight to dusk, no breaks for lunch or anything. We lived and ate in our little dugouts, usually in the side of the trench and roofed over with corrugated iron. We managed to construct beds by making an oblong section and covering it with wire netting. You had to make new places every time you moved. We had two bunks in this particular dugout and I was sleeping in one and my mate was in the other and you occasionally used your revolver to shoot at rats from the bed head.

John Stanley Lattin 1918 at front

(Alf Peacock Collection)

Early in 1917 we mounted a series of blitzes on the enemy and we just about blew the top off a whole hill. There was a tremendous explosion and we were dug in there with literally thousands and thousands of shells all waiting for the attack back from the enemy. But it never came so we hung on about a week and moved down to Messines and to Vimy Ridge, a line held by the Canadians.

In addition to firing on batteries, we had to listen out for planes coming over and if they gave our own battery a call sign, we had to put out long strips of white American cloth about 20 feet long in the form of a letter. K meant 'I am receiving you' and LL meant 'infantry moving'. That was a priority signal. You'd got to get on to the battery major right away. If you missed an LL signal, you were in serious trouble, you could be in for a court martial. In addition we had to listen all day for the planes sending down notice of enemy battery fire, which was NF.

From there we took over a section of French line and moved into an old chateau and into what I suppose was the wine cellars. It was a beautifully built brick building, it'd probably be at least twenty feet wide arched over and the whole ceiling was black with flies. So the first thing we did was set about with torches and burnt them all off. The Germans had been in and the place was a filthy mess. I remember being posted to a battery at Roclincourt, half a dozen miles out of Arras. There was a little bit of life. There were civilians keeping shops open, you could buy postcards and sweets. I remember chocolates cost over a franc each. They clung to these shops to the very last minute. It was in the danger zone.

I got a letter from my brother who was in the Canadians and he was an officer and could censor his own letters. So he was able to tell me roughly where he was. And he arranged to meet me at the Five Cross Roads in Arras. We met there but Jerry was shelling at the time, so we didn't stay long. He'd been out in Canada a couple of years before the war. I hadn't seen him since I left home. He'd been wounded and in hospital and while he was recuperating he did a bit of studying and passed out as an officer. We had a drink up at his headquarters.

French Reconnaissance aircraft

(Daphne Dench)

Flying ace Guynemer with his Spad

(Daphne Dench)

In the German big blitz in 1918, the whole of our batteries were put out of action by 4 or 5 o'clock in the morning but I still went on receiving messages. At one stage my aerial was run down. There was so much shell fire falling all around us. Normally you had to get about three men to get the 30 foot steel aerial up and down. It was in six foot sections. But as there was so much shell fire about, I didn't want to risk that so I just climbed up the aerial and the receiving wire had been cut just near the top so I had to reconnect it. Eventually they were firing on us from behind, so we had to pull back. They started firing high explosive and gas shells together. We were moving forward when the war ended. Our squadron was in Valenciennes. I was very lucky because I moved up and down the line in all kinds of hot places.

William Law served in the army initially and was wounded, but in 1916 he joined the Royal Flying Corps.

I became a pilot and I flew in France. For my hearing test [during training] he talked from the other side of the room, "Do you play golf?" "Yes Sir." "What is your handicap?", and I said "Plus four." He said, "You're a liar, but you've passed". I did five and a half hours flying by myself but there was a Sergeant Cook looked after the pilots. We flew around Brighton and then he got out and said, "Now it's yours. Go right to the back and don't fly it too soon". So I flew around the front, turned at the West Pier, very gingerly, and back again and managed to make a landing. I began with the Farman Shorthorn, then the BE2C, then the Avro 504, a two seater. The observer would sit and watch the sky, take care we weren't attacked or tell me things that were happening. "Steady up I think you're wrong", or, "Fly straight, I want to relieve myself". It's the comedy that keeps you going.

We had an ordinary Vickers gun. It fired through the propeller and if the timing was wrong it shot the prop away so we were very careful. You couldn't fire on anybody from that height. I just went on at my job of ranging the guns, there was an awful lot of smoke and fire went off, not all of it where I wanted it to be.

William got no specific training on aerial combat.

We just had the talk. I got near enough to see the rest of the crowd, they went in great mobs, circled and dived and did tricks. You took off and flew towards the target then turned round and sent a 'G' to the battery. Then you turned about again and fired. They used to send 'CPIP' to say the weather was too bad to fly. The rascals used to say that when it was really quite good. I don't remember being attacked except by flak. I was never attacked directly by a German fighter, *because I'd been told to stay out of the way, it would've been foolishness to risk it with those characters. They were beautiful shots.*

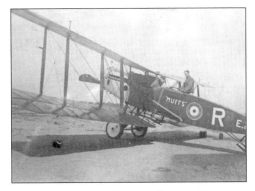

York man William Burley in RFC
(York Oral History Society)

I was spotting at Bailleul. I was too enthusiastic, because I ran out of petrol. Not over the German line but it was so near that when I crashed it, the artillery got on to me. I was supposed to be responsible for the poor soul in the back, he didn't know how scared I was. We came down and crashed a little bit in a shell hole. I had four bombs attached and I had a horrible feeling I had only put down three so I said, "Jump out, have a look underneath and see if I've got a bomb there." He looked out, "No bomb." So I relaxed. After taking me to hospital and being looked at, they grounded me. They gave me a full pension.

After the war William worked on the Glasgow Herald as a journalist until he joined up again in the Second World War.

Charles Beacon was 18 when he

volunteered as a pilot in the Flying Corps. They'd lost so many men and wanted people. I was sent to the Savoy Hotel in London, to go before a board, all looking at you, and asking you questions. We had to wait in a room until we were told to go home.

Charles did not hear any more so he became a rifleman.

The thousand in my unit that were going to France, they were on the train, and I was going with them, but they singled me out to say I was due to go to the Air Force so I didn't go. I heard afterwards that 800 of them were mown down, killed or wounded, on the first time over the top.

I wasn't really looking forward to it, it was a case of you had to go, it's your duty, in those days. At the age of 18 you don't care what happens. You go for the devilment. I went to Hastings. There we did quite a lot of bookwork, including map reading. After that, Oxford University, for an economics course. I was there three or four months and it was extremely nice. I was at Brasenose College, and Earl Haig had previously been there and his room was just over the other side. There was an epidemic of influenza during that period, and everyone was taken down. I was playing tennis, because they said to get out in the open air, so I played tennis practically all the time until the very end when I got the flu. I was down for about 10 days.

We had long legging affairs, leather coats, and flying helmets with goggles. All before I went to 204 Training Depot. My instructor was a Captain Audred, a marvellous man, he stood about 5 feet, or 4 foot 10. He was a Canadian and he had a decoration for bringing a German down in France with a revolver. He was the first man to do it.

We did a certain amount of flying, half an hour a time. On one occasion we were lucky to get down, because something had gone wrong. It was an Avro and those planes had 160 horsepower. I remember going over Canterbury, and I'd had breakfast, and I saw the cathedral going round. We had a telephone from the instructor to my ears. He said, "I'll just show you how to spin", and he did this nose-dive, and all we had in front was a small windscreen, nothing else, and I'm afraid my breakfast came up over the side.

There were a lot of accidents, especially on your first flight out on your own, and a lot were buried in Leysdown on the Isle of Sheppey. The planes they sent us were old ones that had been in France, and a lot of them had shots round about them, but they were patched up. They had an altimeter, a compass, one or two other gadgets.

If the weather was bad we didn't go, we played cards. We did about 10 hours before going solo. The first one was an Avro. They wouldn't allow you on Camels or Pups. When I went to the Camel, you were taught to fight there. One would go in front of you. One would take off, and you would follow it and more or less swoop on it. On the Camel you had the Vickers gun. It had just recently been fitted, and fired through the propeller at 600 rounds a minute, and you could go for short bursts. It had a very bad reputation for stalling, and it wanted very careful handling. The Pup was much easier. I found I had an awful job getting my legs in. My legs were very long, and I had a job to bring this joystick in the centre. The engine was quite good to control.

We also had a Sopwith triplane going up and down the whole time, and we had the camera guns on the ground to fire at. I was aerial fighting in 1918, just before the end of the war.

Gothas [German aircraft] came over mostly at night. There was a Captain Saunders, who had been out to a party. He came home, just getting into his kip, and the Gothas came over, and he dashed out, got in the plane in his pyjamas. And those planes were cold. He brought a Gotha down and he came dashing back, they put him to bed, but he had double pneumonia. He said afterwards, "The day the war finishes, I will take a plane and go under London Bridge".

CHAPTER TWELVE

THE MIDDLE EAST AND NORTH AFRICA

Although the First World War is largely connected with the Western Front in France and Belgium, war also raged in Asia, the Middle East and North Africa.

The Ottoman Empire, with Turkey at its centre, allied itself to the Central Powers, Germany and Austro-Hungary, and the Allies fought the Turks in Asia and Africa.

The Gallipoli peninsula, north of the straits of the Dardanelles, was blocked by the Turks, cutting off access between the Aegean Sea and Russia. Allied naval attacks were a failure, with a lot of shipping being sunk. The land campaign lasted for eight months in 1915 to 1916 and involved the British, French and Anzacs (Australians and New Zealanders, who still mark the day of landing as Anzac Day), but resulted in huge casualties and a Turkish victory. The following year, 1917, saw troops fighting in Mesopotamia (modern day Iraq) and in 1918, it moved to Sinai and Palestine.

Bill Busby

embarked at Liverpool on the Empress of Ireland. We went to Egypt and onto smaller ships. Then my brigade went over to Gallipoli. I was in a place called Horseshoe Bend. And the other people there were the 63rd Naval Division. It was hopeless, absolutely hopeless.

Our first casualty was the scout officer. He was firing through an armoured plate so there was only just room for his rifle and his sights to go through. And damn me, a Turkish sniper put a bullet straight along his sights and into his eye. The stink of dead bodies was absolutely shocking. The place we were told to take was a little hillock called Achi Baba [the main position of the Turkish defences]. Well we never did get it. We were taken out from there, and then we made the landing at Suvla Bay. We met very little opposition and we took some prisoners. The sun was burning down mercilessly and we stopped there for three days. In the meantime the German Commander, Otto Liman von Sanders, got all his reinforcements up and we'd got to go across this flat salt lake. We were trying to take a place called Chocolate Hill. The 29th Division came round from the other side and when they saw that, they said, "That little pimple. We'll soon have that". They damn well didn't though!

My CO and the adjutant were about 15 yards from me and a Turkish shell dropped at their feet and blew them to smithereens. And all the rubbish from it came clean over the top of me. I was laying there firing when a Turkish sniper put a bullet straight through the back of my helmet and my iron rations on my back. We had a piece of tin on the back which the sun shone on, so that the navy knew exactly where we were and didn't drop their shells on us. That was the idea. Beautiful mark for the Turks to aim at!

You couldn't get out of the line. You couldn't get out of shell fire. We'd come down to the beach and have a swim in the sea. One night some Turks were shelling, and they set a lot of low scrub on fire. I was ordered out with some men to beat it out. Then they dropped a shrapnel shell clean in the middle of us and I got a piece of it. I was evacuated to a French hospital ship and then to Imbros where they operated. I was in a convalescent camp. We were sent out on fatigue. And the bloke who took us out forgot where he had taken us and we were all posted as deserters. A telegram was sent to watch out for us at all the ports, 20 odd of us.

Eventually a boat came alongside us, and when we landed we were placed under arrest. I went in front of the company commander next morning and explained the position and we all got off. We were put in a camp at Sidi Bishr, just outside Alexandria. And there I had an amazing experience. I walked in my sleep! And it was the hot sand burning my feet that woke me up. I was in the middle of a banana plantation! I had a hell of a job to find my own tent. Then we went up to the Sinai desert for a time.

We were there from February till August 1915 and then came across to France.

Walter Aust

went to Malta, from there to Port Said. They put us out for the evacuation of Gallipoli, defending the Suez Canal. The Turks were fetching supplies up and *getting ready to attack. We had redoubts through the day, and then at night-time we had outposts scattered amongst the sand dunes. The job was to follow a camel track. Just before dusk they had a camel with a native driver. A plank of wood was tethered to this camel, and it dragged along the sand and when the patrol came in, in the morning, it had to follow this, to see whether anybody had crossed the track. Before long we went to France. We went from tropical weather to snow.*

Arthur Bull recalls

On April 24ᵗʰ the regiment disembarked at Alexandria. August we went to Gallipoli. It was no Cook's tour, none of it was. One boat had sunk the day before going through the Aegean Sea. We landed at Limnos then got taken by paddle steamer to Suvla Bay. The Turks spotted us but they didn't fire their guns at night. Next morning we were given three sandbags and two or three days iron rations, told to get ourselves in. We landed on the rocks. Every time daylight broke, the Turks would be using their guns. They shelled the beaches all the while. They knew some more had landed. We hadn't got a cat in hell's chance. They were led by German crack troops.

We moved up this hill. You couldn't have a bathe because water was rationed. We got two pints a day for everything. We were in the front lines most of the time. The beaches got it and even field ambulances with red crosses on! We were absolute cannon fodder. The casualties, you had to get them under cover and leave them comfortable for when the field ambulance came and picked them up, all that was done under heavy fire. I saw a chap hit, his leg cut off at the thigh and he bled to death. Some men went raving mad. One of the bravest men was Father Henry, a Jesuit priest. He went over the top with us, armed with a walking stick.

Then the evacuation started. It's a good job they did, we were getting less and less, no reinforcements. If you hadn't got dysentery, you'd got chronic diarrhoea. The chaps that had the worst were the machine gunners. They had to stay until we'd gone. Every night they had to fire off five rounds to let the Turks think we were still there. It was blowing a gale, and hailstones. We went down to the beach, they had a motorboat pulling barges and the waves coming right over. You couldn't sit or lie down, you were pleased to get to a ship. They took us to Limnos to a casualty clearing station. We got bread and jam, no flies on it. It was like cream!

We got to Alexandria. The ship had been used for running back and forth to Australia, taking wounded and bringing back reinforcements. We couldn't get to England. We were filthy, lousy and stinking. We weren't allowed to go ashore. Only officers were allowed. We were in the bows, there were a rope down there hanging. Someone said, "How about going ashore and risk it?" I must have been barmy. I went down town, why I didn't get picked up by a red cap! But I didn't see one. I said, "I'm going to the Egyptian quarter". We had a drink, got back as quick as lightning.

There were three sword charges in Egypt and Palestine. I was in hospital. My guardian angel got me through. On Christmas Day 1915 we saw a fixed cavalry charge at Marsa Matrouh. They made a complete brigade of cavalry, mostly reinforcements just out from England, some back from Salonika. Those commanders in Egypt were directing the front from Shepherd's Hotel in Cairo. You talk to the men in the line and the officers, they knew what was happening. It was only when Allenby came and sorted Cairo out and sent them all up the Suez Canal where they should have been.

We got the Turks on the run. They brought practically all the Indian troops from France and relieved us in Palestine. I went to France with the 74th division, dismounted cavalry. I can't forget those lads who died, I don't want to. I swore at the end of the First World War, that I wouldn't put a uniform on again for anybody, not the King himself, for what they did to us, how ex-servicemen were treated.

Bill Hairsine was born in 1894 in the East Riding of Yorkshire.

We went out as cavalry, we all volunteered to go to Gallipoli before it was evacuated. We were equipped with drill uniform, pith helmet then rigged up with infantry equipment. We headed for the open sea. So many bad sailors among us, men and horses were seasick. Those who could stand it had all the work to do. In Alexandria, we were camped along the seashore then sent to the Faiyum

Bill Hairsine on camel
(Liddle Collection)

Oasis, 100 miles south of Cairo, half as big as the East Riding of Yorkshire. One of the outposts was to guard the natives who were Turkishly inclined. The desert dwellers knew where the water was. The biggest requisite of all. It was quiet for about a year then Johnny [the Turks] nearly got to the canal at Kantara. He cut up one or two yeomanry regiments there. The infantry took the brunt of the thing and drove him back. The yeomanry, the Australian Light Horse and Camel Corps had to follow him up over the oasis, near Sinai. I was back on horses then. The infantry had driven them away from the canal bit by bit.

The cavalry had to keep doing patrols. The desert is a heck of a big place. Men couldn't go out on it, the horses had their limitations because you always had to water them. We had some long do's without water. The whole of Sinai was desert, with certain small oases with a few date palms.

The Senussi and the tribes out there were antagonistic towards us. We wanted to keep them out of the line of our communications so our brigade strung itself out in a semi-circle to see that nobody came through in any strength. The Turks had nearly got on to the Canal. They'd got pontoons up and then they'd made an onslaught on three yeomanry regiments. They'd really given them a rough ride and killed a lot of horses and men, and they sent for our brigade to reinforce them. Khan Yunis was a desert contacting station. Get off the Sinai Desert there and you were in the old caravan route up into Palestine and branching off to Iraq. The infantry were going to make an attack on Beersheba. There was nowhere they could really entrench to be comparable to where the Turks were.

The whole brigade plus a brigade of guns got right round behind the Turks. We were three days away from base in enemy country and the evening of the attack came. The infantry were shelling from the front. Our battery of guns was covering us. We had three horses to one man and we had to lay down where we could and keep advancing bit by bit. Then we got the orders to shift back, the Turks were more than we could ever overcome. There was a heck of a rumbling along the road and it was the Turkish reinforcements going from Beersheba to Gaza. And in the early morning we set off back to camp so they never saw us.

In four days we got among the Judean hills. The Turks were on a plain. They'd got a few machine guns and a few men in a rear guard. They told us we were going to charge. They started shelling and gave us a bit of stick and we started galloping.

My horse wouldn't charge back and it galloped into the village of Ramleh. But they hit me, and she got a bullet through the nose and went down. I thought, "I'm in for it now. The rifle's in the bucket and the mare's on the floor", but in another second she showed signs of getting up, which she did. One man got a bit of shrapnel through his knee, his horse had to be destroyed. They got the field ambulance and by that time we'd taken seventy men and four machine guns.

Bill Hairsine on motorbike in Egypt

(Liddle collection)

Eventually we got north of Jerusalem. We didn't know where the rest of the brigade was. There was no communication at all, we were near the end of our tether when up come the Scotties, the 53rd Division and took over. We were taken back to refit and by that time the infantry brigades had taken Jerusalem, which was done absolutely peaceably in the finish. Allenby walked in through St. David's Gate, and accepted the surrender. [Field Marshal Edmund Allenby, 1st Viscount Allenby, who led the British Empire Egyptian Expeditionary Force, capturing Beersheba, Jaffa and Jerusalem in 1917].

Victor Shergold on left

(Enid Worrell)

We got the order that we were going back to France as machine gunners.

Victor Shergold recalls

It's a six days trip on the Aquitania. I'd never been on a sea voyage before. One of the old chaps, a stoker, got me a clay pipe. He said, "That'll righten you". He got this tobacco, cut it up and I just managed to get a pipe-full by the time we finished the journey. Destroyers took us from the Aquitania to Mudros. We only had dugouts, the Turks had trenches.

We were taking turn on guard. But most of us had dysentery straight away. I volunteered to go down to the beach to get water, which was pumped into a canvas bag. That would be about half a mile. And the snipers were sniping at that point, all the time you were going down. One of our poor old corporals used to parade out in the middle of the night. He had malaria. And it affected him every night about midnight.

Victor Shergold and friends
(Enid Worrell)

We got the sandstorm, and we got the heavy shell fire from Achi Baba. We were told to make the line up and start digging ourselves in. Then one of the Turkish snipers got me through the liver and lung. They helped carry me to the base with a stretcher. They treated me at the base, and we went to Malta from there.

British troops at the Dardanelles
(The Graphic)

I was discharged. I was on food production.

John Edwards was in the 1ˢᵗ/8ᵗʰ Manchesters and went to Gallipoli.

The Australians, they were tough. They used to be fighting the Turks up in them hills. They had no discipline. They had to acknowledge officers sometimes but not like we had to. If it's left to a man's own discretion I think it's a better system. That iron discipline is no good for nobody. But there's one thing, how England was loved by these colonial troops. They might have been fighting for their own country, they were fighting our battle. They were real good soldiers, there's no doubt about it. We should be proud of them.

George Ashurst

Furness of Khartoum 1914 depicting tropical uniform
(Borthwick Institute)

went to Alexandria. Straight away we got off the boat onto the train and all across Egypt, a hundred mile or more. Then to Port Suez and there we found the Anzacs. We encamped there, had a glorious time going out on the town, boozing and dining and fighting. They hated the mortal sight of us, the Egyptians. The soldiers had to go out with a bayonet. One or two was missing and we knew where they'd gone, these buggers had snaffled them. Robbed them and killed them.

There was some fun. You could get a fellow blind drunk and put him on a donkey and take him a mile back. He's falling off at this side and falling over that side, these gruff fellows shooing him on and then when he gets to camp, he has to fall out and go to the officer to get his sixpence.

Then we got orders to move across the Canal into Sinai so we got on a little railway there that took stores and munitions. We went about three mile further in the desert with camels carrying

Royal Australian Artillery
(Mike Race)

Australian Infantry
(Mike Race)

our kitchen stuff and blankets and we dug trenches there. They could do it better, them young camels.

Reg Gifford

Reg Gifford seated and friend
(Julie Gifford)

was at Sidi Bishr and then we went up on the Western Front of Egypt to Palestine and that's where the fun began.

As we was up in these hills, we could see Gaza down there. They was shelling that from the sea. Our people made a feint attack, and the Turks mustered their men. And the Australians went round to close them in. It wasn't on such a big scale as France. We lost a lot of men because you were out in the open, and I remember a young lad beside me got shot right through the head. I reached out and got his paybook and after we got somewhere nice and quiet I wrote to his mother.

The first time I ever saw a tank was outside Gaza. They shelled it and a direct hit at the tank stopped it. The name on the side of the tank was Nellie, but poor Nellie didn't get very far.

Eventually we got to the Judean Hills and it was certainly cooler there, with mist on the summit. On the other side on these redoubts, I saw natives and they had got skins and old biscuit tins, carrying water. We went and holed our well there. It was so cool and clear and I hadn't had so much water for a long time.

I got wounded on 9ᵗʰ December 1917. I lay unconscious and there was a sergeant named Austin from Bury St Edmunds, he took the stretcher bearers out and fetched me. I went down to Kantara on the Suez Canal and by train up to Cairo. If I hadn't had a tin hat on I shouldn't have been able to tell the tale today.

Reg Gifford at 90
(Julie Gifford)

CHAPTER THIRTEEN

ROYAL PIONEER CORPS

In 1917 the Labour Corps was formed, though labourers had been involved in the war since the beginning. Over 300,000 British soldiers were part of the Corps, as well as a large number of African and Chinese troops. Some were also part of the Royal Engineers or the Royal Army Service Corps, helping to construct bridges, breastworks in trenches, repairing barbed wire. There were eventually 68 battalions of pioneers and eventually the Royal Pioneer Corps was formed.

Frank Arnold started out in the cavalry but by 1918 he was on the Somme.

We disbanded and I got sent to the Pioneers and the job was burial party. There was poor lads only been out a month. I had six weeks on it and with hot weather and crows, it were a sickening job. The first task was to collect a soldier who had been out in the sun for a long time, you could pick them, nothing else but bones. Someone's son!

West Yorkshires 1916, Robert Hope right. 'This is us digging a trench, can you see me with little glengarry cap on'.
(York Oral History Society)

Ernest Newsome joined

The 16th Royal Irish Pioneer Corps. We weren't in the trenches, we were digging, making reserve trenches.

Ernest Newsome, son James, granddaughter Marian Tate & great grandson Nic

(Marian Tate)

You'd leave your billet at Dranoutre [11 kilometres from Ypres] *about six o'clock, go in marching order to a certain point and then break into single file. You had your picks and shovels and all your tackle. When you got to the place where you were doing a dig, it was marked out with tape. And you'd to dig it four foot six wide at the top, to finish at two foot at the bottom, and about four to six foot deep. We had to leave room for your duckboard.*

You'd go back single file because there were that much firing going on. You'd get back two or three o'clock in t'morning and then have your breakfast and be off again next night, same performance. I was on a burial corps as well. We was coming back one night and they dropped some of these shells and you went, "By that's a nice smell". You were sniffing, you didn't know it were gas. By that time it were too late. I finished up in a hospital. It affected my eyes. This sergeant walks in and says, "I've to find somebody for a job in brigade headquarters". And so I were sent there. I were writing, I were on the crime sheets.

But the war, it wasn't worth it. Wasn't worth the loss of all those lads. Life's too precious.

CHAPTER FOURTEEN

THE SOMME

The Battle of the Somme is renowned as the biggest disaster for the British army. It began on 1ˢᵗ July 1916 and continued until November. On the first day alone there were 60,000 casualties. Over a million soldiers fell in 1916, and whole battalions, such as the Pals battalions, were wiped out. By the time of the battle, nearly all of the regular soldiers of the original British Expeditionary Force had gone and in 1916 the war was being fought by Kitchener's Army, a civilian army. The battle saw a new kind of warfare appear in the shape of the tank, but this was not without its problems. Of the 49 tanks sent over in September 1916, 31 broke down. Aerial reconnaissance was essential at this stage of the war but the Royal Flying Corps lost 782 aircraft.

Hundreds of mines were exploded in France and Belgium, the main one at Beaumont Hamel. The debris from the La Boiselle mine rose 4000 feet into the air.

William Angus explains

When 1916 began, the Germans opened the fighting with a large scale attack on Verdun which the French held off. Then the Allies took the offensive and on 1ˢᵗ July they attacked on the Somme, with a very heavy artillery preparation which it was hoped would do the trick and enable the infantry to break through. At first success was claimed, but the German defence held. We nibbled off a mile or two here and there and suffered very heavy casualties. It was clear that a long struggle was going to take place. Conscription was introduced in this country in May 1916. Munition work mopped up most of the surplus labour and in December Lloyd George ousted Asquith as Prime Minister.

At that stage I realised that I might be in the army before it was finished. So far my chief object in life had been to get a scholarship at Oxford or Cambridge. Now there came the added question, could I get a commission in the army?

Arthur Gladwin

joined the line on June 29th 1916 and on June 30th the extra equipment we would need for an advance was brought, such as rations and reserve ammunition. It was obvious that there was something going to happen, but of course we didn't know till within a few hours. We went up by stages through various villages, some of which, as you got nearer the front, were deserted by their own populations. Just here and there you could see a few civilians.

There were several woods and in the centre were all these ammunition pile ups. They were screened from the air. You didn't see much of the terrain round about and there was no horizon more than woods in the distance. "Your aim is to get over the top. Follow the chaps in front of you and make for that wood and you don't want to expose yourself to rifle fire. We think we shall surprise him". But of course all that proved to be absolute nonsense, they had dug 30 feet down into brick trenches. There was no sign of them on the surface but as soon as they saw there was something serious they had that terrific barrage. They were ready for our coming.

Our barrage began about 10 o'clock at night and went on until six or seven in the morning. I remember it being absolutely deafening and, we came to the conclusion, nothing could live in that, and it wouldn't have done if it hadn't have been so deep. We had 20 rounds of ammunition, two great bandoliers of it, your rifle, bayonet and three or four Mills bombs.

They had the Engineer Corps there. If a bomb or heavy bomb or shell fell and blasted a length of 50 yards of trenches, they would get to work as quickly as possible and scoop out enough for fresh troops to get in and be hidden.

Then the barrage lifted and the troops who were in the front actually 'standing to' at that time were given the order. And suddenly these chaps started forward. We were out in the open. Anything beyond the trench we'd been in overnight, was all pounded up to a terrible mess. Our particular battalion didn't get orders to move at the time. Just by the toss of a coin, our battalion was the one in reserve and to follow up later in the day. Then the order suddenly came that we were to move back.

Of course they brought up reinforcements to replace those chaps that had died. It would be about the 7th or 10th of July we went over in the same early morning conditions. We got so far and there were terrific bursts of rifle fire facing us and there was a tendency to get into one of these shell holes. While I was there, I heard a groan and I saw the legs of a wounded officer. He was sufficiently conscious to cry out 'water, water'. It was obvious that he was near dead. I unscrewed his water bottle and gave him a drink. Then he flopped down and at that moment a shell burst over us and I got hit in the leg and the buttock.

Nobody had ever had experience of the thing before. You can go out onto a parade ground but when you get onto a battle field and all that terrible barrage of fire from the enemy, it's different. The Red Cross people got me onto a stretcher and they did magnificently.

We went for several miles and found a field hospital. There were a few British nurses, they were really brave, it was far from a comfortable life for them. I was put on the rail head and shipped back to England.

Arthur was soon sent back to the front line, but

in November I was hit again, and it blew out the inside of my thigh. I was scuppered. I lost consciousness, but the Red Cross people picked me up and got me onto a stretcher. By 1917 I was at St Thomas's Hospital. My younger brother, in the Northumberland Fusiliers, had written to say he was going over to France. I managed to get out of the hospital and got a taxi to London Bridge station and found where the train was. Because I still had an officer's uniform on, I could get through and I managed to have a brief word with him until the whistle blew. He was killed in a very short time. My parents lost one son and the other one twice wounded, that must have been a difficult time for them.

Claud Hey explains

the French fortress was Verdun and it had been shelled for months and the French lost thousands and thousands of men. They needed us to attack somewhere to draw off the Germans. A lot of Kitchener's Army were inexperienced, they weren't regular soldiers. Delville Wood [the scene of battles on the Somme in July and August] was captured and recaptured. I've never seen so much carnage in my life. Hundreds of legs, arms, heads all sticking out. Then they brought in the new

Claud Hey

(Robert Hey)

weapon, the tank. These things were going slowly and you couldn't see anybody in them. The soldiers got behind the tanks, because the Germans had rapid fire and the whizz bangs were going over. My section of machine gunners walked beside them. You walked criss-cross, if you walked straight you were liable to get a bullet. It was the queerest thing, it had caterpillar wheels. We did look into one and it was absolutely boiling hot, like an oven.

The Germans fired point blank at the tanks and we lost a lot there. That's where our colonel was killed.

Alfred Chapman

had a little Testament and a bullet hit it, it was in my breast pocket. The Earl of Feversham was on the Somme and I remember seeing him stand up in a field of corn and he was killed. At certain times when it rained and rained, it was a horrible place. The mud would be above your feet and up your legs and you used to have to waggle your foot to get it liberated.

We came to the conclusion that war's a mad idea at any time.

Eric Haylock

recalls the mining which had gone on before the battles started. Tunnelling was done by British miners and 'sewer rats' who had built the tunnels for the London underground. On the morning of 1st July, the explosives were detonated at Beaumont Hamel where a huge explosion took place.

The Royal Engineers were carrying a lot of explosives and were mining under a village. I never dreamt of how much stuff they'd put in, but when that went up, it was a sign for us to go over the top.

They said it would rock the trenches, which it did. From then we clambered on the parapet. I was company range finder as well. I had to measure the distance. I had only got five rounds of ammunition in the revolver.

Our wire had been blown away by the Germans. Our field artillery was firing over our heads into the German front line. Then the Germans come out of the dug outs and got on the machine gun. Well after that they was going down like corn in a field. I looked to see who was with me, and there weren't anybody within the length of a cricket pitch either side. Then I felt this thing in my leg. There happened to be a little tiny shallow and I sat in it and put my knees up to protect my face. The bullet had exploded and I sat in this hole until 11 o' clock at night. I'd lost so much blood and instead of undoing my trousers and wrapping it up, I laid there for about an hour. Eventually I got to our line. A few minutes afterwards, another boy fell on top of me. Then a shell come and hit the front of the trench and buried the pair of us. We had to wriggle our heads to get out. Then a couple of chaps with a stretcher came along. "All right chum, we'll pick you up". I said, "I've been crawling for nearly two days, I can do another twenty yards".

Nelson Drake recalls going over the top.

At Peronne Wood on the Somme we were 360 strong and only 12 of us come out. We met the Prussian boys and I got shot. We lay there for two hours. Then I had to crawl back six and a half miles. The Canadian Hospital took us in. I went to King George's Hospital in Waterloo for six months then my arm broke down and I had to go back and have another operation.

At Hellfire Corner I lost my speech with the shock. It was hell on fire. Sometimes men wanted to get sent home. If you fire a rifle that'll leave a black mark behind. So they used to tie an old sand bag round and fire. I saw it lots of times. Some of them got found out, they'd go mad. They'd run all sorts of places. You see we were only 19.

Len Cavinder was on the Somme

in the winter of 1916, wading into trenches deep in water. I was supposed to be on sentry and I was standing in a bay of a trench with the light on the fire step to keep it out of the water, when up came the sergeant major. (Just before we had got into the line another religious chap had asked me to help him at a little meeting he was having in a tent. I spoke on how a man would sell everything to buy the pearl of great price, meaning Jesus Christ). I didn't know that sergeant major was in that meeting. The first thing he said was, "Where is your pearl of great price now?" I said, *"It would be 'God help me' Sergeant Major if I didn't believe in him", and for the first time I saw fear on a sergeant major's face. He said, "You reminded me of my mother, she was a Salvation Army woman".*

Ted Green

joined the 4th Army Corps, under Sir Henry Rawlinson. I was a gunner. We used to do shifts on the guns, they were always manned because if they weren't firing there was ammunition coming up which we had to unload.

On the Somme on 1st July at 6.25am there were thousands of guns. The record shows that there was 1,508,652 shells in that battle, of all sizes. The howitzers suffered the most, they lost a lot of their gunners through prematures and faulty ammunition.

Ted Green 4th from right at back
(Borthwick Institute)

We didn't know there were 60,000 casualties. When you came off duty, you'd go and have a chat with our signaller. He used to get all the news through. And we saw a lot of the walking wounded coming down. A lot had to be carried, the ambulances couldn't get up the road.

A gunner will only fire so many shells and then it wants re-rifling, it has to go down while the Ordnance Corps put a new muzzle piece on. There was dozens of guns being done. Each gun had its own set of six horses. There were times some of the horses were sick, so they didn't have a full gun team.

Ted Green on right

(Rita Freedman)

Arthur Britton remembers,

We had been told that, "Eventually you'll be given zero hour". Then so long after, the Leeds Pals were going to take the first line of German trenches, then the First Bradford Pals were going to take the second line. Then the Second Bradford Pals, which I was with, were going to get the third.

On July 1st I was stood with Alan Craven, he was a grand lad, Bradford boy. I was talking to him and this terrific barrage was on, then a colossal explosion, and the next minute, he wasn't there, he was down on the ground. I turned him over and he'd been sniped clean through the heart.

I had a couple of stretcher bearers that wouldn't turn out. They got scared to death. I didn't want to be responsible for them being shot. They would have been. I was three short, which made it difficult. I concentrated on the wounded in the trenches. That kept me busy.

You had to be ruthless because at first these stretcher bearers were bringing people that were dead. I had to get quite callous because it were wasting lives. It were no good to you if you got your stretcher bearers killed because you'd no-one to replace them. I were going all over, having a look to see who you

Advert for Oxo

(The Graphic)

could save, who was too far gone. I'd given morphia to a lot of them. You were under fire all the time. There was no safe spot. You'd just got to say your prayers, trust in God and go.

A while after that, my parents wrote to the army authorities and sent my birth certificate and claimed me out of the line. I'd said I was 20 when I enlisted, I was 16.

James Arthur Atkinson was born in Scotland in 1896 but later moved to Bradford.

I joined the Bradford Pals. We went to Skipton then to Ripon and eventually to France. July 1ˢᵗ, the Bradford Pals were all washed out. We were signalled to go over by whistles or flags. I got a few hundred yards, that's all. Hundreds of our lads were shot down.

I was one of the lucky ones. We came back in a pantechnicon. I had one wound in my head, a really bad wound on my leg. [As well as wounds in the stomach and arm]. I'm holes all over. There were seven of us left out of the whole battalion.

Stanley Bewsher was a machine gunner. He went to Egypt initially, then France.

Stanley Bewsher
(Borthwick Institute)

We got into the trenches at dusk. It was just like a newly dug garden, no man's land. At half past seven it was time for the advance. We had our watches, and the NCOs had stop watches. All at once the artillery stopped, and up went the mine, Beaumont Hamel. It just took the soil and all the lot. Then the whistles blew and over we went.

All at once out comes Jerry, he stood on the parapet and he lobbed bombs at us. They were potato mashers, bombs with sticks in. Then we got the machine guns cracking and the lads in the front all in a line. They dished us out with Lewis guns. There were in six in a team. Number one and number two were in charge of the gun. Number three had all the spare parts, number four was the range finder.

Stanley Bewsher, 5th from left, front row Egypt before transferring to France
(Andrew Jackson)

They said it'd be a walk over. 'There won't be a living thing when you get there'. But it was slaughter, men fell like nine pins. We were pinned down. I'd lost my number two, I was on my own. After an hour I picked up the machine gun and I set my stall up. Stretchers were running about picking men up. Wounded fellas were shouting. I waited until three o'clock and then everything was dead silent. I lay in no man's land and I saw the Jerry stretcher bearers. I started to use the gun on them. I fired my volley, picked my gun up and run towards our trenches. I got about 20 yards and bullets came flying over my head so I dropped down again into a shell hole, then I made a dive for it. Just as I got in to our trenches, there was a sap, [narrow trench at angle from existing trench] *and there was our signalling officer and the colonel and a lot of signallers. "You'd better get back my lad, you've done enough. There'll be reinforcements coming up soon". I said, "No, they might counter-attack". They took my name, rank and regiment. I went back into the fire pit, set my gun up and this went on all afternoon. I must have been hit by a shell, but I didn't remember anymore until I were woken up in hospital in Etaples.*

Stan Bewsher
(Alf Peacock Collection)

One of our sergeants came, "You've been recommended". And I didn't get to know I'd got the Military Medal until about a year after. I went to

Manchester in a command depot, then I got a job as chauffeur to a colonel. They started to shift all us fellows to relieve fit men out of non-combatant units. So I went to motor transport, on convoy work, moving lorries from different places to the south coast.

Every dream I've had every day of my life, I think about the Somme. And some part of it comes back into my head. I've never forgotten it, never can. All the machine gun company that I belonged to were killed.

Bill Hayes found that

On the Somme you stood no chance. A lot of the wire wasn't cut. You got a drop of rum every morning. You used to get extra when you were going over. But you'd see blokes going mad, they'd look terrible, used to go clean off their rockers. Some of the youngsters used to cry. They didn't know where the hell they were going to!

Maurice Jowett recalls

They had a church service before you went into the line, and it were like lambs going to the slaughter. I think the secret of the whole job, they underestimated the German strength in their own lines. It would have to be a change of tactics to get past them.

Archibald Kirk

marched from Ypres down to the Somme during the night. We were going along singing and they passed a message back from the colonel, "Be quiet, the GOC will be in bed". Anyhow the men kept on singing and I think there was always that streak of mutiny in the ranks. We were in the 8th Brigade, and still in reserve. We went over on the second Battle of the Somme in September. We finished up on this ridge and Delville Wood was on our right. And on that day the Gordon Highlanders took it. One of the most heroic actions I seen in my life.

Len Lovell recalls

The big attacks were in daylight. We bombers were called upon to try and clear Jerry out of the last corner of Delville Wood. The colonel had given his instructions and had disappeared and off we went, maybe a dozen of us, with bombs. When *we got near, I gave the signal and then we crept back on our tummies until we got about 20 yards off our shell holes. I saw one fella make a dash for it, he'd hardly got to his feet when a machine gun shot him in the head.*

York City Council Chamber 1965. Archibald Kirk (2nd from right in row facing front), Deputy Lord Mayor, later Lord Mayor

(RIchard Pollitt, York Mansion House)

I was the gas tester, the one who would lift his mask off his cheek and take his nose clip off and if I smelt gas, "Leave your masks on". We'd been given instructions that this attack was going to come off, and our colonel said, "At six in the morning, you creep to the edge of the wood and you'll wait there until you see the Super Land Dreadnought"! (The tank). They were as much of a shock to us as they was to Jerry. This thing came wobbling over tree trunks and in and out of shell holes, just like a ship at sea. And we had to continue bombing to our right. The tank's machine guns opened fire on the two German machine gun posts, and then it just squashed them out of existence. We was crowding behind and enjoying the spectacle. We were supposed to bowl a Mills bomb like you'd bowl a cricket ball, it was all a load of bunkum. We used to throw them, pelt them. And somebody popped up and fired and it hit me in the arm, spun me round and I fell in the shell hole with another fella who'd been hit in the arm and a fella who'd been hit in the ear, half his ear had gone. And I'm nursing my arm with this flaming Mills bomb in my hand, I didn't know what the hell to do. This other fella with half his ear off, he was drenched right to his boot toes with blood, and he's screaming, and we ended up throwing the bomb over the top of the shell hole. I wanted to get rid of it and it could explode, which is what it did. We got our rations out and had a bite or two, and I said, "I'm off, are you coming?" Because everybody was on their own. Once you get wounded it's up to you then.

Thomas Nixon

Thomas and Lilian Nixon 1975
(John Ayers)

was one of a draft of about 40 who left for France on 3rd July. Within three days we were told we would be going into trenches first thing in the morning. All our guns were firing and we could hear the sound of the shells falling. When nearing the front line, I could sense the smell of death. Very soon we saw the dead and wounded being carried out. Daylight was breaking as we entered the trenches which were badly broken up. Two of the soldiers from our draft were killed by a direct hit. I was with an officer and sergeant in no man's land putting barbed wire up. All this time the Germans were sending Very lights up and one dropped close to me. I immediately dropped flat on the ground and into a little hollow. They machine gunned over and around me.

For over 20 years I occasionally had a dream and could hear the machine guns firing and shells dropping.

George Robinson recalls

I went over as an officer's servant, and I kept with him. My instructions was, if your officer or any officer near you gets wounded, you must get him into a trench. We got so far across no man's land to where the Thiepval memorial is now. He got a tremendous piece of shrapnel, it nearly took half his back away. A stretcher bearer was near and we bandaged him up and had to stop there until dark. We got him to the dressing station, he was between life and death. I got a letter from his mother a week later to say that she'd been called over to France to see him. Eventually he did recover but he never went abroad again, I don't see how he could with a back like that.

Then George himself was wounded.

By stages I got on a Red Cross train. This Australian chap says, "Let's have a look, I haven't time to give any anaesthetic". It was only a piece of shrapnel, he yanked it out and he said, "See that ship, it's yours, going out 10 o'clock". I don't remember anything until we got to England. They sent me down to Eastbourne, it was heaven. I joined the battalion again on May 6th near Poperinghe.

I've thought about why someone didn't find out about those deep German dug outs [on the Somme]. We were told it was going to be a walkover. I couldn't understand why intelligence didn't know about it.

Walter Smalley joined the Bradford Pals.

I went to Liverpool and sailed to Egypt. We saw a submarine by the side of it, I machine gunned it myself. I was always in the machine guns. You got hardened to the job. You were there to kill or be killed.

Walter later went to France and was on the Somme on 1st July 1916.

It was a lovely morning. Birds singing, a perfect day. Birds doing a bit of courting, flying about, excited. They knew what was happening.

We didn't get a yard or two. It was like facing a fire brigade with all their pipes firing at you. Why a thousand more men weren't blinded that day I don't know. You just saw fellas stand up and take two paces forward and they were all on their faces

Walter Smalley (standing)
(Stuart Bradley)

again. Some cocky general thought it would frighten the Germans if we walked to them!

I got one in my right leg, below my knee was smashed. And something came through my tin hat and dented it. If I hadn't had my tin hat, I wouldn't have been living.

Norman Tetley recalls

Leeds Pals, 1ˢᵗ Bradford Pals, us, then the Durham Light Infantry. That was the order of advancing. The Durhams were a fine body of men, they were six footers. The first time I saw them come out of the trenches, they were nearly on their knees with trench feet from standing in water. There were duckboards but they used to break up.

We were in fairly tight trenches and we'd got a ration of rum. A billy can passed along the line, "Just have a swig, pass it on". I had no feeling of being afraid. It was just a matter of duty. My first impressions as I got over the top, I could see shells bursting. Flashes of fire. I only got 20 or 30 yards before I got caught. When I crumpled up, they helped me into a bit of a depression and moved on. I rolled over and I was quite near to a communication trench full of fellas. I hadn't been in there very long before I heard bullets hitting the ground. I saw the earth just being strafed.

Norman's mother had actually been trying to get him out, as he was under age.

Looking back it was damned nonsense, a fiasco.

CHAPTER FIFTEEN

THE NAVY

The British navy, comprising the Royal Navy and the Merchant Navy, has long been the senior service.

Norman Rogers was born in 1898 in Stockton on Tees, the youngest of seven children.

There were five of us served in the war. My eldest brother was commissioned in the Green Howards and was taken prisoner in April 1915, and returned more or less a broken man.

My youngest sister went to Red Cross classes and then volunteered for service. She went on the hospital ship Britannic. It was sunk in the Aegean Sea in 1917. She was safe and landed home after some time with nothing but her pants and a greatcoat. She then was re-kitted and went out to France as a nurse until after the war, and she came home and qualified as a health visitor.

I left school in 1913, sat the exam for the Post Office and was a sorting clerk and telegraphist and I learnt Morse. When war broke out, Stockton-on-Tees was the headquarters of the 5ᵗʰ Durham Light Infantry Territorials. And on the Sunday, the day before war broke out, the police were called out to open the pawn shops for the soldiers to get their kit out. It was worse than the crowd coming out of a football match. Everybody was seeing the lads out. If you joined the army you got a khaki armlet with a crown, but if you volunteered for the navy you got a blue armlet with a red anchor on.

I was in charge at nights when I was 17. An edict then came out that they wanted telegraphists. I registered in the Royal Naval Volunteer Reserve and got my blue armlet. I went down to Crystal Palace, did my training and served on the Doon, a destroyer. I'd never been to sea. We were on convoy. It took us nine days to go up to Lerwick, and there was rough sea all the time. We were slung in hammocks in the mess and I was sick all the way up and I hadn't anything to eat.

We were held up in Lerwick two days because Mary Rose and Strongbow were sunk. I did two trips on the Doon and I came back to Chatham and went on the Elegant, an old turtle back. We were on patrol from Immingham to Spurn Point backwards and forwards, four hours on and four hours off, which was pretty heavy going.

I went to Hampton-on-Thames to wait for a coastal motor boat being built. They were submarine chasers, they carried armaments, or they had two Fiat engines and they could do forty knots. And the crew was a lieutenant, sub-lieutenant, a wireless operator and two mechanics. The armament was two 18 inch torpedoes, a couple of machine guns and two depth charges. We couldn't go out in very rough weather. We'd do two nights in Dover, and one in Dunkirk looking for submarines. I rather felt that I was in a secluded job.

British mine sweepers clearing mines
(Mike Race)

Things hotted up in April 1918. We were losing a lot of shipping and the scheme was to block Zeebrugge and Ostend so that the submarines couldn't get out. I was on a coastal motor boat, they set off about four o'clock to join the fleet from Harwich and when they were about halfway, they got the propellers tangled with a rope and were towed back with a trawler. They managed to get the thing free and set off again. It was all a smoke screen [to distract the Germans from the real action].

The Vindictive was the ship that took all the troops and the losses were very heavy on it. It was a miracle that she ever got back. The return of Vindictive to Dover after the operation was a most inspiring sight.

John Teal was born in 1897 and was apprentice to an electrical engineer and was involved in a secret operation.

A naval lieutenant was going round all these electric firms to get chaps who knew what they were doing, and he came to our place. I kept getting papers to join the Duke of Yorks, which I didn't want. The infantry were getting blown to bits so I signed up for the navy.

Our job was to look after the electricals. They attached us to the Royal Marines. Gosport was where I was stationed.

This business of submarine mining, they were going to build 16 towers and plant them across the channel, about a mile and a half in, to go across 22 miles. They were seven decks, four below and three above water, and the walls were 11 foot 6, thick concrete, shaped like a thermometer, a big bulb at the bottom so they were buoyant. You towed them into position and pulled the plug out to make them sink. If they sank and they came to rest at anything less than 15 degrees, they were going to leave them. If it got to 15 degrees, they would send divers down to try and tilt them up a bit. Attached to each was a minefield at each side. There was all the electric gear. But we had to have dynamo. They'd one complete when the war finished but they completed two after the war. One was towed to the Solent defence.

These minefields were connected to a keyboard like a piano and if you pressed that down, it would blow that section of minefield up. It was secret work. If you'd have passed over that mine, you'd have been blown up. The only defence we had was a little pom pom gun.

Charles Minter was born in Kent in 1897.

I worked on the railway in Margate as an engine cleaner. I was there when war broke out. I left and joined the navy in January 1915 as second class stoker.

We had to do working parties while waiting for a ship. One afternoon about Whitsun we were taken to a merchant ship in the Medway. One of the lads says, "This ship's full of mines". Next morning we went straight to Sheerness. She was secured to a buoy and they were unloading these mines onto barges. We hadn't been there long before there was a terrific explosion. We saw this liner blow up. Everything was a mess.

My pal and I both climbed out and laid on the deck. When it had cleared away, we looked at the stern. There was a bargee there, with his little boy and his father, an

Charles Minter after war
(York Oral History Society)

older man with a beard. He'd been hit by something, he was bleeding. We went along the deck of this barge and jumped into this dinghy. This was a fair drop and we were in a bit of a panic. We started pulling away with the oars. A torpedo boat came alongside us, took the man and little boy but said to us, "We don't want you". So we rowed round the harbour till we thought it was safe and then went back. When we went on board this merchant ship, we were run in for being improperly dressed, lost our caps and smothered in oil! Another ship had been blown up a few months before, HMS Bulwark. This explosion released bodies and they were towing up and down the harbour picking them up. We were turned into funeral parties.

Very soon a good many of us got a battleship called Hibernia. We were detached along with another one and sent to the Dardanelles. I was in the engineer's office as messenger. We got up to Scapa on the Saturday night and attempted to go to Milford Haven. But we met such bad sea, we left it. We lost some stuff overboard and went back into Scapa. The wind was screaming. When we went to the Dardanelles, we met more bad weather in the Bay of Biscay. All we could do was keep ahead. The sea came over and caught the main derrick, bent it like a twig. We eventually got to Gibraltar for repairs.

We used to go bombarding Turkish positions in the afternoons. They had a gun causing trouble and we went to try and find it and a big shell went through the funnel. We took the Anzacs [Australian and New Zealand soldiers] when they evacuated. These lads were in a terrible condition, dirty and worn. Finally they went on another ship and we came home and joined our squadron. Most of the crew went. I was left on board with a care and maintenance crew. I became an engineer's writer, the person looking after registers and records. I was 20. One morning the engineer said, "There's an examination for petty officer. Go and do it". And I passed. That really gave me a start.

I was put on draft to a destroyer. She was up in the Tyne been built. She was lovely, one of the W class, Warwick. She did 34 knots. We went on a steam trial *at the end of the Tyne one day and I wondered what was happening with these seamen with hoods up and duffel coats. 34 knots is pretty fast! She had some defect and had to go back into dock again. The engineer said, "Get a big spanner and sit on the upper deck where two stoke holds join. If they make black smoke, bang once, if it is white smoke, twice". We had to get her ready and used to do patrols at night, but lay in harbour all day. Some people thought we never went to sea. We went out at dusk and back at dawn. When we had a break it was to lay wire on a buoy out in the channel ready for immediate action.*

I liked this life, it was all right. Then the skipper told us we were going to take part in a naval raid on Zeebrugge. All ships were assembling and one afternoon, 22ⁿᵈ April 1918, we went up channel and found all these ships in anchorage in the Thames estuary. Two ferry boats were there and Royal Marines and sailors, all rigged up for this raid.

About 3 o'clock we started off, at the speed of the slowest one. The skipper told us we were going to arrive off Zeebrugge at 11.20 and stay to 12.40 because of mines. Just after 11 we saw the Vindictive. She fired a Very light. I went scurrying down. Everything began happening. I used to take orders down from the bridge to the engine room.

We were doing such things as full ahead, full astern. We were going where the last salvo of shells had dropped. There were four of us – Warwick, Deluxe, Trident, North Star. The North Star got out of step and sunk, the Vindictive got away.

Finally we got to sea, four of us keeping together, in the early hours of the morning, smoke was coming out of holes in funnels,

The Queen Elizabeth in action in the Dardanelles

(The Graphic)

and a great heap of casualties. The Zeebrugge raid was a complete success [though at a heavy cost for Britain and only a temporary blockade of the port]. *We were there before they knew about it. A submarine full of explosives was towed over, the crew were going to get out, abandon it and it was going to blow the lot up. A German regiment was coming along and it cut that off. We didn't surprise the people at Ostend. They had searchlights before we got there.*

I was standing on the upper deck at 20 to 4 in the morning, terrific explosions. We'd struck a mine and she started to list a bit. A ship astern came alongside and passed a wire to get us towed, next one came alongside and the fourth went round for submarine protection.

Charles Minter's wedding in 1920s
(York Oral History Society)

We got a great hole in our stern, two bows wrecked and put into dry dock. Next thing I heard I was on draft again for a ship called Alexander. We got to Hull and couldn't get a bed anywhere. Somebody said, "There's a Seamen's Rest", and we went there. The chief petty officer talked to the lady there, she said, "I can take you in if you're merchant men, not if you're navy". He said, "We're merchant men", and gave us a kick to cover our collars up. We had a good sleep and a nice breakfast. We went to the docks, and made up our minds it was a cruiser, the Alexander. On the other side of the dock there was the dirtiest looking old crock you'd ever seen in your life, black and rusty. They said, "Don't you want the Alexander? That's it". It was a Russian ice breaker.

I was a leading stoker by this time. We did some trials, started off again in rough weather, putting in here and there for shelter and finally got up to Cromarty and joined a convoy going to Russia. We were such an ungainly thing, they left us at it, went off. She was a queer ship.

It was rough weather. The ship's carpenter came along. He said, "It's a poop sea. We can't get over that wave in front, if it breaks on us, we're pooped. If you're alive tomorrow at this time, you'll live forever". We got to Murmansk and it was all lit up. We didn't know the war was over. The Armistice had been signed while we were at sea. But we stayed there till 1919.

We ran over an uncharted reef. They found that there was a leak under the engine room. We opened all the bulkhead valves and let the water go through. Had a great big piston pump, huge thing, and they started that and it shot a jet of water out of this ship's side. Never stopped till we got back to England. It had bent the propeller shaft and broken bolts off holding the shaft down. We came home with a tug. That pretty well pulled us home. For safety we came through the Norwegian fjords. A lovely trip really, across to the Shetlands and down to Chatham.

After the war Charles stayed in the navy and became a petty officer. He went to Russia, China, Cyprus and Palestine. He eventually moved to York and became City Engineer in 1935.

Naval observation balloon
(Daphne Dench)

CHAPTER SIXTEEN

PRISONERS OF WAR

During the First World War, over eight million men were held as prisoners of war. The Russians had 2.5 million taken prisoner, (mostly by Germany), and the Austro-Hungarians had 2.2 million (mostly taken by the Russians). 1.2 million Germans were captured by the Allies. Britain only had 0.2 million men in prisoner of war camps.

There was much harsh treatment, particularly in Germany, partly because of the situation in that country, where the people were virtually starving. When prisoners were captured, they became the responsibility of their captors and therefore had to be housed and fed. About a quarter of prisoners held in Russia died in captivity, of starvation or diseases such as smallpox and typhoid.

Alfred Bracewell was born in 1897 in Bradford, and remembers,

At 12 o'clock at night Jerry opened his bombardment. As it was getting to daybreak, I've never seen so many Germans in my life! Just coming up out of the ground. All our front line had got flattened, and we were on these reserve trenches so they'd made their way up the communications line.

They lobbed a hand grenade over, and all I remembered was seeing a cloud of dust and hearing a bang, and when I woke up in the evening, the sun was shining and all quiet. A German ambulance fella came and bandaged my leg. Then they sent me to a rail headway. There were a hundred more wounded, and we were behind their lines for ages and they put us on an ambulance train. We finished up in Bayern.

It was a kind of hospital and there were British, French, Belgian, Italian, all dressed alike. The only man that looked after us was an Italian corporal. He'd shake hands and say, "Can I ask a few questions?", right sociable. He'd start

pumping you, "How long have you been in France? Where did you do your training? Which way did you leave England to come to France?" Writing all this down, he'd say, "I bet you'd like your mother and father to know that you're a prisoner safe and well", and he'd give you a card. One of the older prisoners said, "Tell him a load of baloney. They sift it all out till they find out which ships leave so and so, at what ports and what time. The submarines are waiting for them". So we used to tell them a pack of lies. (It was really a shame, the generals didn't know what they sent us into because they'd never come near to see).

In the prison they'd give the Russians the dirtiest, filthiest jobs they could find. If they were on for tea and this fella wasn't walking fast enough, (he was injured), they'd give him a right crack to walk faster. Because they'd no government to stick up for them. In our camp we had representatives from the neutral countries, Switzerland and Holland, and they'd ask if we'd any complaints, were we getting our parcels all right? Were we getting our clothing?

Russian Prisoners, photograph deposited by Walter Greenhalgh
(Liddle collection)

The conditions were terrible, you were just out in the open air. After I'd been there so long, you got a box with biscuits in. We'd open it with a knife in the middle, put it under a tap and let water drip in and it'd come up like a little cottage loaf!

That would last you a fortnight. You'd get fellas who were fit and well go down the station and pull a cart and load it up with all these Red Cross parcels. You'd get a parcel one week, and you might not get another for five or six weeks. So we'd make little cliques, pals of different regiments, so you were sure of somebody getting a parcel and there were lumps of bacon, chocolate, cigarettes, all kinds of stuff. They were lovely. If it hadn't have been for the British Red Cross parcels we'd all have died.

We were all badly wounded. You couldn't escape from that camp. Every so often we'd have a medical inspection on a Sunday morning. There'd be a German doctor and we'd go on the parade ground in trousers and a shirt. You stood there in the rain, lifted your shirt up and he'd look at all of your body then tell you to turn around. What he was looking for was infectious diseases. When you'd get back to your hole you'd find the Jerries had raided it, upset all your bed, looking to see if you'd any compasses or anything that would help you to escape.

There were so many tricks that they did. The night Armistice was declared we were all in bed and a German officer come in with his sword dangling. "Englander wake up". Then he read this paper out about the Armistice and we said, "It's one of their tricks again". It was only two or three days after, we found that it were true. They'd given up sending us Red Cross parcels. Now the revolution broke out in Germany and different mobs took control and they come and saw us. They'd have us standing out in the snow saluting. We took a vote and decided we wouldn't meet them. They wouldn't give us any paraffin for the lamp, they wouldn't give us wood to cook our meals. We had shutters outside, down comes the shutters, smashing them up, down goes the doors till eventually we'd start taking the floor boards up so we were just walking on rafters. We were told we were going to move off, and next morning we set off and we sang all the patriotic songs we could and the Germans were coming to the window shouting about Englanders.

We got aboard this German train and got to Basil, Switzerland. I must have collapsed, when I woke up I were in hospital in Calais. When I was fit enough to travel, I went to hospital in London and then transferred to Bradford. What they did was they offered all prisoners two months leave then back to your unit to get discharged. I got a medical board and got a pension. I had half my foot blown away. I got eight bob a week and I've no use in my foot!

Ernest Brook was born in 1897 and joined the Second Bradford Pals in 1915.

It were a gimmick, the Pals, all the young fellas joined. We formed up in the roller skating rink on Manningham Lane. Eventually they put us under canvas and there were wounded there who said, "Whatever you do lad, don't go to France". Well of course I went.

Three of us were down this deep dugout, and we went up and there they were. Hundreds of them all advancing in sections. We put our hands up and they come over and took our gas helmets and we had to go back over the German lines. They collared me and I had to help carry a wounded German in an oil sheet back to their trenches. All the artillery had pulled out and left us in the front line. Well I saw my school pal, and we stuck together. We slept in a field all night and got some dirty white flour soup. And next day we marched 16 mile and the day after we did another nine mile. We got to a village, the Germans had a light railway that run up to their trenches and they wanted some men to stay behind. Me and my pal stopped. And they took us into Germany. We were there about a month.

You were up at 7 o'clock every morning and you went to this rail head unloading trucks. There were four of us and we were at it while 3 o'clock in the afternoon, we'd nowt to eat. There were crab apples in the tree and we were plucking the lot and eating them. Guards took shovels off us to get coal out, but my pal were on a truck loading Demerara sugar. I had my field dressing in my pocket and he filled it with sugar and tied it up and I put it under my tunic. A German spotted me and he sent a guard to look and he wouldn't give me away. We took it back to the camp and we were eating Demerara sugar all night.

Eventually they left this village and we had two or three days on a train and they gave us three quarters of a dark coloured loaf. We got to a camp, there were Italians, Americans and Poles. I saw a human skeleton there because they were only giving us soup. It was the straining off potatoes and they thickened it with meal.

They sent me to a mine, nine mile off Dortmund, and they could take 40 men down and bring four tonne of coal up. You were down seven hours. I thought we were never going to get to the bottom when I went down first time. He had a pitch corkscrew had the German and we used to be laid on the rock screwing this into a seam of coal, then they packed it with gunpowder and blew it out.

Len Cavinder was born in Hull in 1897. He got captured.

There was my officer down in the bottom of one of the slip trenches and a Jerry was on top of him with his rifle and bayonet. That was Lieutenant Hatfield, he'd just come from England. He said, "Do you know sergeant, I would like to win the VC". And I said, "You will get a WC, never mind a VC", but there he was at the bottom of the trench crying his eyes out with a German on him.

We were marched away by then and we had not gone very far before one of our planes swooped down and fired at us. They didn't know the difference between grey uniforms and khaki. It was a hazardous trip, back to a cage. They'd already made lots of cages in which to put POWs. Eventually we came to the front line that we had lost and there were our lads laid out with no boots and stockings, the Germans had taken them off because they were in a bad way for footwear. They replaced the jack boots. Later on when I was working with the Germans, they told me they had no leather on their soles, they were wooden soles and socks were made of calico, they were in such dire straits. But it was sacrilege to see these fellows laid out with boots and stockings off.

I was there nine months. On 26th March I sent my young lady a blue postcard saying I was a prisoner and that I was well. She got it in the August! My mother had said, "He'll be dead because they'll torture him. His tongue will get him". Well it nearly did. We were on the way to the camp and French people were throwing food to us. A lady threw a little paper bag to me, there was an egg inside. But the German turned his lance round and pinned her up against the garden fence with the butt end of his rifle. I shouted, "You dirty dog", and he brought his lance up and I thought I'd lost all my teeth. He hit me on the head with that lance and a pal of mine said, "Keep your mouth shut Len".

For the next nine months we were subjected to two slices of black bread a day and sauerkraut at dinner time. We never saw meat of any kind. We never saw jam, marmalade, butter or sugar. One fellow died of malnutrition. If we could have got our parcels we would have been all right. My wife [his girlfriend at the time] used to take five shillings to a place in Hull where they sent parcels to us. We never got them. I did get a parcel towards the end of the war. There was a scarf, a tin of Andrews liver salts, a tin of toffees and a safety razor but they had taken the blades out.

I was at the rear of the party of 15 men. As we marched through a village [a woman] *came along and walked with me and told me her husband had been killed in the French army. She was only 19 and I asked her if she could give me a piece of soap and she gave me her little ration. We hadn't been washed from March to August. Then a German knocked her down.*

And I knocked him down, and picked her up. He put his bayonet on the end of his rifle and chased me down the village. Fortunately there was a German officer coming and I told him about this. Then the officer berated him right and left. After that I bucked up. We were working behind the lines but all the sergeants from the camps were sent to Germany. We marched to Mauberge and to Charleroi and

Pears Soap advert
(The Graphic 1915)

entrained for Westphalia. We were sent ostensibly to be cleaned and have a better impression of Germany. We were given a British Red Cross parcel, butter, jam, hard biscuits, we had our first good feast.

You can tell how bad things were, when we emptied our tins of butter and jam and threw them over the wire, German civilians in high silk hats were probing about among the tins. On the train journey we stopped at different stations and we saw people queuing up for soup.

[When we arrived] *our heads were shaved and all the hair on your body, for hygienic purposes. Mine never came back on for years. And one fellow's hair came back white.*

Lewis Holt was one of the

prisoners behind the lines. There was some terrible guards. Young ones was okay, old 'uns was bad 'uns. We used to get a slice of bread in a morning and a bit of sour jam. We was picking up rifles and working all day. We got back, got a bit of soup, might be a bit of bread. We left there and we finished up loaded into wagons.

I was there nine months. If we'd stopped another one. I should have been dead. There used to be a German come round in a morning to rouse us with a stick. They come round second time and if you weren't up, he'd lay the stick across you. Some of them was that poorly they died.

They used to search us. I had two ounce of bacca and I'd fastened it round me. They pulled me trousers down and give me a slap at side of the face. Our lads would come over bombing and Jerries used to get away in the dugouts, leave us there. They knocked my shoulder out and they wouldn't help me. It was very bad.

After the war I got a pension for so long and I had to see the doctor. There was five or six and one said I was fit. They sent me £80. I took bad and I saw my own doctor. He said, "You damned fool, why didn't you come to me? I'd have sent that cheque back. You'd have got a pension all your life". I should have been getting a pension all them years but they sent me £80.

German POWs at Chalons 1915

(Daphne Dench)

William 'Pop' McPherson was taken prisoner to Germany.

They were having an inspection knowing that the war were going to finish, and the men were in a shocking condition. I were like Robinson Crusoe, hair down to here, I hadn't had a wash for two or three months. I were lousy, had no underclothes, all I had were a tunic, a pair of trousers and worn boots. I were as black as hell fire, whiskers and all.

We got on a truck to Paris. And were outside Paris four days, and never got nowt to eat. There were a train coming up to the Yanks. It had everything on. Our lads got to know and they broke into these trucks with cigars and nuts and pineapples and give it a right doing. They ate everything on board.

Vernon Rhodes was taken prisoner

about midday. We marched to a cage, barbed wire round a field, prepared for prisoners and we were put in there for the night. We'd had to carry a wounded German officer, four of us. It was very cold and I'd no overcoat because they'd made us take our equipment off, so just my tunic, trousers and puttees. They made us throw away our gas masks, but they'd got their own.

On the following day we were put into box cars, packed solid, and taken to a railhead. It kept stopping and there was no toilet. Fortunately, the people with bully beef, they'd emptied their cans and we used those and a hole in the floor. It was rather distressing. Eventually, we arrived and were marched into a kind of castle in Chambery and put in a cell for a week. We were worried that the war was going to be over and we were going to lose it.

We were taken back to Péronne, they'd built a camp. We'd go out on working parties, building things up and digging. I had to help once at an aerodrome to push German aeroplanes back into the hangar.

Several times chaps escaped because these camps were mostly temporary affairs. They weren't those great big things where you'd sentries on a tower like Colditz. But all these chaps who escaped came back. And they only looked a shadow of the men who went out because they really put them through it. They liked to put people underground. We were at a mill and there was a very dark basement. If anybody did anything wrong, down they went on bread and water.

We went back until they came to Montebourg, where we heard the church bells ringing, the Armistice. The officer said, "You will all be taken back to Germany, ready for being sent back home". I happened to be with the interpreter. He said, "I'm not going back to Germany. The ration cart comes in at five o'clock and there's only one sentry, I'm going to rush it". Eventually there's half a dozen of us. We just stood about innocently, waiting for the gate to open. Sure enough, the cart came in and we made a dash and the sentry shouted 'Halt' but he didn't fire. The next largest town was Chéraute. We had to keep dodging because German troops were coming back. We got arrested by the police and taken to the town hall. Some civilians came in. And one happened to be the mayor and he took two of us to his house. We had a lovely night's sleep. We were told that we must stay there because it was dangerous to go out until the Germans had gone. On the third day, we went out and when people saw us, they danced rings round us and we ate some lovely meals in spite of the severe rationing. And we went to Maubeuge. We met some troops and a band playing. And it was the Scots Guards and they looked lovely, all cleaned up. We saluted and they stared at us because we were a scruffy looking lot, our uniforms had got battered and torn.

Then we were put on a hospital train. It was delightful, we had nursing staff and we were looked after. At Boulogne we were put into a camp and had medical examinations. We were given beer and cigarettes and it was heaven!

We were taken to this cross-channel steamer to Dover. I think we must have been among the first prisoners to return home. When we went into the harbour, there was such a hullabaloo. Sirens and hooters were going in the factories and car hooters were going. And on the dock there were tables laid out with food and the Women's Institute gave us a good feed. I was a skeleton when I got home but in a week or a fortnight, I was beginning to look myself.

Cecil Slack was a captain.

We didn't know where the hell we were and eventually we found that the Germans had broken in and they'd bayoneted these boys that had just come out from Hornsea and the battalion was wiped out. From our shell hole where the Major and I were, we saw the Germans behind us and my assistant adjutant, Thompson, shot one of them in the back and they were right round us. We got ready to get out of this shell hole. I stayed behind a moment or two destroying recent orders

I'd got. Anything that might have been of value to the enemy. Then I got out and there was a shallow ditch and in it was a squad of Germans ten feet away. They signalled me to take my pack off.

Cecil Slack

Our four people were in the other direction with their hands up, and this German who had been shot was pointing his rifle at them. The corporal was restraining him, and then he saw me coming and he turned his rifle onto me. I walked up to him and his finger was on the trigger and I was looking right down it, his finger quivering all the time. I thought, 'This is the nearest I've been to death'. If I hadn't been able to speak a little German he'd have done it. I spoke to him in German, sorry for him and so on, and 'one didn't shoot prisoners'. I kept on talking and I walked slowly away, waiting for a bang in the back which didn't come, so that was that. The first camp we got to, we were given a loaf and the fellows who drew it cut the middle out before they cut it up.

When the Armistice came we were in the barracks in Cologne and a fellow prisoner called Hicks, cousin of an actor called Seymour Hicks, said, "Look here Slack we've won the war, will you come round Cologne with me?" We polished our buttons up, went straight out past the sentry and got to the cathedral. [Interestingly Seymour Hicks and 'his entire London company' were appearing at the Theatre Royal, York

Cecil Slack's wedding

at this time!]. *We came out on the banks of the Rhine near the Hohenzollern Bridge and I said, "Shall we cross the Rhine?", so we did. There was a song, 'When you wind up your watch on the Rhine, everything will be damn damn fine'. So we stopped in the middle of the bridge and wound up our watches on the Rhine, crossed over, came back by another bridge. I think Hicks and I were the first two of the allies to cross the Rhine.*

CHAPTER SEVENTEEN

PUNISHMENT, EXECUTIONS AND MUTINY

Punishment was often severe in the First World War. It was not until many years later that the public learnt of the extent of the brutal punishments and executions carried out on soldiers for 'cowardice' or being absent from duty. Mild punishments would consist of being put in 'the glasshouse' or given unpleasant duties. But the Army Field Punishment Number 2 consisted of ordering a soldier to run round a field with his full pack on, for a certain length of time. This had replaced flogging in 1881. Occasionally it would include the soldier being tied with cuffs on hands and feet, though he could still march.

Field Punishment Number 1 was much worse, and involved the offending party being tied to a gunwheel in the crucifixion position. This could only be ordered by an officer and would be up to 28 days, although a court martial could mete out a punishment of 90 days. It was not supposed to happen in England but only on the front line, though not within range of enemy fire. But there are many examples of these rules being ignored. This punishment would also include loss of pay. Richard Holmes in 'The British Soldier on the Western Front' states that Field Punishment Number 1 was carried out on 60,210 occasions.

The most severe punishment was, of course, execution. By 1917, due to campaigning by several MPs in England, the authorities cut down the number of death sentences imposed. But as a result, the offending men were often sent over the top on the first available raid.

Over 3,000 British and commonwealth soldiers were sentenced to the firing squad, but only 306 were actually executed. Officers were not punished in the same way but diagnosed with shell-shock and sent to hospital. The well-known poet Siegfried Sassoon was sent to Craiglockhart Hospital where he met poet Wilfred Owen. Sassoon wrote to the Times in July 1917 stating that 'the war is being deliberately prolonged by those who have the power to end it'. Had he been an enlisted man, he would almost certainly have been shot.

During the 1990s families of men who had been executed, for what is now known to be post-traumatic stress disorder, campaigned for a pardon but this was constantly refused. Eventually in 2006, the government agreed to give a blanket pardon to all men executed during the war, regardless of reason. Whilst this was considered unfair by many, because it also included those punished for offences like murder, it did mean closure for families of those who had been genuinely suffering from shell shock or other illness.

FIELD PUNISHMENTS

William Simms

was in Amiens one night, looking round the town. I'd got a hand in my pocket and the regimental sergeant major saw me. He made me take my tunic off and do six laps round this square with all crowds looking.

Donald Berwick recalls that

they used to make them run round the field. I remember a Sergeant Major Sweeney, he was a devil, he used to relish the idea. He would go, "Come on, come on", making them move all the time and he didn't finish till they nearly dropped down dead. I have known people who had been shot at dawn for disobeying orders. All these things don't get into the press, it's all gagged.

Nelson Drake had been wounded and in hospital in England for a year before returning to the front.

They was ever so brutal. We did twenty miles a day in full marching order. I got a little thing on my heel, my leg swelled up and I reported it. I could not march. This officer come on horseback and he whipped me across my face and kicked me up the backside and left me there. I crawled to a French village and found a little old lady and she got a knife and cut it and poured some iodine in. I lay there for two days. I thought to myself, 'I can't go no further'.

But then Nelson met up with members of the Veterinary Corps and

He got his knife in and got it out. He put some salt in, banged me up and I crawled back to Bouzincourt.

Herbert Cussons

had a court martial for moving away from my post [in England]. *Major Gane says, "What were you doing neglecting your post?" "I had a touch of neuralgia and I'd come to warm me handkerchief", and I got 28 days in York Castle.*

Hubert Johnson felt that

Field Punishment was over hard. It was very humiliating. One man, always a bit on the scruffy side, if he had the chance to wash and clean himself up he never did. So the battalion officer said, "Right you've had many chances, so we'll do it for you." They got a big metal bath, stripped him naked and they had two men with hard scrubbing brushes. They scrubbed him until he was bleeding on the back, legs and the arms. He was yelling and screaming all the time. Now that was a punishment for being scruffy.

Fred Horner

got seven days CB [confined to barracks] *for missing saluting an officer. I went out with one or two pals and he was on the opposite side of the road and I hadn't seen him and he come over to us, give us a right dressing down and reported us. I got seven days then went round the barrack square with full pack for two hours 'at the double'. There was too much bullying. They'd get a bit of authority and they'd damn well exceed it all the time. We were barrack room fodder.*

Most of them were sergeant majors what had been in the regular army. And every little thing, if you give 'em a look, they'd have you off at the double. It got so bad at one time, we didn't get to know till afterwards, there were a damn mutiny. And I don't wonder at the conditions they were on.

Bill Smedley was

out at rest at Toutencourt, [a village on the Somme], *a mile down the line, at a field kitchen in the woods. I was hungry and the cook said, "Get some timber, get these fires going". I got some timber and a tin of bully and I shared it with a pal of mine from South Wales. As soon as I opened that tin and ate it, the whistle blew for a ration inspection. I thought I'd started a war, the officer was going blue in the face. "Take his name sergeant".' The sergeant said, "I'm sorry I couldn't do anything. I told him you'd just come from the South Wales Borders". But the following day, I'm on a charge. You're not supposed to eat unless it's by order of an officer of field rank.*

It amounted to five days penal punishment and I paid for the whole caboodle. I was confined to the camp, and if I went to the latrine I was escorted with an armed guard. Queen Mary's gifts to the troops came out but I missed those. I had to go up to the front line every day digging trenches. And it was only eight pence, this tin of bully beef.

Arthur Bull thought

It was inhuman to be tied to a gun wheel. I knew one bloke, he wasn't even 16. He was found asleep on duty. They had to court martial him. That was the Red Caps [military police].

There was another man tied to a wagon wheel. The Australians went and cut him down, took him to the canteen, and got him drunk and took him back to the commander and said, "You so and so's, if you do that again, we'll do you".

Arthur Abel recounts a tragic story.

One officer had a batman, and this chap had been up to the front line observation posts, and he came in at 3am. His batman had been on duty for 24 hours without a wink of sleep. He'd just lain down when this officer came in, and demanded he should get up and make him coffee. He took him his coffee and says, "Here's your coffee, I hope it.... chokes you." For that, he was court martialled, and got Number 1 Field Punishment. He was tied to a gun wheel, spread eagled, and suspended, and it was the bitterest, coldest day you can imagine. He spent hours tied by his wrists and feet on this wheel. Well, it would have killed lions, never mind anything else. He had two days of this, and at the end of the second day, got pneumonia and died. There was merry hell about it, and a lot of people threatened this officer would probably run into a bullet. He never did.

Arthur Pierse was at

Vimy Ridge. We had a driver and he lost his nerve. They called him Slater and every now and again he was missing and he always seemed to be found up the line. When they brought him back, they give him a court martial and sentenced him to crucifixion. They took him up the line and fastened him onto an ammunition box, and they were firing with him like that. He was trapped on there.

We moved from one place to another and we found ourselves in pitch darkness in a place where there had been an ammunition dump. We got an issue of raw oatmeal. I boiled our biscuits up with them as porridge. All of a sudden there was an explosion, there must have been a hand grenade or something under there. Poor Driver Slater was killed of course. He was blown to bits boiling oatmeal.

Harry Kilkenny

did twenty-eight days field punishment myself. Crucifixion for answering an NCO back. It's disgraceful. The bloody big birds dropping on your face, and mosquitoes, you're blowing them off. Then they took you off and you'd have to run round the barrack square with your full pack on.

Harry Mellor

had a cousin, he was out there at the same time as I was. We came on leave together, and I went back. He was 24 hours absent, and he got seven days punishment on the wheel, and it broke him. He was in Macclesfield Hospital for 52 years, forever shaking. He said, "They murdered me." And he never spoke another word to me.

Michael Regan

landed on Salisbury Plain. I was made up into one of these companies with vehicles and drivers and a workshop section. We managed to find an old building that had been a mill and we got enough cover to put our beds in there. We were working on different vehicles and they said we must finish these wagons and have them ready for morning. In the middle of the night we were all tired, so we laid down, but it was six o'clock when the sergeant came round, and he finds us in bed. One fella got away with it, two of us got No 1 Field Punishment.

We were fastened to the fence twice a day. And instead of being put back onto the essential work which we could do, they put us on cleaning the rooms deep in mud for a fortnight. The Australians who were further over from us, heard about this and they came over, "Where's that so and so that's given this field punishment?" They were going to mop him up. He'd have got mauled.

We were going across to France then, 100 vehicles and men, separate from the rest of the camp. We went to the canteen at break time and when we got to the door, one of these police sergeants says, "Nobody's coming in here, until you get lined up two deep". I said to some of my mates, "Come on, let's go to the Salvation Army, there's no red tape there". So we set off.

We got a fair way and I got hit on the face. You know them canes they carry? Well this sergeant hit me from behind and he brought blood down. He grabs me by the shoulder, "I'm going to run you in". I picked him up and threw him in the ditch. My friends stood by me. They witnessed what had happened at the trial. And they had him [the sergeant] up next day. He was never seen on that camp again.

It should never have happened. They expected men to do things that weren't human. To live in trenches in the winter and no shelter, and the gas damaging their lungs, it was wicked.

Clarence Ward also had problems with a sergeant.

Sergeant Lawson was arguing over something and I told him what I thought, and I was given the gun wheel. We had a regimental sergeant major, he came back and, "Who's tied you there?" "Sergeant Lawson". He went and fetched him and he didn't half give him it. "Give that man something else to do without playing that game here. Never let me see you tie a man up again".

But sometimes the ill-treatment and brutality by certain sergeants and officers became too much.

Alfred Bairstow recalls,

You won't believe this, we put a bullet through one of our officers at the Bullecourt sector. He were really bad to us. And we shot the sergeant. He were that hard on us. It were done by lots of the lads. If you didn't do it they'd do it to you.

Henry Bendall remembered how on the 1st July 1916, two young men from the 11th Suffolks had refused to go over the top.

So the colonel shot them. One had five or six children. The colonel became deranged as a result of the experience.

John Graham recalls how, when others in parliament tried to put an end to it, Earl Haig said that Field Punishment Number 1 was absolutely essential.

We looked upon Earl Haig as 'the butcher'. He would have put his grandmother in the trenches if he'd had to.

If a man was fastened crucifix fashion on a big wheel of a wagon, and it was hot weather, you wouldn't stand much of it before you fainted. The Aussies wouldn't suffer this at any price. They cut our chaps down and then there was a devil of a row and our people couldn't do anything. Nobody dare say, "What are you doing?", or there would have been a fight on the spot.

Sometimes it wasn't just the Germans who were the enemy.

One of the bombardiers knew what he was doing. He took a pin out of a Mills bomb and chucked it down this shallow dugout where the telephones came in, and it blew the roof off and it came down on this officer. They hated his guts.

They had to dig him out, he was bleeding terribly. He died three days after in an advanced field dressing station. He went down as killed in action. And there was no inquest, we were too near to Jerry for there to be a court martial.

Alf Peacock tells his father's story.

Alf Peacock Senior
(Alf Peacock Collection)

As they paraded ready to embark, a soldier with several wound stripes stuck his bayonet into his rifle and chased the regimental sergeant major around the parade ground threatening him. The two had apparently served overseas together. The soldier had suffered at this man's hands without any doubt at all.

But he was overpowered, stuck on the troop ship and the next time my father saw him, he was chained up in the crucifix position to a gun wheel. That must have been a traumatic experience for a young man just going abroad.

I don't suppose my father would have left Cambridge even for holidays. The furthest they went, even later on, was Hunstanton and Yarmouth. Try as hard as I did later on in his life, I could never persuade him to come abroad with me and have a look at the battlefields. He'd had his experience of cross channel steamers and he was never going to go through that again.

Alf Peacock Senior *continues,*

That sergeant major turned out to be one of the lousiest cowards ever. When we went into the trenches he would get himself into the first dugout and remain there the whole of our stay. One night the colonel came up on a tour of inspection and had this animal go through the trenches with him. He was petrified. When we went out, however, he reverted to type. As we got further and further from the front line he became the parade ground bully that he was. As we got onto a high road, our spirits revived and we were asked to chuck our Mills bombs into a canal. On one occasion we did this and he was with us, back to his old self, shouting, swearing, cursing, when out of the sky came a little German aircraft. It flew along our column and machine gunned us, and, do you know, the only person hit was that sergeant major. A bullet went straight through his head.

Sometimes we went out into no man's land, crawling to see whatever there was to see. I'd done this fairly frequently at one time and had got to know the land in front of our trenches well. One night I went with a new young officer. We laid in a shell hole when he said, "Man on the horizon". I tugged at his sleeve and told him it was the stump of a tree with broken branches that certainly did look like a man. This officer said, "Don't you think I know a man when I see one?", and threw a grenade. Then all hell broke loose. Machine guns opened up and we were pinned down. We were very lucky to get back.

Rations often came up in sandbags and water in petrol tins. Many is the time I had rice pudding from a sandbag. I remember one night carrying water in two cans slung across my back. As I got nearer and nearer the front line I felt my back getting wetter and wetter. When I eventually arrived back I found the cans practically empty. Bullets had pierced them.

Bill Kitching

first went out from Le Havre to Harfleur. There was a camp there for prisoners. Our King and the big man in France [Joffre] were walking by and saw the lads that was doing time, with their thumbs fastened up in barbed wire. They would see this but they didn't care.

Walter Watson had a different experience, and an understanding officer turned things around for him. He was sent into the glasshouse a few times.

One morning the sergeant said, "You're going out today. Smarten yourself up a bit". And he marched me on the square. They was all there, the whole battalion lined up. "Private Watson, you are accused of throwing a boot at Sergeant Major Cooke". "Yes I did Sir".

I got 21 days. I had to run, everything was on the double, the sweat was rolling off me. They used to bring the food round, dried bread and water. When I come out, I could hardly walk.

The captain said, "When you came here there wasn't a better lad than you were and now you've started this game". I said, "You started it". "Look, will you be my batman". So I were his batman after that. He used to come in and say, "You having a beer? There you are, get what you want. Get 20 fags".

EXECUTION

Horace Calvert recalls,

We had one shot for cowardice in the face of the enemy. We were in farm billets just away from Poperinghe getting ready to go to the Somme. I was on sentry at four o'clock in the morning, outside the entrance to this farm and there was a firing party, six men, an NCO and officer. They were very incensed were the French, they'd been saying 'shooting comrade', and they pointed to a quarry. And apparently one had been shot in this quarry for desertion. The military police in charge of that area were there to see the sentence had been carried out.

Edward Cooper explains,

Any trivial offence on active service was frowned on if it came to the notice of the higher authority. I was sent out to give evidence against a man who'd gone absent without leave in the previous attack. He was in my company and I was the only senior NCO left and my evidence was vital, but all I could tell them was that word was passed along that this man had gone absent without leave.

He was sentenced to be shot. And when I rejoined the battalion, after 15 days in England, my name was down to be in charge of the firing party. I went to see the sergeant major, "Is there no way I can get out of this?" "If you can get somebody to do your job. I'll not demur". I had a bottle of whisky in my pack that had been given to me at home and I went to the sergeants' mess and said, "Does anybody fancy taking my job over in battalion orders? There's a bottle of whisky for them." Sergeant Smith said, "I'm your man." And of course I got out of it. But the battalion was paraded that morning, and the man was marched out and shot. The order was 'about turn, quick march', and off we went.

Jack Morris saw

two who were shot, they were Bradford Pals, I went to school with them. We'd promised not to divulge it but Herbert Bradley's letter was in the paper and he mentioned about two of them being shot for desertion.

Richard Hopkinson recalls

When we'd gone up for the 1st July job [on the Somme] *they'd disappeared* [two men in his unit, Bradford Pals] *and then they found them. They were tried and sent up the line. I was ordinary duty man and these two were told to fall out by two fellows on horseback. They were shot the next morning. They took them into a field behind the church and then in five minutes we heard these rifles. The French people in this village thought it was disgraceful.*

Archie Kirk was not happy about Field Punishment.

I didn't like it. If you got shell shocked and you were walking away from the trench, you was arrested, taken out and shot. We had a chap in C Company, he'd been shell shocked and he was only nineteen. The sentence was to be carried out on a certain morning. It was all paraded in the square, a chair was placed there and then this lad stood up. He said, "I'm not a coward. I can face this". Took the bandage off his eyes and threw it away and just stood there. And they shot him like a dog. Oh it got me. The only one I've seen and I didn't want to see another.

We all felt bitter. All these things that built up led to the trouble at Etaples. They can say what they like, blaming the Canadians for what damage was done there. But this was a real mutiny, and the war could have finished then. It was a pity it didn't.

Len Cavinder recalls an execution in 1917. The man in question was from Hull, Private McColl.

Leonard Cavinder Hull 1915
(Jane Chimes)

When I went through my platoon, I realised that Private X, (afterwards we were told never to mention the man's name) was missing and I reported it. That was July. In December, my C.O, Major Jackson said, "He is going to be shot for desertion. I want you to help him to find God". He was a religious chap, a lovely old man, Major Jackson.

There was the Black Hand gang in my platoon, seven men who just did as they liked, mainly because they were so fearless. When they were out of the trenches they'd commandeer an empty house and live in it. I don't know where they got the paint from, but they'd plaster on the wall a hand with seven digits and the names of each chap. They didn't know what fear was, whenever we had to have a raiding party or a party to cover the bombers in front, these seven men were chosen. The officers couldn't do a thing with them because they knew they had to depend on them for good coverage in the line. These seven men and three others were the firing party. They were sent out of the line to practice firing at a piece of paper, about four inches square. They were good marksmen.

[Private McColl] *was 30 and a little bit backward. The sergeant major said, "He doesn't know that he's going to be shot, so be careful". He'd gone ten miles into a village, and lived with a French woman. And then was caught. [In the prison] there was a sandbag with a bottle of whisky, Laudanum tablets, and bread and butter. But he was off his food. At midnight in came a long string of brigade officers and the captain in charge of the firing party, and I was told to stand him to attention. And they read out the sentence of death, signed by King George V. I'll never forget that. He nearly went raving mad, but they left him and about turned.*

Len Cavinder 1982

(Jane Chimes)

From midnight until daylight, Danby and I were pacifying this fellow. He got his photographs out and then he started singing, then he started to cry. The priest ordered myself and Danby out of the cell, and I heard him say, "You'll have to ask God for forgiveness for your sins".' I broke in and I said, "Excuse me but I've been asked to help this fellow to find his way to God and that's not the way". He says, 'I'll report you, sergeant". I says, "You can just do as you like".

Within the next two or three hours I tried to get that fellow on his knees, and he very haltingly said the Lord's Prayer. Then the two military policemen came and manacled his wrists behind his back. I shook hands with him as they led him out and there the ten men were. They put an old gas helmet over his head and pinned this piece of paper over his heart, then five stood and five knelt, and ten shots rang out. The two men detailed to bury him just put him on a stretcher. They left the bag on his head. Everybody was in a state of nerves. They left it to Danby and I to drop him in the hole that had already been dug. It was December, the ground was frozen, and I couldn't break a piece of the clay as I said the words 'Ashes to ashes, dust to dust'. There should have been a parson there.

He was one of those cases that in [the Second World War] would have been dealt with psychologically because he wasn't 99 % really, you couldn't make a soldier of him. The men who shot him, they were given an extra dose of rum. But after that we never mentioned it.

I'd seen signs of other fellows breaking up, in fact one fella gave me his rifle and asked me to shoot him, because he couldn't stand any more. I got one fellow off being shot. I told a lie about it, though I was a Christian. This fellow was a very fine chap. His brother had just been killed in another battalion and I was real sorry for him but when we took part in the Battle of Arras, he'd escaped. I had to go to the court martial. I cracked up a yarn that when we went over the top, he'd behaved very creditably and had shown no fear. When it was all over he was let off.

Service in a French casino, with army chaplain
(The Graphic 1915)

But the regimental sergeant major who had it in for me because I was religious, says, "You bloody liar". This man had been away only a few hours. I was glad I had got him off. He'd go to a military camp. I never saw him again.

MUTINY

Early in the war there were mutinies by the French army which were sorted out fairly quickly, but the British largely accepted their situation. But in 1917 there was a mutiny at the Bullring training and transit depot in Etaples.

Etaples was on the coast, five miles from Boulogne, and surrounded by sand. The camp stood on a hill. Wounded men on their way back to the front were sent there for a short time, after which they were delighted to return to the front line. The treatment was described as 'punitive not therapeutic'.

Poet Wilfred Owen was at Etaples on his way to the front. He wrote to his mother, *'I thought of the very strange look on all the faces in that camp; an incomprehensible look, which a man will never see in England. Nor can it be seen in any battle but only in Etaples. It was not despair, or terror, it was more terrible than terror, for it was a blindfold look and without expression, like a dead rabbit's'.*

In September 1917, there were strikes in Boulogne by members of the labour corps, mostly Chinese and Egyptians. Some tried to leave the camp but were shot down, though they were unarmed. 23 men were killed and 24 wounded at the first strike and another took place a few days later resulting in four deaths, 15 wounded and others being imprisoned.

William Gray went to

the Bullring at Etaples. I got seven days for speaking my mind there.

The Canaries [instructors] used to wear a yellow band. This sergeant said, "You're not at home now. You want to realise where you are". "I'm quite aware of that Sergeant. It's my second time here, not my first". Had up for insubordination. Seven days in the yard.

As well as the bullying which took place at Etaples, the other problem for the troops was that, unlike the officers, they were not allowed over the bridge into the town. On September 9th 1917, a New Zealand private was arrested for attempting to cross over, and a large crowd began a protest. Military police came and tried to break up the crowd. One of them, a soldier from the Boer War, Private Reeve, shot a corporal named Wood and wounded a French woman nearby. The fuse had been lit and hundreds of men began to pursue the military police. They went to the commandant's office and bore him on their shoulders through the town. More police were drafted in but the men continued demonstrations. Men from the Honourable Artillery Company, armed with staves, were sent in, along with Hussars on horseback, and some of the Machine Gun Corps. 300 men were arrested. The commandant's diary attributes responsibility to the military police.

Edward Cooper recalls,

There was some of them bloody Red Caps, stopped us going over. Some of the Australians come to where we were camping and said, "Any of your lads coming over tonight?" So we went across. They would have slaughtered the damned lot of them if they'd stopped there long. But they moved us out, onto the Somme.

Stephen Palmer was also

in this camp at Etaples. We was marched up to the Bullring morning, noon and night and we had to drill up there, and hell it was with these instructors. After we'd done our quota of drills, we were marched out onto the road and these damned instructors stood on the roadside, "Pick your feet up, swing them arms properly", enough to drive you mad.

This trouble broke out on account of these damned instructors. They were pigs. A lot of fellows decided they were going to do a bunk, so they went over the bridge into Etaples and the man in charge of our lot said, "Any of them you see, shoot him, because he's a deserter".

Gunner A. J. Healy, a New Zealander belonging to No. 27 Infantry Base Depot, went into Le Touquet which was out of bounds. His son recalled,

Graves in France
(Daphne Dench)

It was the practice for those who wished to visit the township to walk across the estuary at low tide, do their thing and return accordingly. In my father's case the tide came in, and to avoid being charged as a deserter, he returned across the bridge and was apprehended by the Red Caps and placed in a cell. When news reached the New Zealand garrison, the troops proceeded to the lock up.

Gunner Healy was released but within a short time over a thousand angry men were pursuing the military police, who fled to the town.

Frank Wood was actually in hospital there.

The Bullring was right at the side. You could hear 'em shouting and balling and the chaps really were done up. We used to think what we'd like to do to some of these canaries. It was terrible. They were bullies, there's no doubt about that.

As soon as the mutiny started, we were put on full alert. I was taking a message from the unit down to Etaples. We had to cross this railway bridge which was the centre of all activity. It was bad, because the troops were agitated, making speeches, all stood in one mass near this bridge. It was really dangerous for anybody to go unless you was on their side. I don't think the troops had been looked at as human beings. You'd hear them shouting at these chaps who could hardly walk.

Frank Wood far left back row Etaples
(Borthwick Institute)

Frank Wood, football team 1919, far left front row
(Borthwick Institute)

By this time there were deserters living in the sand dunes.

I suppose that's when they broke into canteens to get food. It was a disaster that it happened just before the Battle of Passchendaele. If this had burst, they'd have had to take about two hospitals for casualties. The camp commandant was a bad one. He put more coal on the fire. They were so hard, there was no humanity about them.

The cemetery at Etaples now has 12,000 allied graves.

There were more mutinies after the war, when men were desperate to get home once hostilities had ended. In late 1918 there were some riots, and on December 10th, men burnt down depots in Le Havre.

Arthur Bull was born in Birmingham, 1895, the son of a manufacturer of chemicals. When the war ended he was in Germany as part of an occupying force.

We got shoved in this pub. Next to the pub was a separate building, a gallery round and evidently a dance floor. No heating and no lights, all the bulbs had been taken out. They got annoyed because we'd turned the picture of Little Willie, the crown prince of Germany, to face the wall. We were fed up, on stew and bully beef and it was Christmas. We refused to march one day. Everybody was fed up. The orderly sergeant was a regular and he talked to me quite a lot. "Why don't you complain? Get them all to stand by you". So I went round the lads, "Yes corporal, we'll stand by you, don't worry".

Round come the colonel, the quartermaster, the sergeant major, more brawn than brains. "Who's the corporal who's complained?" "I did, sir, on behalf of my men". "Pick the men out who complained". "It's every man". We got back to the headquarters of the brigade and very soon after we were in billets. Catholic padre had permission to have midnight mass in the church. I went to the service, and just going to the billets and a little fella, "Hey camarade, come". We went to his house and they couldn't give us much food. Poor devils I was sorry for them. But we had schnapps with them.

They decided to move us to the next village where there was billets. I'd got no boots to my feet, they were worn through. The sergeant major told the colonel that he could hardly be responsible for us chaps. The war was over and they couldn't do what they liked to us.

CHAPTER EIGHTEEN

FRATERNISATION AND TRUCES

The incidents of fraternisation during the war are well documented. The most widely known are the Christmas truces of 1914 and 1915, which were later condemned by the hierarchy. On Christmas Eve 1914 the Germans began to put up Christmas trees along parts of their front line. This was later followed by German carols such as 'Stille Nacht' (Silent Night), and in response many British soldiers also sang. Alf Peacock reports from a letter written by Private James Pettigrew to his parents.

'On Christmas Eve we were entertained by 'our friends' to a sing-song which kept us cheery. Then what appeared to be Yule logs were held up frequently. This, together with the frost, made it quite Christmas-like. On Christmas Day they went a step further and came out of their trenches without arms, and exchanged greetings with some of our men. Private John Fraser and I went out and met them, and had a great 'parlez vous'. I shall never forget it. For once there was no treachery'.

In one area, the Germans had raided a brewery and had beer, and some fine wines. The British responded to their gifts with jam, bully beef and gloves.

Private W Weir of the 18th Hussars had been stationed at York. In 1914 he was attached to an Indian cavalry regiment.

I was in the trenches with the Maxim gun on Christmas Day. The German trenches were only about 60 yards away, and they called out to us, "A happy Christmas". About 1.30pm we looked out and they were all standing on the top of their trench. They started to cheer and shout, "Here's some cigars for you". We could hardly believe our eyes. At first we thought it might be a trap. I climbed over the parapet and we met in the middle and he handed me cigars. I shook hands with him and wished him the compliments of the season. The other Germans cheered like mad. They started to come out and our boys started out to meet them.

Official sources number the troops involved in fraternisation and cease fires at something like 100,000. When the truces were reported in the English press, many letters condemned what had happened. The government decided that it was actually treason. General Sir Horace Smith-Dorien, commander of the British II Corps, issued an order forbidding any more friendly communication between the English and Germans. The following year, artillery bombardments were ordered at Christmas to ensure that there were no further truces.

Khaki Chums Christmas Truce 1999

The provincial press played down the truce. The Yorkshire Herald in York, for example, stated that 'the guttural chanting of the Boches was invariably the signal for a deeper outburst of chorusing on the part of our men to drown out the sound'!! (Not the same as the two sides joining in carols together!) The Herald went on to say that 'the overtures in the direction of fraternising on the part of the Germans were but slight and faint-hearted, as though their contemptuous rejection by our men were a foregone conclusion'.

There were other spur of the moment shorter truces which gave men time to bury their dead. The sheer numbers of men who took part prevented what would have been punishment on a grand scale, ending in the firing squad. These truces only illustrate the absurdity of war.

In 1999 a cross was erected near Ypres, at the place where the first truce took place, with the epitaph, 'The Khaki Chums Christmas Truce', as a mark of respect for those who fought and died in the area. Local residents treated the cross with wood preservative and set it in a concrete base.

George Ashurst was born in 1895 near Wigan. He recalls,

It was Christmas morning and everything was quiet. A German lad was playing carols on a cornet. It was lovely to hear him, he was a grand player and we were singing. Just before 11 o'clock a Jerry appeared, walking towards us. He stops when he gets half way. And this man goes out to meet this German. He had a message, asking for an armistice of two hours. But we had to keep that fellow as a prisoner.

He played hell for a while and then he settled down and we sent him down the line. Then our fellow goes back [to say] that we will agree to the armistice for two hours. Eventually one would venture out, then another fellow, and we were all on top at the finish. We were glad to get out of those holes and stretch our legs. We were kicking a sandbag about with puttees on and balaclavas, we'd no tin hats then. The ground was hard, with a little bit of snow on, but we played football.

George Ashurst
(Andy Simm)

George Ashurst 1915, Eastbourne convalescent home
(Andy Simm)

Anyway, 1 o'clock comes and we're still on top. The armistice is over and the fellows keep running about on top, and now Jerry puts a pole over with a white rag on it. I'm sure it was 5 o'clock in the afternoon, three or four hours after the armistice was finished. The fellows behind in the chateau gave orders for a battery of artillery to open out, when they saw what was happening and machine gunners in the line to blaze away, to start the war again. So Jerry of course had to do the same. When we got news from home, everybody was saying, "Fancy, our soldiers fraternising with the Germans, on a day like Christmas Day!" But had not the big heads started the war again, if it had been left to the lads on both sides, German and English, that war would never have gone on anymore.

Jack Bouch was from Braunds in Northamptonshire. He was on the Western Front in

1915 at Christmas. Our platoon, about 11 of us, were detailed to go off with a machine gun to a point slightly offside of the line. On Christmas Eve, the Germans put up a sign, 'No firing after midnight'. And it went quiet. At daybreak a German popped up and down, and another, then one or two popped up on our side. Before you knew where you were, it was just like a football match. It was one roaring hullaballoo all along the line and the officers were rushing about, ordering them back and threatening to shoot them. And all leave was cancelled.

Harry Christmas was in Italy.

The Austrians was one side of the river and we were the other. One night we would go there, and then the next night the Austrians would be our side. Our machine gun sergeant started it. He sees some of our blokes trying to talk to the Austrians and that's how they palled up.

You could tell what it was like, we had two casualties in four months, they were both accidents. The Austrians didn't want it no more than we did.

Edward Cooper recalls that

the Bavarians were inclined to be more friendly. They put notices up, "We don't want to fight, why don't you go home, Tommy?" We used to fire shots to try and hit the notice boards. It was frowned on by the officers who used to retaliate by putting something rude up and shoving it above the trenches. In 1915 there were very strict instructions about fraternisation. We never met with the Germans, but we never fired a shot for all of that week between Christmas and New Year. [A couple of officers were court martialled because of this].

William Gray was born in 1897.

On Christmas Eve 1914, we'd only be about 250 yards from their barbed wire to ours, and we could hear these Germans singing and playing mouth organs. All at once different coloured Chinese lanterns come up on top of the trench. They shouted, "Merry Christmas to you Tommy. Come out in the morning and meet half way. No rifles, no ammunition". We agreed. An hour after dawn, every man has to stand to. That's when they were likely to attack, either dawn or dusk. When the time came, they got through the barbed wire and we done the same. We had no equipment. They'd got their pouches full of cigars. That went on till the next day. But about eleven or twelve, they found out at GHQ!

Fred Horner explains that,

In the line they had the Prussians, the Bavarians and the Saxons. The Saxons were just the same as us, they didn't want to fight. In 1915, Christmas time, we were talking to the Saxons. I was sitting on a trench and this fella were telling me he had been a waiter in London.

If the end had stopped there, I don't think there would have been a damned war. We kept on our side, but they were fairly close, you could talk to one another.

The Saxons used to say, "Save your ammunition for the Prussians, they'll be in tonight." And when they come in, it would open up again. There was no fraternisation after that, the Prussians were vicious and damned big fellows. We were like kids to what they were.

Maurice Jowett was in the trenches at Christmas 1916.

There were about a dozen Jerries, all stood up in front of their own line with their hands up, shouting out, "Merry Christmas". Then they started walking towards our line and they asked us to come over. Some of us were cautious but they were shouting out, "It's Christmas Day. Goodwill". So our lads went out to them and they shook hands and, slapped them on the back, and then walked back again.

They stopped firing entirely. We could stand up above the parapets and you wouldn't get hit, all these pack of Germans and a pack of our lads all shaking hands and dancing around. Then they came back, as though nothing had happened, and started firing at one another.

Peter Mason was

quite close to the Givenchy Front when this fraternisation commenced, with the coming up to our lines of a German soldier wearing a Red Cross armlet, practically opposite our Lewis gun post and speaking just as good English as I could speak and perfectly unarmed.

They had beautiful trenches, things we were never accustomed to, beautiful duckboards, clean, well-made trenches. And he was shouting, "What sort of a breakfast have you had this morning?" And the man on the fire step, a lad from Leeds, said, "Look there's a few more coming up Peter". I said, "I'll stay here with the Lewis gun, you ask Captain Foster to come to the post quickly". And Captain Foster said, "Mason, put a couple of Mills bombs in your pocket and come over with me, we'll go out and see them".

In no man's land there might have been a dozen Germans. 'A' Company followed us out after a minute and Captain Foster started to speak in German, with the result that after ten minutes there must have been a hundred of us and the Germans. We talked about the war and the rations and when was the war going to finish. And then one of our men happened to notice a very big hulking sort of a German that was making menacing signs to his men.

[The message from Captain Foster came] *in two words, 'disengage unobtrusively'. Very soon after we'd got the message and passed it on, the Germans opened up from every direction and we all went down like rabbits to ground. Some of their own men were killed, we had a few casualties but the Germans got the brunt of it. They fired on their own men.*

I finished up in a shell hole with one of our men, and about 14 Germans. I said, "We've got to get back to our lines, we can't stay here all day. Look after yourself and keep leapfrogging from shell hole to shell hole until we get back to our lines". What happened to the Germans I don't know. Most of us got back but, as a result of that fraternisation, two or three days after that we were relieved.

We did get a rocket. Instead of going back into support we were lined up on parade in a square. Brigadier General Price with his staff and two gallopers rode into the square and addressed the troops, standing in his stirrups, 'Alexandra Princess of Wales Own West Yorkshire Regiment, I'm ashamed of the way you've behaved with the enemy. You've stained the escutcheon of the regiment and it's a most dishonourable thing that you have done. Words are difficult to find to define your behaviour but I've put you in a place where you'll only be too glad to fight for your lives'.

Albert Smith was

out on the barbed wire patrol one night, and we got within about ten yards of Jerry's trench, and just alongside of us there was a dry dyke. We slid into there and had a good view. There was a couple of fellows down there, and we got pally with them, we gave them tins of jam and they gave us tins of sausages, sauerkraut and cigars. It happened several times, we did these swaps with them.

They could talk English as good as we can. One was a pork butcher in Blyth. I had to look after him until the military police came and took him away.

CHAPTER NINETEEN

PACIFISTS

Standing out as a pacifist or CO (conscientious objector) during the First World War took courage and resilience. In some ways it was easier to enlist in the army, and those who, for various reasons, would not fight, had to accept punishment and humiliation as a result of their stand against the war. They were often labelled cowards or 'pro German'. Many of them held strong religious beliefs, but there were also political and moral reasons why some men refused to fight.

There were about 16,000 COs in Britain during the war. Although the Society of Friends or Quakers, had an ethos of pacifism, their individual views varied. Some actually did join up to fight, some would not actively fight but did other things to help the war effort, such as joining the Friends Ambulance Unit, and some (absolutists) refused to do anything at all remotely connected with war. The Quakers, whatever their stance, worked tirelessly to support and help refugees. The Clifford Street Meeting House in York, for example, housed 450 Belgian refugees from October 1914. In January 1915 part of the building became a hospital for wounded soldiers, under the auspices of St John Ambulance Association and the VAD (Voluntary Aid Detachment).

Probably the most famous case of COs was that of the Richmond 16, pacifists from the North of England who were taken to Richmond Castle in May 1916 after defying the new conscription law. After suffering ill treatment there, they were shipped out to France, court martialled and sentenced to death for refusing to obey orders. Kitchener had personally decided to make an example of them. Before this happened, Kitchener died and the Prime Minister, Herbert Asquith, changed the sentence to ten years hard labour. Arthur Rowntree, the Quaker MP for York, campaigned for the release of the men. One of them was also from York, Alfred Martlew, a clerk at Rowntree's and a Quaker. He committed suicide in July 1917.

Alfred Higgins was a trained teacher who gave up his career because of his beliefs.

It was a case of considering that there was a difference between right and wrong, and things would be a jolly sight better if people did the right thing instead of acting selfishly. That was the whole idea behind socialism, that we should get a better world where people would act more honestly and there wouldn't be class distinctions. It was based upon Christian teaching.

My brother was working in Leeds and he was in the No Conscription Fellowship. When I was called up in 1917, I was teaching, and I left and went to live in the Brotherhood Church in Beeston, Leeds. There was a man called D B Foster who was a Labour man and a Christian. He offered his shop to workers who were defeated in a strike. A few of them started doing electrical work, repairing and making bicycles. The group in Beeston established themselves with stocking machines, and a little later flat machines for doing garment work, and made a living that way. My job was knitting stockings.

My brother had been arrested and taken to York Barracks and I was sent there too. I was hunger striking for five days and then I went to the commandant and said, "I want my freedom". They packed me off to Pontefract Barracks and billeted me in a tent there. They left me alone so I hopped over a wall and walked home. I just cleared out and I was never arrested again.

During the war, quite a lot of COs came to Beeston. There were 11 police raids altogether. There was an attic, but the police must have got a tip that they were hiding there. One man, who was actually a deserter who'd become a CO, got behind the chimney breast and got clear. We had some cellars and there were stone steps down. We ripped the wooden top off and hinged it so they could lift that, and dumped a palliasse down there. And on one occasion this man was caught, and he went down through the cellar door. They looked for him all over but couldn't find him. He made a living by repairing boots. We had a Quaker halfway up Beeston Hill who had a boot repairing business and he gave him quite a bit of repair work when he found he could do really good work.

After my brother was captured a second time, he spent a long time in jail. He accepted the Home Office Scheme where you were allowed more freedom. You had to work and there was a roll call at night but you were allowed to go out in the evening. He spent the rest of the time hunger striking off and on but he was forcibly fed. Another man, Sidney Oldbury, was taken to West Hartlepool and there court martialled and given one month's imprisonment. He was hunger striking in Wormwood Scrubs. His mind controlled his body and he could reverse the peristaltic action and as soon as the food had got in, he could throw it up again, even though they strapped him down. And it reduced him from ten stone to about six.

John Kay, far left at back, and family
(Jasper Kay)

John Kay was born in 1901 and was a master at Bootham School in York where he eventually became acting head. After the Second World War, he worked in France as part of a Quaker team of relief workers.

My father was a schoolmaster in York. He joined the Society of Friends some time before 1914. The Quakers of York, the Rowntrees especially, were closely associated with the Adult School Movement and my father became involved. I went to the Quaker Sunday School. I can remember August 4th and the paper coming, 'War declared against Germany'. And my father said, "It's an absolutely shocking thing to happen that war should break out between ourselves and Germany".

Arnold Rowntree (2nd left on front row) with his wife and family 1933
(Mike Race)

It wasn't like 1939 when the clouds had been looming for years and we were all more conscious of it. Things were happening in the Balkans and it was so far away and we hadn't the radio to give us up to date news. The whole thing was remote. I learnt afterwards that the British Navy had been playing football against the German Navy at Kiel two or three days before the war broke out. The traditional enemy was France not Germany.

I was a boy at Ackworth School and we got very little information about the war. I learnt afterwards that the staff were divided between those who favoured the war and those who didn't. Two or three joined the Friends' Ambulance Unit and we had conscientious objectors. In the Second World War I registered as a conscientious objector.

Andrews Britan was a master at Haxby Road Elementary School, I remember him well. He was engaged to one of the teachers and when he became a conscientious objector she threw him over and married a wealthy shopkeeper. People remembered him being driven through York on something like a corporation refuse cart. There were conscientious objectors that were submitted to the most humiliating and degrading treatment.

My grandfather was a magistrate and said that, irrespective of the fact that he wasn't a conscientious objector himself, "This man is so utterly and genuinely sincere that there's no case against him and I'm not going to send him to the military". He discharged him. But another magistrate took a different attitude and the man was sent in to the charge of the military and suffered consequently.

He was sent to Richmond Castle where he was beaten and humiliated. He was kept in prison until April 1919 and later emigrated to Tasmania. A letter to the Yorkshire Herald in 1916, stated that,

'Such brutality is a disgrace to our country. We are fighting for freedom and justice, and to crush brutality. The treatment of Mr Britan, being beaten, knocked down and stripped almost naked, is not going to help our cause in the eyes of neutral countries. Let us remember the military authorities are the servants of the state and are paid by the state. Prussian militarism is a brutal, cruel and loathsome thing'.

In the same week a letter from ten people in Canada said they 'read with shame of the treatment of conscientious objectors in this country'.

John Kay continues,

After the war we had two wives of conscientious objectors living with us in New Earswick. One of the men was Jim Ward Roper. He'd played rugby football for York, was a very well built man and he was dropped from the team as soon as he declared himself to be a conscientious objector. The directors were of that type of mentality. He also went to Wakefield and after the war he rose very quickly in the Rowntree hierarchy and became manager at Toronto. But he had to associate with people to whom the words 'socialist' and 'conscientious objector' were absolute anathema, and he had almost to deny his past in order to do his job properly. It was a great tragedy.

My wife's family in Bradford is a completely different kettle of fish because her father was born in Germany, Dr F W Eurich. And he'd become naturalised before 1914 but kept his name. He lost all his patients but he set to work to solve the anthrax problem in the wool industry. His father and mother returned to Germany straight away but he and his two brothers had been naturalised and they remained in England. My wife and her sister were completely put into coventry at Bradford Girls' Grammar School.

John's wife **Guendolen Kay** recalls that her father

John and Guendolen Kay

(Jasper Kay)

joined the Society of Friends when they found there was so much hostility and jingoism and such a wave of anger against many German citizens in Bradford. My mother became very involved in pacifism and befriended several people that had taken up a pacifist view of the war. As a child of seven when the war broke out I remember her taking in two very charming, handsome young men. One had been music critic of The Times for years. They'd had court proceedings in Bradford and they'd been found guilty of refusing to enlist and were sent for prison sentences. This upset my mother and father very much. I can remember our house being raided by the police. They thought that my mother and father were spies.

Guendolen Eurich on left and family 1916

(Jasper Kay)

There was a man called Herman Schmidt who had a bakery up Oak Lane. He was a marvellous baker and he used to make birthday cakes on special occasions. He had to close down because all the windows of his shop and all his machinery were smashed and he was hounded out of the town.

George Hutchinson was born in Haslemere, Surrey in 1896, into a Quaker family.

I was always interested in politics. I have a vivid memory of going home by train at the end of July '14 and reading about the murder of the Archduke at Sarajevo. I don't think people realise how far war was from our thoughts. The Boer War was over and it was far away. I was quite enough of a Quaker to make up my mind that I wasn't going into the army. We all thought the war would be over in a month or two. I was due to go to Saffron Walden as a student teacher in the September and just before Christmas the school was turned out by the military. There was a bad epidemic of diphtheria due to crowding too many men into barracks and we were bungled out

George Hutchinson

(Liddle collection)

at twelve hours' notice and the soldiers took over. I went with a few bigger boys to Leighton Park as refugees. The committee that was looking after my bursary said, "You can do what you like. You needn't finish your year at Saffron Walden". I wanted to serve my country and the Friends' Ambulance seemed to be the way of doing it. The FAU was a civilian thing, it wasn't military.

They had an office in London. There had been a second Battle of Ypres and the FAU work behind the lines in Belgium was thrown into disorder and they only accepted half a dozen of us. I was told to do my own training and get a first aid certificate. I spent about six weeks being seconded to the YMCA, running a recreation tent in Portsmouth. We had a sort of officer's uniform, breeches, puttees, a khaki shirt and a tunic with an open neck.

There was a tremendous amount of criticism of Friends' Ambulance Unit members from soldiers who said that they looked so like officers that they saluted them.

It embarrassed us very much. As time went on and our uniforms wore out we were wearing the ordinary British Tommies' uniforms. We did not get paid, just board and lodgings. Our expenses were almost nil, particularly later on in the French convoy, there was nothing you could buy. We were then given the pay of a French soldier but the FAU took that. We never saw it. And they issued it to us in extra rations such as jam. Later in the war the Sidcot Old Scholars' Association started a fund. And I remember getting a grant from them for my uniform and a little pocket money.

I got a telegram to report to London and we went to Dunkirk. Those of us with no special skill went as orderlies to the Queen Alexandra, a typhoid hospital for soldiers and civilians. Then I was sent up to help in Dickebusch. Our base was Poperinghe. There were about five of us, headed by a doctor who had a medical orderly, a driver. The typhoid among the civilians was very bad. We did preventative work, milk testing and taking patients in and out of the hospital. King Albert of the Belgians had made a special request that the civilians in that little Salient should not be evacuated. The military didn't like them because they said they were all spies. But there were many civilians getting wounded too. We did get shell-fire. I was cooking supper one night and the wall was blown straight in, glass all into the omelette.

Towards the end of 1915 I was taking milk from a big Catholic farm to children. Then I was put onto Number 13 Section, and I stayed for the rest of the war. There were 20 ambulances, a 30 hundredweight lorry which was my job, a mobile workshop, touring car for the officer and a motorbike. That was the standard convoy.

We never saw the really bad side of the war such as the soldiers. In 1916 conscription came in and a little group of FAU men came round. They wanted us to go before tribunals and take the extreme position. But I think most of us felt we were doing something to relieve the suffering.

You had to staff the Aid Posts at night. They were as close to the line as could be got. We weren't allowed to use the top storey because it was in sight of the lines. We had a big dugout. Harry Locke and I slept in that quite a long time. He was the driver. There was endless traffic, particularly at night. We were driving very often with no lights and there was endless shelling.

An ambulance would bring down whatever casualties there were. You could get four stretcher cases in, one above the other. We were very busy doing ambulance work from the trains that came in, and taking them round the hospitals near Compiegne, then further south to Champagne. And we had some very active periods. All war is chaotic. When you're in the middle of it you don't realise. You know your own little bit. We had two or three ambulances smashed up and one man killed.

We thought the tanks were a horrible nuisance, they blocked up the roads, they were always breaking down. One of our drivers got stuck behind a tank and he got out and addressed the tank in thoroughly obscene French and a head popped out of the top, "Who the bloody hell are you talking to?"

When the Armistice came, we were demobilised in classes according to occupation. The first class was miners, the second was teachers and the third was students. I was kicked out of the FAU almost at once.

Harry Locke was the son of a London policeman. He went to college in Birmingham and when war broke out, joined the Friends Ambulance Unit. After the war Harry was head of the education staff at Rowntree's in York and on the governing body of Joseph Rowntree School.

I joined the Christian Socialists. I had pacifist attitudes. There were a lot of young Friends who wanted to be doing something, but not fighting, and this voluntary movement was just the thing. In fact we were afraid the war would be over before we could get there. We were trained in ordinary ambulance work. We used to march through the roads of Beaconsfield, and one time we saw a hansom cab with a great fat man sitting on the back seat and he saluted us. It was G.K. Chesterton [the famous writer] *going for a carriage ride through the country.*

We were trained for first aid work and they got us linked up with the French army as a voluntary body. We didn't have an easy time of it, the people who wanted to be nasty were nasty. Going over was eventful because a ship was torpedoed on the way and our people were involved in rescuing some of the shipwrecked. Then in Dunkirk we immediately found heaps of ambulance work. The French had no ambulances, they'd got wooden carts to carry the wounded. English people set up funds to provide them with proper ambulances, and the Durham Miners supplied a complete unit, 20 ambulances, a workshop and a meal van. They wouldn't allow civilians up at the front, but our organisation had permission from the British army to work with the French. We had a helmet with a Red Cross at the front. We lived on French rations, but our unit used to make good the rations with things like porridge.

By this time Harry had lost a brother, a regular in the King's Royal Rifles.

The wounded had been dumped in railway sheds where they stored goods. They didn't have any attention and the wounds simply festered. It was a foul place, it stank awful. We were put to work in the huge goods sheds. They hadn't got any proper equipment, we had to do the best we could. In the beginning it was very primitive, but we were kept busy day and night. The wounded were taken either across the channel or to the south of France. There were a lot of voluntary people to help.

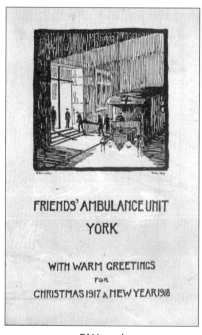

FRIENDS' AMBULANCE UNIT

YORK

WITH WARM GREETINGS
for
CHRISTMAS 1917 & NEW YEAR 1918

FAU card

(Mike Race)

I was driving an ambulance at this time, and teaching other people to drive. We took every opportunity to get up to the front. The roads were very primitive, six feet of pavé and on either side just loose soil. If you slipped off the pavé, your wheels were covered with mud. You couldn't put a jack up unless you'd got a solid basis. It took us hours sometimes to do two or three kilometres. And we'd been blocking up the troops going up the road while we were trying to go the other way. We were in Ypres a fair time, Poperinghe and Nieuwpoort on the coast. A chunk of the line was allocated for ambulance work, and we had to serve that district and remove the wounded and bring them back to Dunkirk, where they'd be properly treated and sent to hospital.

It used to be a devil, driving along a rough road at night, because you weren't allowed headlights, we had to go in complete and utter darkness. There were a lot of these Very lights, which were up in the air most of the time. We saw the first phosgene gas attack. People were blinded by the gas, the only mask they had, they used to pee on their handkerchieves.

We did a certain amount of work with the British troops, largely emergency work, no one else was trained to do it. We spent most of our time in the Ypres area, which was always under shellfire. I remember going to collect some wounded and we had to turn up a road and there were a line of 12 dead men, they'd all been killed with one shell and were left. We had to drive over them. There were rich Belgian families living in their houses, but after the evacuation of Ypres they all had to go. Rats were a problem, typhoid fever was a great problem. The people had no food, they just scrambled as best they could amongst the ruins. There was a huge building which they used before the war for insane people, and we used it for our headquarters. There was two Belgian nurses working in the town and one or two Belgian priests who stayed behind to look after the civilians who refused to leave. Well I suppose it was their home.

I'm rather thankful that I took the opportunity to use French as much as I could. If you didn't speak French you were cut off. Our job was to move the wounded out of the danger areas as quickly as possible, and it wasn't pleasant.

My ambulance was set fire to near Rheims. That set fire to a wood, of course it lighted up the whole countryside. They gave me another ambulance and that was knocked out the next night and I was knocked out in April 1917. I was hit with a piece of heavy explosive collecting wounded off the battlefield. I was put on a stretcher and left for a fair time with an old army blanket just outside an Aid Post. I recovered after three or four months. I went down to Limoges, a French hospital. [Harry then got the Croix de Guerre].

I don't think it shook my belief in pacifism. It made me believe in it all the more.

Robert Rose was born in 1900 in St Albans.

Robert Rose
(Alf Peacock Collection)

I was in the park. There was some jollification on there, August Bank Holiday. Then they came along and announced that there was likely to be a war and it staggered me. The fact that the nation was at war was wrong. It only dawns on you when you get to about 16 or 17 and you know the day is coming when you have to decide. I decided I wasn't going to take part in a war.

It wasn't till 1916 that they had conscription. I was working at Vauxhall Motors, Luton, as an apprentice. It transferred to war work. And then I left and worked with my father in his shop. I was called up at 18. Conscription age was raised to 40 and my father was included. My father, my uncle and I went to a tribunal in St Albans on the same day. Father wasn't sent because he'd got to keep his business going. But one of the requisites was that he should join the Auxiliary Police Force and he accepted that.

The tribunals consisted of a man who represented the army, and other local people. The rule was that the military man was not to oppose your application. It was left to the local people to decide whether you really were a conscientious objector. It was easy because I was a Quaker. They obviously knew my past history. I wanted to join the FAU, and they said, "We'll have you if the tribunal agree". I had to go for training for five weeks. They sent two of us with a stretcher out into the country and we'd find a man lying down with a label saying what was wrong with him. We'd bring first aid to him and brought him back. And then the doctor would criticise what we'd done. It was fun.

I was sent out to Dunkirk, the headquarters, and was met by Lawrence Cadbury. The Cadburys helped finance the Friends' Ambulance Unit. Because I was an apprentice at Vauxhall, they put me straight into the garage. And I never handled a stretcher after that unless it was to sleep on. We were repairing vehicles.

Arthur Rosewarne talks about his father, York man **Percy Rosewarne,** whose situation was a little different.

His family were ultra patriotic, everything about them was for God, King and Country. His father joined the Boer War. My father was brought up that this was the thing to do.

Arthur Rosewarne
(David Rubinstein)

They put him in the army, between the age of twelve and thirteen, as a band boy. He played the cymbals in the Green Howards. These huge cymbals weighed about fourteen pounds each and the clanging of them going up this blooming hill was nobody's business. He was five years in the colours, seven years on reserve and he came out at the beginning of 1914 so he was still in the army about six months before the war broke out. There was an old sweat who took pity on him because he was so thin and tried to build him up and scrounge extra rations. He took him under his wing and then disclosed to him that he was a socialist. He had a book which was one of Ruskin's, 'Unto This Last'. And he gave that to my dad and that started the process of turning my father from being a staunch Conservative to international socialism in a philosophical sense.

When the war broke out father was extremely patriotic. There were three of them, a friend of his and a cousin, they said they would only go if all three were in the same regiment. But only my father was chosen and he said, "If you aren't taking all three of us, you're not taking me". He began to think and eventually he became an absolutist, he wouldn't take part in the war effort in any form whatsoever. He was a fireman on the railway, a reserved occupation so he hadn't to go. But when conscription came they decided that all the railwaymen should work two hours a day longer so that younger men could be put on the military register. And my father refused. He worked his eight hours and then went home.

All his family were very pro-war, and when this happened he was living with an aunt and they just put all his things into the street and wouldn't let him in the house. He was courting my mother at the time and her father took him in. He had two sons that had already joined up, so it was a courageous thing to do. It was the people that didn't go that gave the white feathers. They were either too old or in reserved occupations or medically unfit [or were women]. My father was suspended and put on the military register. He refused to register, was arrested and taken to the barracks at Fulford then transferred to Hartlepool.

After a month he was court martialled and sent to Salisbury Plain and given six months detention. He was in his railway uniform with a donkey jacket and railway cap, and he went with the other prisoners to where they were training new recruits. They put him on the parade ground and my dad refused to march. He just walked at a normal pace with his hands in his pockets. He was just strolling across and they had to mark time all the way which disrupted the army discipline. In the end they said, "We can't do anything with this man", and they sent him to jail in Wandsworth. At the end of six months he came out. An escort was waiting for him and he was taken back to the army and they decided to make another impression on him. He was at another court martial and was given two years hard labour. He was at Wandsworth, Wormwood Scrubs and Pentonville.

Conditions were bad for all prisoners. The cells were usually twelve feet long, six feet wide, had a small window high up which you couldn't see out of, and just a bed board with a mattress and a couple of blankets. The first month you were in solitary confinement. In the depths of winter you just froze. You were only on bread and water for the first month and the conditions were quite grim because you were in your cell 23 hours a day, only allowed one hour for exercise.

In Wandsworth he was told that he had to undress in his cell and put on uniform because they still tried to make you become a soldier. They would physically strip you and leave you for days and the uniform would be there and you would shiver. But if you put it on, they handed you back to the military authorities. My father refused and they thought they'd make an example of him. Six warders came in and they tied the whole of the uniform and the equipment with flex round his neck and then they threw him up in the air and he hit the ceiling and crashed onto the floor with all this equipment tied round his neck. It was about a year before the cuts in the neck were made better. It swelled up. Of course the six warders were ones that hadn't been in the forces.

It was Percy's strong faith which kept him going. He wrote to another Quaker, 'We rejoice in our sufferings as God is always present with us'.

The commander [in another prison] *asked him to move a huge pile of coal and he moved this in half a day. The man was absolutely staggered and asked him what he was in real life. "A railway fireman". He said, "It's remarkable, it would have taken the whole battalion at least a week". My father was given the job of being boilerman because the prisons were always cold. Food was bad naturally. They did get on occasion a little bit of bacon, usually never cooked and usually completely fat. One day he got his little bit of meat, put it on a shovel and cooked it, wrapped it up in his handkerchief and took it back to his cell and had it with his bit of bread. The smell went right through the wing and they allowed him to do that whenever he got bacon. This was wonderful for him because this was his job again and he took a great relish in it and the prison was warmer than it had ever been before.*

When the war had finished, all or many of the COs never got back to the position that they had, especially on the railway. I think everyone was demoted because of their stance. [Percy did not leave prison until July 1919]. *But my father was a rebel, he had more one-man strikes than anybody I know and won practically all of them. He said, "Unless I go back in the position that I should have been I'm not coming back". He stood out for six months and eventually they gave in. He'd lived by buying old crocks and making them into good bikes and selling them.*

He became chairman of the 'No More War' movement, that gradually became the Peace Pledge Union, which hundreds of thousands signed, prior to the Second World War.

Arthur Rosewarne himself was a CO in the Second World War. He was imprisoned in Leeds and Wakefield. The Yorkshire Evening Press reported his story, and how when he refused to pay a £100 fine, he was told 'It looks as if you are going to spend the rest of your life in prison'. Arthur had more support than his father had had, with sympathetic family and friends. He went on to carry out relief work in Europe after the war, and was part of a team visiting young Quakers in Germany.

Arthur Rosewarne
(York Press)

Those who stood out against the war, refusing to fight, were also punished in other ways. Often ostracised by their friends and neighbours, and sometimes their families, becoming social outcasts, they often also lost their jobs. And there was another punishment. The Yorkshire Evening Press reported on 19th July 1918, that women over 21 had become part of the electorate, but that '48 conscientious objectors were omitted' so not allowed to vote! There was a lot of bitterness directed at pacifists by those who had lost their loved ones in the war. They resented the fact that the pacifists had not had to fight, not realising that the fault lay with those who had started the war and kept it going for four years!

CHAPTER TWENTY

YORK IN WORLD WAR ONE

The city of York is an example of a provincial town or city during wartime. Newspapers were filled with the latest details of the war (though heavily censored) alongside rabbit and pigeon shows, and the winners of a flower competition. In the Yorkshire Herald, recipes for roly poly pudding were printed beside the 'Mode of the Moment' latest fashions, with a list of those killed in France on the following page. Ordinary life had to continue alongside the war.

But the war affected everyone, young or old. Many schools and workplaces raised corps to go off and fight, including Haughton School Old Boys, York Gas Works, York Waterworks, York Corporation, the York Co-op and Rowntree's Cocoa-works. Many York buildings were used for military purposes. Poppleton Road, Scarcroft Road, Fishergate, Park Grove and Shipton Street schools were all used for billeting of troops, as was the Picture Palace on Fulford Road (400 were in the ballroom).

Troops on St George's Field, York
(York Oral History Society)

GERMANS IN YORK

One of the first things that the government did was to round up 'enemy aliens'. Outside Clifford's Tower, the grass (now the Eye of York) was filled with tents where aliens were detained. A new camp was later built on Leeman Road with armed guards patrolling. Unfortunately anyone with a German-sounding name was immediately thought to be a spy. Sometimes these people were Danish, Russian or even French, but they were still treated with hostility and suspicion.

Over 1400 York men were killed during the First World War. Many more were wounded, either in body, mind or spirit, or perhaps all three. There were also those killed on the home front during Zeppelin raids.

ZEPPELINS

When newspapers reported Zeppelin attacks, they did not pinpoint the exact locations. In a raid on 2nd May 1916, one of the places hit was Nunthorpe Court, later Nunthorpe Grammar School, now Millthorpe School. The school has a plaque remembering the nine people killed that night, who are all buried in York Cemetery.

Poppleton Territorials, York.
Joe Blades on front left

(Josephine Clampitt)

Joe Blades was born in York in 1900.

I got a job in 1914 at Thomas Cooke's on Bishophill, making war instruments, gyro sights for guns, telescopes, range finders, anything appertaining to the military. I was going to work and a chap came rushing past, and he says, "War's broke out". I wasn't really interested, being 14. Well after that, everybody was joining the army. All the Territorials was called up, and they mostly had red uniforms but that didn't last because they was too conspicuous. It was very soon changed to khaki. I remember reports in the papers of Germans mounted on horses with spears.

We could see the Zeppelin in the sky with a light shining on it, and they dropped bombs. As kids, we'd go round and see the big hole. It knocked a house out, the railing had big dents where shrapnel had knocked lumps out. I remember everybody shaking at the knees with these bombs dropping. It was something we'd never experienced before.

In April 1915 it was announced in the Yorkshire Gazette that air raids warnings would be given by gas lights being dimmed. But in September 1917 warnings were to be made by rockets fired from certain points in the city, the Railway, Rowntree's Cocoaworks, the Electric Generating Station, the Ordnance Stores and the Police Station yard. At the end of 1917, quite late in the war, the chief constable reported that he was preparing a list of places to be used as shelters against air attacks. DORA (the Defence of the Realm Act) meant that occupiers of city centre premises with cellars or basements had to allow them to be used.

Zeppelin
(The Graphic)

John Kay recalls

the Zeppelin raid which removed a few tiles from a house in Fountayne Street. We all went to have a look at it afterwards. The war had come to us.

We lived in Penley Grove Street and my brother always liked entertaining and was a member of a little concert party, run by a chap called Duke. They were giving a little concert in the Leeman Road area and the air raid warning came. I remember my mother standing at the door waiting for them to come back. And an uncle who was a special constable described to us, "The thing was like a great big cigar up in the sky".

Seebohm Rowntree, well-known for his study on poverty in the early part of the 20th century, lived at the Homestead in Clifton. While he was away with the Friends Ambulance Unit, his wife Lydia sent a letter in November 1916, describing the Zeppelin scare.

Dearest One

Last night we had a Zepp warning about 9.30pm. The maids went onto the nursery verandah and the wretched thing was upon us before we knew. It came so quietly that there was only time to snatch Doo [youngest son Julian aged 5] and go down to the passage by the dining room door. Our one searchlight was on it most of the time, and the gun going for all it was worth. We put Doo to bed but in half an hour we heard another one in the distance. I went to put a light and some rugs in our junk hole, telling the others to follow with Doo. I stood at the door and watched. The gun was splendid, it hit more than once and seemed to turn turtle. There were enormous cheers from the crowds which made one feel awfully bad. Then they came and told us it had been brought down. There was a great rush of motor cars down Skelton Road.

After this we heard bombs in the distance again. I decided it would be well to go to our little hut. We covered Doo in my Jaeger dressing gown and got him across the garden quite safely. By this time I had fallen down some frost-covered steps and sprained my ankle, but the girls were splendid. They flew back to the house and got cups and boiling water and we had a cosy cup of tea. When all was quiet at 2.30 am we came back.

My ankle is bruised and swollen but I shall be quite spry before your return. Doo is no worse for his midnight adventure.

WHITE FEATHERS

As excitement and hysteria were whipped up about the war, any man who had not volunteered could find himself the butt of ridicule and even worse.

In November 1915, a letter to the Yorkshire Herald, signed simply 'Tommy', protested about the 'objectionable recruiting methods' being used in the city. He had returned from the barracks to be accosted by four young women near Lendal Bridge who 'began bawling and shouting in anything but a ladylike way', supposing him to be a civilian. 'The younger of the four began to throw stones'. One hit another young lady passing by who tactfully told them to go away. He asked, 'Why do they not go and do something, as thousands of their sister women are doing, instead of shouting and making a fellow's life a misery?'

Another letter signed 'Fairplay' objected to young women and girls insulting 'young men who do not happen to wear khaki'. He had witnessed a young man, who had been passed for the Army Service Corps, being called 'slacker'.

Another target was Arnold Rowntree, one of York's two MPs, a member of the Rowntree family and a pacifist. In December 1915, a letter to the Yorkshire Herald, signed 'Briton' stated that, "I strongly resent Mr Arnold Rowntree as a fit representative in parliament for the city of York and the British nation. Instead of weighing up love, faith, haunting fear of great industrial struggles, he ought to do his utmost to beat the Huns at their own despicable and brutal game". Rowntree had given a talk on the anniversary of the Adult School in which he mentioned comradeship and peace.

WAR WORK AND MUNITIONS

As well as asking men to enlist in the army, there were also advertisements for 'skilled workmen' who could

> Become war munition volunteers
>
> Get into the factory line and supply the firing line
>
> Every shell shortens the war, every hour you work shortens the war
>
> Every man capable should become a war worker
>
> Millwrights, tool-fitters, turners, tool makers, fitters, boilermakers, shipwrights and other skilled workers are wanted
>
> If you are not engaged on war work, enrol today
>
> Free training at the Technical School in Clifford Street.

Of course as the war progressed, women were taken on in these roles. For the first time in history, women were doing what had been 'men's work', which enabled those men to enlist.

Bert Kendrew

was 14 in 1916. I went to work at Gray's in Priory Street, the joiner's shop. In the middle of the war, shops closed down, business people were cut down and you couldn't get work. I started at six o'clock in the morning and went on the tram.

Then came this government contract of making mallets for the troops. They were made of greenheart wood, about 8 or 9 inches long, and 6 inches thick, and they were used for staking the horses in France. They couldn't have stables for hundreds of horses, they just drove the stake in the lines and tied them to it. We made about 30,000 greenheart mallets. It came from Cattley Ernest in Skeldergate in the raw state, it was exogen, and we bored a hole right through the middle, started from the circular hole and worked to the big shaft. We had a steel template from the government, marked with War Department. When we finished, they sent a government inspector round. If they weren't up to standard they used to throw them out. We were all on war work, you aren't making fancy things for people to buy. Everything's at a standstill.

MILITARY HOSPITALS

The War Hospitals Depot in Museum Street was opened in the autumn of 1915, to co-ordinate the work of the British Red Cross Society and the Order of St John of Jerusalem.

St John's VAD Hospital
(Hugh Murray Collection)

York Workhouse on Huntington Road, Nunthorpe Hall, St John's Teacher Training College, Rowntree's Dining Hall, and a large hall at Naburn all became hospitals. Askham Grange, now a women's prison, opened as a military hospital in 1915 with 10 beds, increasing to 30, closing in 1919. It was the home of Mr and Mrs Wailes Fairbairn who actually equipped the hospital, refusing a government grant and VAD allowances. They treated 441 British and 16 Belgians. Clifford Street Hospital opened in March 1915 with a convoy of soldiers direct from the Front. It was part of the Friends' Meeting House and was lent by the trustees. There were 56 beds and 819 men were treated there. The commandants were Mrs Lycett Green, Mrs Watson, who were both made OBEs, and Miss Helen Argles. St John's Teacher Training College opened part of its site as a hospital in November 1916 with 45 beds which increased to 164. When it closed in April 1919 it had treated 1,252 patients. A massage room with electrical apparatus was arranged. Mrs Eardley Wilmot, who received the OBE, was the first commandant, succeeded by Miss Ethel Leetham of the Leetham flour mill family, who received the MBE. Other places, such as the Settlement, St Mary's, were used to house a stream of Belgian refugees. York people also took them in for meals and social occasions.

Staff at St John's VAD hospital 1917
(*Hugh Murray Collection*)

York lady **Ada Cade** remembers

Belgian refugees coming. We only had a little house in Ebor Street and they all sat round by the fire. Mother made them cups of tea and Father went to the corner shop and got beer in a jug. They were always helping people.

Red Cross Ambulance in York. Driver is Frank Walker, chauffeur to the Gray family of Gray's Court.

(Malcolm Walker)

The York Motor Ambulance Section undertook the transport of the wounded of all York hospitals (11,375 cases). The orderlies also cared for the dormitories for stranded soldiers and sailors installed at the Assembly Rooms where men were fed and housed free of charge. They had a recreation and games room, and in the first four months of its opening, 43,320 men had spent time there. The commandant was Captain Anderson of the St John Ambulance Association, who donated the chairs and sofas himself. By May 1916 more were needed so there was an appeal for easy chairs.

The West Riding War Depot was established at St William's College, and the ladies of the St John Ambulance Association despatched comforts for the troops overseas, sending 238,011 articles out over the course of the war. The Queen Mary's Needlework Guild produced many of the garments. The depot later amalgamated with an East Riding Depot and moved to Park Street.

Tank Week York 1918

(York Oral History Society)

As well as buildings being requisitioned by the army, they also required stabling for horses. Elizabeth Bramfitt of the Lion and Lamb Inn on Blossom Street agreed to 'let His Majesty's Secretary of State for War stabling for 68 horses on a weekly tenancy at a rental of one shilling and ninepence for each horse. Also two pounds, three shillings and ninepence for accommodation for 50 men'.

Soldiers at Lion and Lamb 1916
(York Oral History Society)

YORK SCHOOLS

Archbishop Holgate's Grammar School for Boys had its Cadet Corps officially recognised by the War Office in September 1915, affiliated to the 5th Battalion, Prince of Wales's Own (West Yorkshire Regiment). Boys went from there into the army and navy. One of them, Lieutenant T W Hardwick, was awarded the Military Cross. Others from the school got the Croix de Guerre and Military Medal. By March 1918, 46 old boys and masters had been killed on active service. There would be more before the war ended.

The boys at the school also undertook cultivation of part of the playing field as allotments, and sold the produce in aid of York County Hospital. In 1920 a trench mortar was donated to the school 'as slight recognition of the work performed by old boys and masters during the war' and it was mounted on a permanent concrete bed. In 1921 when the staff considered having a war memorial to the boys and masters, they felt that the new library would be a fitting tribute, and so the 'School Memorial Library' was formally dedicated on 5th October 1923.

REST AND RECREATION

Despite the war, entertainment continued. It was necessary for morale. In York the Empire held concerts with comedians and music hall acts. The Theatre Royal offered light plays. Victoria Hall in Goodramgate showed films, which later included documentaries and news about the war. The Hippodrome and Electric, and the Picture House in Coney Street (opened in 1914) also showed films supplemented with music.

The YMCA hut on St George's Field had seating and recreation for 500. The erection of the building cost £1000, paid for by the citizens of York. There was a café, billiard room, writing room, lounge and concert hall. There were free writing materials and 7000 letters a month were written. When the Lord Mayor formally opened it in late 1915, he said that it 'was doing a wonderful job, providing a home from home for our fighting men'. The YMCA also had a 'soldiers' home' in Clifford Street, and in the first year, over 250,000 soldiers had availed themselves of the hospitality there. There were also bathing and laundry facilities. There were many YMCA huts in France and Belgium, Gallipoli and Salonika, with motor kitchens 'taking the men Oxo and so forth'.

The Exhibition Building, today York City Art Gallery, was initially a recruiting office, but later became a social centre for troops, and the Presbyterian Church, Wesley Chapel in Priory Street and Clifton Wesleyan Chapel opened recreation rooms for soldiers. Miss M Whitehead, commandant of the Red Cross hospital in Escrick, asked

York Military Hospital Ward 14
(Hugh Murray Collection)

the public for gramophone records for the wounded men. 'Nothing gives greater pleasure than a new record, and our present stock they know by heart', she said.

Rowntree's Cocoa-works had a wounded soldiers' committee and dispatched boxes of chocolate, cigarettes, tobacco, matches and fruit to the various hospitals, as well as weekly parcels to their wounded comrades, and grants to the Stranded Soldiers' and Sailors' Fund. At Christmas 1914, all York soldiers were sent a tin of Rowntree's chocolate from the Lord Mayor, J B Morrell. A collection of letters sent back from the front to thank him, still exists in York City Archives.

A wounded solders' club was opened in Dringhouses in June 1917, and provided whist drives, golf, bowling and croquet competitions. The club was free and there were 'illustrated papers, magazines, writing materials, cigarettes and a good tea' donated by the public. These clubs were also set up to discourage the city's drinking problem. New laws in 1915 reduced the opening hours of public houses to 12.30 to 2.30pm and 6pm to 9.30, 9pm on Sundays.

One facility which became very popular was the British Women's Temperance Association canteen at York Station. Gertrude Wildon was one of the regular volunteers.

I felt it was important to provide our men who were going off to war with some refreshment. It was something small that we could do for them. We might be the last friendly faces they saw before they left home, and the first when they returned wounded.

Soldiers' and Sailors' Buffet at York Station. Gertrude Wildon in white in centre

(Van Wilson)

The city tried to provide entertainment in other ways. Soldiers in York could ride without charge on the pleasure boats on the River Ouse. In November 1915 it was announced that there would be Cinema Day on Tuesdays when local picture hall managers would 'make the effort for a fund to provide 50 motor ambulances for the Red Cross'. The Music in Wartime Sub-committee arranged for touring parties of national artistes to appear in the provinces. In late 1915, the hospitals in Fulford, Haxby Road and Clifford Street, and the military wards at the County Hospital, all held concerts. A doctor stated that men recovering 'did not need soothing music but music which was spirited and rousing, which would lift their spirits'. A concert took place in October 1915 at Fulford where 'Miss Guy's Ladies' Orchestra rendered several pieces in exquisite style. The men sang with great zest several of the popular songs'.

The Lady Mayoress held flag days with about 300 young people collecting in the city. Some of the funds went towards 'smokes for wounded men in York'. Over 30,000 cigarettes a month were being distributed to the military hospitals! The city held a Tank Week in Parliament Street in 1918 to raise badly needed funds.

Calpin brothers

(Raymond Calpin)

'PATRIOTIC FAMILIES'

The newspapers in York made much of any families whose sons had all enlisted. In December 1915, the six sons of James Linfoot had all joined up, with two more waiting to be called. George and Albert Linfoot enlisted in the West Yorkshires and James junior joined the Leeds Pals. Ernest joined the Royal Army Medical Corps, Jack joined the South Staffordshires and Fred enlisted in the Royal Garrison Artillery. The two younger sons Edward and Harry Linfoot attested under the Derby scheme.

The family with the most sons at the front was the Calpins, with ten boys fighting in 1914, John aged 39, Patrick aged 36, James aged

33, William aged 32, Martin aged 29, Thomas aged 27, Arthur aged 24, Henry aged 22, Ernest aged 21, and David aged 18. The family had come over from Ireland during the potato famine in the 19th century. All the men returned though three died later as a result of the war. John received injuries from gas at Loos and was one of the men commemorated at a memorial service at St Margaret's Church, Walmgate, in May 1917.

Outhwaite grave at York Cemetery
(Mike Race)

The Outhwaite family had five siblings in the army. Arthur Outhwaite was a well-known stationer and newsagent who also produced collections of postcards, including rolls of honour for various areas of the city. His son Edward, of the Machine Gun Corps, died in Egypt from shellshock and pneumonia in 1918, Jack died of wounds in 1917 and Harry died at only 18. Arthur junior was in the 104th battery of the Royal Field Artillery and was complimented for conspicuous gallantry in the field in October 1918. Their sister Miss H M Outhwaite was forwarding supervisor in the Royal Army Service Corps. The war took its toll on the parents, and Arthur died in 1919 aged 56. He and his wife Hetty had lost three boys to the war and two girls in infancy.

Alex McTurk, York man who was in the Machine Gun Corps and survived the war.
(Van Wilson)

In 1916, Jackson Street in the Groves, claimed to be 'a patriotic York street, every mother in the street having given a son to the colours. Nearly 50 men have joined from the street'.

NATIONAL KITCHENS

Rationing was introduced quite late in the war. Unlike the Second World War, when preparations were made in advance, the food shortages seemed to come suddenly. York's first national kitchen was opened in Clarence Street by the Lady Mayoress in May 1917, where 200 people were served on the first day, followed by others in Walmgate, Leeman Road Adult School and Layerthorpe. Food cards were introduced in early 1918, for butter, margarine, tea, bacon or ham, lard, cheese and meat. Posters encouraged the population to eat less meat and less wheat. Parcels of frozen steaks were sent over from New Zealand, as well as parcels from the USA, Australia and Canada.

In Spring 1917 land was taken over for allotments and in February 1918 York Race Committee leased eight acres of land at £5 per acre to the Parks Committee. By then it was estimated that over a million tons of vegetables had been produced on the allotments of England and Wales.

SERVICES FOR THE FALLEN

At different times during the war, but particularly in 1918, churches held memorial services for their area. A big service in January 1918 included men from Wesley Chapel, Southlands Chapel, Skeldergate Mission, Acomb Chapel and Holgate Chapel.

Acomb war memorial 1920
(York Oral History Society)

A roll of honour held in January 1916 for the free church in York had 32 on the list. By January 1917 at a service at Salem Congregational there were another 53, and in January 1918 another 61 names of Methodists, Baptists, Presbyterians and Congregationalists were added. The Anglican and Roman Catholic churches had their own services.

One York man who died less than a month after arriving in France in 1915, at the age of 19, was Lance Corporal Edwin Lofthouse of the Kings Royal Rifle Corps whose parents lived on Bishopthorpe Road though they came originally from Blackburn. His was one of Kitchener's New Army battalions. He is commemorated on the Menin Gate Memorial in Ypres.

YORK MEN AND THE VICTORIA CROSS

There were only three York men who received the VC during the First World War, the highest decoration. Lt Colonel Bertram Best-Dunkley was born in York in 1890. He was an officer in the 2/5th Battalion Lancashire Fusiliers and was killed near Ypres in July 1917, awarded the VC posthumously for 'leading his men into assaults under heavy fire'.

Edwin Lofthouse medals
(John Lofthouse)

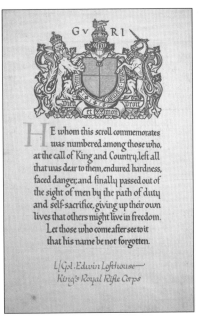

Edwin Lofthouse scroll
(John Lofthouse)

Corporal Harry Blanshard Wood was born in Newton on Derwent near York in 1882. The family moved to Strensall when Harry went to school and later to 13 Grange Street, Fulford Road. Harry's mother was related to the Lord Mayor, James Melrose. Harry worked at York railway station as a cleaner before joining the Scots Guards. He received the Military Medal for capturing a prisoner who had important papers and in 1918 he received the Victoria Cross for driving off enemy counter attacks against his platoon. In 1919 he was still in Grange Street but later moved to Bristol where he died in 1924.

The King's Book of York Fallen Heroes in York Minster also lists Captain Arthur Forbes Gordon Kilby who won the VC in 1915 and was a descendant of York Lord Mayors.

PRIME MINISTER VISITS

In November 1918 the Prime Minister, David Lloyd George, passed through York on his way to Newcastle. He came to the window of the saloon at the railway station and addressed the crowd on number 5 platform. He said that the country owed a great deal to the North of England 'not merely for the great part which the gallant troops from that part had taken, but also for the contribution which it had made in munitions and otherwise'. He added, "I thank you from the bottom of my heart for the share the North of England has taken in the glorious victory we have won'. After this, Lloyd George was offered the Freedom of the City of York.

CHAPTER TWENTY ONE

ARMISTICE AND AFTERMATH

Although the armistice took place at 11am on the 11th November 1918, it took many months for the troops to return and for life to get back to normal. Of course life never could be normal again, as people from every town and city, every village and community, counted the cost of the war. Street parties took place throughout the country in 1919 to celebrate the end of the war and within a few years memorials would be erected to remember those who did not return.

Peace celebrations Moss Street York 1919

(York Oral History Society)

Street party in Lowther Street, York
(York Oral History Society)

Memorial to Able Seaman James
William Sharp drowned 1914 and
Private Albert Edward Sharp killed
on Somme 1st July 1916, uncles of
Peter Sharp

(Peter Sharp)

The 'Death Penny' presented to families of
those who died. James William Sharp

(Peter Sharp)

The war was responsible for the deaths of ten million soldiers worldwide as well as several million civilians. And in 1918 another enemy swept the world, killing further millions, and that was influenza.

Oscar Bell recalls

When I first got news of the Armistice, I was in hospital with the flu. We got it from the Germans. All our unit went down, one after another. It was a rough do. I was glad [the war was over] but there were nowhere to celebrate.

William Marsh was wounded at the end of the war.

I was taken to No. 4 General Hospital Etaples. I was in there when the Armistice was signed. The nurses came round every bed and kissed all of us and said, "The war is over".

Marching Home sheet music
(Mike Race)

Delville Wood cemetery
(Alan Milner)

Thiepval Cemetery where 73,367 British and Commonwealth troops are buried

(Alan Milner)

Some troops were sent to Germany as an occupying force in 1919, including **Arthur Bowerman.**

I stopped in a little bit after t'war because we got in to Germany, I thought I'd like to have a look at it before I come home. I had a billet in a shoe shop in Cologne. You had a lovely bedroom and I used to leave it and when I come back it was all nice and clean again.

Although men rarely talked to their families about the war, they took comfort in reunions of 'old comrades'. A club for 'York Comrades of the Great War' was opened in November 1918 by Sir Frederick Milner, Bart. Membership totalled 200. They met in 'the spirit of comradeship to talk about a new after-war England'.

The York Press reported Sir Frederick's speech, in which he said,

There was nothing more scandalous throughout the war than the apathy of the House of Commons toward wounded men. They were content to take their £400 a year, and did not seem to care what happened to the men who were fighting their battles and suffering tortures for it. Whenever a pensions debate was on, the House of Commons was empty, and not more than a dozen members showed any interest in it.

Much has been written about decorated war veterans returning to 'a land fit for heroes', only to find there were no jobs or homes for them, and that their bravery and sacrifice were quickly forgotten by the powers that be. On 7 September 1921 the newspapers carried this story, one amongst many,

Arthur Bowerman on far right in 1920s
(Don Bowerman)

'Ex naval man, L J King of Hoxton, stated to be the sole survivor of the blockship at Zeebrugge, could not obtain work and had to pawn his medals and sell his furniture. He was among the applicants for relief at yesterday's meeting of the Shoreditch board of guardians, who decided to allow him 26 shillings in cash and 19 shillings in food per week for one month. King aged 31 had the DCM and MM, and had a wife and three children'.

Colonel Innes Ware

was very fortunate in the little staff job I had at the end of the war, I was in a very interesting mess with a man called Blanko White, who became a judge afterwards. Those of us who came back, said, "We want a better England". And we set about it. Quite frankly I think the men who came back from the war altered England.

I can remember the poverty. In York, Rowntree discovered what poverty was like. I think the first Labour government really changed the life of this country. You go through a thing like the war and then start right down at the bottom. You see the ugly face of capitalism. I don't know how far the generals felt it. A lot of controversy on that. They had a job to do. Their job was for the top man to win the war and we were merely pawns in the game.

'The war to end all wars' was not the end, for in another twenty years, the flame would be ignited again. Many of those who fought bravely in the First World War, who had vowed never to fight again, would find themselves drawn unwillingly into another conflict.

Sgt Jim Melody takes wreath from the 5th West Yorkshire Comrades Association to the York city war memorial, on his right is Walter Davy

(Mike Welsh)

The veterans whose experiences are recorded here were ordinary people drawn from all walks of life. Many of them did not choose to take part in the war, or were brainwashed into thinking it was a great adventure and 'would all be over by Christmas', but they <u>did</u> take part and were never the same again.

In this centenary of that terrible period in our history, we commemorate these men. All were survivors, though they witnessed their comrades and friends die beside them, and all found their lives were changed forever, as they carried memories too painful to talk about for over half a century.

This book is dedicated to them.

Joe Blades and his great grandson Joe. The survivor and a new generation

(Josephine Clampitt)

BIBLIOGRAPHY

Sagittarius Rising	Cecil Lewis	Peter Davies 1936
Gunfire magazine	A J Peacock	G H Smith
York in the Great War 1914-1918	A J Peacock	G H Smith
York Absent Voters' List 1918-1919		
York Hospitals in the Great War		
Yorkshire Evening Press 1914-1918		
Yorkshire Gazette 1914-1918		
Yorkshire Herald 1914-1918		

Recommended reading about the First World War

The Monocled Mutineer	William Allison and John Fairley
Forgotten Voices of the Great War	Max Arthur
Regeneration	Pat Barker
Letters from a Lost Generation	Vera Brittain
Testament of Youth	Vera Brittain
Collected Poems	Rupert Brooke
Goodbye to all That	Robert Graves
Forgotten Voices of the Somme	Joshua Levine
Collected Poems	Wilfred Owen
All Quiet on the Western Front	Erich Maria Remarque
Collected Poems	Siegfried Sassoon
Memoirs of a Foxhunting Man	Siegfried Sassoon
Memoirs of an Infantryman	Siegfried Sassoon

LIST OF THOSE INTERVIEWED BY DR ALF PEACOCK

Arthur Abel	Easingwold
Sidney Allison	York
William Angus	York
Frank Arnold	East Cottingwith
George Ashurst	Wigan
James Arthur Atkinson	Bradford
Walter Aust	Hull
Arthur Aylett	Allerthorpe
Alfred Bairstow	Thornton
George Barker	Pocklington
Hawksworth 'Oxy' Barker	Pocklington
Charles Beacon	Harrogate
Oscar Bell	Pocklington
Tom Bell	
Henry Bendall	Cambridge
Donald Berwick	Manchester
Stanley Bewsher	Markington, Harrogate
Joseph Bircham	Horbury nr Wakefield
Joseph Blades	York
John Blakeway	Alne
Edwin Bond	York
Jack Bouch	Alne
Arthur Bowerman	York
Isaac Bowman	York
Alfred Bracewell	Bradford
Wilfred Braithwaite	Leeming Bar
Arthur Britton	York
Ernest Brook	Bradford
James Brown	Millington, Pocklington

Victor Brown	Histon, Cambridge
Johnny Buckle	Cawood
Arthur Bull	York
William Burlison	Howarth
William Busby	Seaton, Devon
Fred Butler	Willesden
Horace Calvert	Bradford
Irving Camplin	Bradford
Miss Hilda Carr	York
Harold Carson	York
Leonard Cavinder	Hull
Alfred Chapman	Crowle, Lincs
Harry Christmas	Histon, Cambridge
George Clark	York
Harry Cockerill	York
Joseph Coe	Bradford
E E Connolly	Hull
A P Cook	Cambridge
Edward Cooper	Stockton on Tees
James Cowling	Raskelf
Herbert Cussons	York
Jack Dawson	Histon, Cambridge
Arthur Deighton	Horton
Ernest Deighton	Tadcaster
Gerald Dennis	Hull
Arthur Devereux	Stockport
Tom Dolphin	Otley
Ernest Done	York
Ernest Doy	Hatcheson, Suffolk
Nelson Drake	Newmarket

James Dunnett	Mildenhall, Suffolk
Reg Dwyer	Baildon
Harry Dyson	Ripon
Ernest Easton	Histon
Bert Edwards	Wythenshawe
Elijah Edwards	Pontypridd
Alan Ellison	Keighley
Herbert Evans	Brierley, Bradford
Duncan and Marion Fearn	York
Joseph Fell	Bradford
Tom Fidler	Ridgeway, Derbyshire
Thomas Flint	Pocklington
Horace Frost	York
Percy Fuller	Histon, Cambridge
Reg Gifford	Cottenham, Cambridge
James Gill	Haworth
Arthur Gladwin	York
George Gledhill	York
Adam Gordon	Helmsley
John Graham	York
Duncan Grassby	Cottingley near Hull
William Gray	Potton near Sandy
Edward 'Ted' Green	York
Walter Greenhalgh	Willerby, Hull
James Greenwood	Bradford
Maurice Grisdale	Shipley
William 'Bill' Hairsine	Wheldrake, York
George Harbard	York
William 'Bill' Harrison	Millington, Pocklington
Arthur Hart	Longstanton, Cambridge

William 'Ted' Hartley	Wyke, Bradford
Eric Haylock	Newton, Cambs
Victor Head	Bradford
Robert Headley	York
Arthur Hemp	Bradford
Claud Hey	York
Alfred Higgins	Stapleton, Pontefract
Chris Hill	York
Harry Hodgson	Willsden
Lewis Holt	Ripon
Richard Hopkinson	Malton
Fred Horner	Bradford
Rowland Horsfall	Baildon
Edward 'Ted' Howard	Histon, Cambridge
Samuel Hoyle	Bingley
Wilfred Hunt	Calverley
George Hutchinson	Harrogate
Harry Innis	Doncaster
Arthur Jackson	Bradford
Fred Johnson	Bramham
Hubert Johnson	Northallerton
Maurice Jowett	Bradford
John and Guendolen Kay	York
Johnnie Kerr	Baildon
William 'Bill' Kershaw	Bradford
Gaythorn Kettlewell	York
Harry Kilkenny	Wythenshawe
Archibald and Sarah Kirk	York
Bill Kitching	York
Tom Knowles	Halifax

Stanley Lattin	York/Bingley
William Law	Ripon
John George 'Algy' Lawson	York
Harry Lister	Ripon
Cyril Littlewood	Histon, Cambridge
Gilbert Loadman	York
Harry Locke	York
Edwin Lofthouse	York
Len Lovell	York
Edwin 'Ned' Lovely	York
Ernest Mackinder	Bradford
Jim Manby	Ripon
William Marsh	Cambridge
Peter Mason	Raskelf
Paddy McLoughlin	York, previously Ireland
William 'Pop' McPherson	Bradford
Harry Mellor	Stockport
James Melody	York
Harold Metcalfe	Halifax
Dick Mills	York
Harry Mills	York
Charlie Minett	Cherry Hinton, Cambridge
Ernest Moorey	York
Jack Morris	Bradford
Herbert Mouncey	Ripon
John Mylne	Halifax
Ernest Newsome	Bradford
Ernest Nicholson	Beverley
Thomas Nixon	Wyke, Bradford
George Oakman	Histon, Cambridge

Tommy Oughton	Wombwell
Stephen J Palmer	Cambridge
Alfred Peacock	Histon, Cambridge
Angus Peake	York
Arthur Pierse	Richmond
William 'Bill' Poucher	Newark
Wilf Powell	Raskelf
John Pratt	York
Robert Preston	Normanton
Hugh Price	York
Percival Reeves	Heaton Chapel
Michael Regan	Stockport
Ernest Renshaw	Girton, Cambridge
Vernon Rhodes	Wibsey, Bradford
Charles Richardson	Pocklington
Tom Richardson	York
Percy Roantree	Holme on Spalding Moor
George A Robinson	Harrogate
Stan Robson	Pocklington
Chris Rogers	Histon, Cambridge
Norman Rogers	York
Robert Rose	York
Arthur Rosewarne	York
Ernest Rudd	Beverley
Frank Saville	Sessay
Alfred Scott	Bradford
Tom Scott	York
F E Seely	Alford, Lincs
Charles Seymour	York
Harry Shaw	Nawton, Helmsley

William Shaw	York
Harold Victor Shergold	York
William Simms	York
Cecil Slack	Beverley
John Slingsby	Willerby, Hull
Walter Smalley	Bradford
William 'Bill' Smedley	Stockport
Albert Smith	Hull
Dick Smith	York
Harry Smith	Micklethwaite, Bingley
Len Steele	Helperby
Matthew Stevens	Bradford
William Stubbings	Cambridge
George Sutcliffe	Halifax
Fred Syson	York
Harry Tate	Kirk Deighton nr Wetherby
Herbert Taylor	Pudsey
John Taylor	Bradford
John Teal	East Burn
Alfred Terry	Leeds
Norman Tetley	Menston
William Thomas	Baildon
Alex Thomson	Horsforth
John Tompkins	Bradford
Ernest Took	Hull
Joseph Trelford	Derby
Chris Waite	Bradford
Henry Wakefield	Cambridge
James Wakefield	Histon, Cambridge
James Walton	Barnsley

Clarence Ward	York
Innes Ware	York
Arthur Watkinson	Yeadon
Walter Watson	Willingham, Cambridge
James 'Jock' Watters	York, originally Scotland
Arthur Watts	Beverley
Norfolk Weatherhead	Bradford
Harry Webb	Haverhill, Suffolk
George Webster	Drighlington
Tom West	Bradford
Hugh Whitehead	Calverley, Pudsey
William 'Bill' Wilton	Ripon
Frank Wood	Manchester
Lewis Wyrill	Bradford
John Yates	York
Herbert Young	York

PUBLICATIONS BY THE SAME AUTHOR

The History of a Community : Fulford Road District of York.
University of Ripon and York St John. 1984. Reprinted 1985.

Alexina : A Woman in Wartime York. *Voyager Publications.* 1995

Rich in all but Money : Life in Hungate 1900-1938.
York Archaeological Trust. 1996. Reprinted 1997. New edition 2007

Beyond the Postern Gate : A History of Fishergate and Fulford Road.
York Archaeological Trust. 1996

Humour, Heartache and Hope : Life in Walmgate.
York Archaeological Trust. 1996

York Memories. *Tempus Publishing.* 1998

Number 26 : The History of 26 St Saviourgate. *Voyager Publications.* 1999

Voices of St Paul's : An Oral History of St Paul's, Holgate. (Edited).
William Sessions. 2001

Rhythm and Romance : An Oral History of Popular Music in York. Volume 1 :
The Dance Band Years. *York Oral History Society.* 2002

Something in the Air : An Oral History of Popular Music in York. Volume 2 :
The Beat Goes On. *York Oral History Society.* 2002

Rhythm and Romance CD of the York Dance Band Era.
York Oral History Society. 2003

The Walmgate Story. *Voyager Publications.* 2006. Reprinted 2009, 2011

Something in the Air. CD of York Music in 1960s.
York Oral History Society. 2006

Rations, Raids and Romance : York in the Second World War.
York Archaeological Trust. 2008. Reprinted 2009

Stonegate Voices. *York Archaeological Trust.* 2009

The Story of Terry's. *York Oral History Society.* 2009

The Best Years of our Lives? Secondary Education in York 1900-1985.
York Archaeological Trust. 2010

The Changing Face of Clifton. *York Archaeological Trust.* 2011. Reprinted 2012

It's How You Play the Game : Olympic Sports in York.
York Archaeological Trust. 2012

York's Golden Half Mile : The Story of Coney Street. *York Archaeological Trust.*
2013